Ethnographic Research for Media Studies

DAVID MACHIN
Lecturer in Media,
University of Wales, Cardiff

A member of the Hodder Headline Group
LONDON
Co-published in the United States of America by
Oxford University Press Inc., New York

First published in Great Britain in 2002 by
Arnold, a member of the Hodder Headline Group,
338 Euston Road, London NW1 3BH

http://www.arnoldpublishers.com

Co-published in the United States of America by
Oxford University Press Inc.,
198 Madison Avenue, New York, NY10016

The advice and information in this book are believed to be true and
accurate at the date of going to press, but neither the author nor the publisher
can accept any legal responsibility or liability for any errors or omissions.

British Library Cataloguing in Publication Data
A catalogue record for this book is available from the British Library

Library of Congress Cataloging-in-Publication Data
A catalog record for this book is available from the Library of Congress

ISBN 0 340 80687 7 (hb)
ISBN 0 340 80688 5 (pb)

1 2 3 4 5 6 7 8 9 10

Production Editor: James Rabson
Production Controller: Martin Kerans
Cover Design: Terry Griffiths

Typeset in 10/13pt Utopia by Charon Tec Pvt. Ltd, Chennai, India
Printed and bound in Great Britain by MPG Books Ltd, Bodmin, Cornwall

What do you think about this book? Or any other Arnold title?
Please send your comments to feedback.arnold@hodder.co.uk

Contents

Introduction

What is ethnography?

Ethnography is a way of doing research into what is going on in the social world. It is, those who use it believe, a powerful method of revealing why people do the things that they do. At the heart of the idea of ethnography is the act of observing and listening to people as they go about their everyday lives in order that we can understand the way that they behave or think on their own terms. This can be contrasted with the process of either theorizing about the reasons for a particular behaviour or composing a questionnaire, and therefore asking the subjects of our research to respond to a set of assumptions that we have already made about why they behave in a particular way. Thus, ethnography aims to gives the researcher access to the way that people's lives are meaningful to them on their own terms.

One way of thinking about ethnography is as 'hanging out', in that it involves being with people as they go about their ordinary everyday business. In fact, ethnography is very much like the way that we go about our everyday lives, except that the ethnographer has to become finely tuned to the patterns and processes that make up the social world. Being finely tuned to how people negotiate their social world means that ethnography makes everyday life problematic. In other words, instead of seeing how people live their lives as natural or inevitable, as people generally do as they go about their business, we examine the very way by which they accomplish that sense of naturalness. We look, therefore, at everyday life as an arbitrary thing, made negotiable by socially constructed standards, rules and meanings. One obvious example might be why we might have different dress codes for men and women. A less obvious example might be how we negotiate starting and ending conversations on the telephone. Both of these social phenomena are governed by rules, which we have learned and which seem natural. Ethnography allows us to look more closely at these rules that make people's lives meaningful. It can therefore help us to create a picture of the way that social life is assembled for people.

Ethnography involves making the assumption that for the average person simply getting through the day is a complex achievement that requires an incredible amount of knowledge. Imagine trying to program a computer not only to get through breakfast but to also know why it is meaningful to make the comments we do to other people, why going to work and supporting a football team are important, or why we think it is lucky to put the left shoe on first.

The most important part of doing ethnography is that the ethnographer has to take a view of people's behaviour as being determined largely by the culture in which they live, through which they acquire a repertoire of tools for making sense of the world and themselves. If I wanted to understand why a young man is aggressive in a bar in the centre of a city on a Friday night, for example, I would need to find out how such behaviour was meaningful to him in the context of his cultural tool kit. Even though at the end of most Friday evenings he usually ended up fighting, I would have to resist dismissing him as being a mindless, violent person who behaves without motive. I would look into the whole culture of drinking alcohol and what that has come to mean for this man. I would also have to understand some things about masculinity in that particular culture, about definitions of assertiveness and about power. How have these come to inform this young man about what he is doing and what it means? While things, such as constructions of masculinity involving shows of strength, may seem ridiculous to the researcher, it is important to remember that these are behaviours that the young man shares with his friends that allow them to behave as if such things were real and important. Therefore, the ethnographer must try to see the world through the eyes of this young man.

The ethnographer must also realize that people are so highly engaged with each other that the only way to really understand what they are doing is to approach even behaviours which seem very private as fundamentally interpersonal. Life is always carried out with an intense mutual gaze. It is a fantastic thing that humans can share common complex ideas such as ways of raising children, fashion industries, local cafés, etc. All of this has its basis in our mutual responsiveness. Even getting drunk with friends on a Friday night requires an intricate and delicate knowledge of what others know and think. It involves a vivid awareness of how the people around us are responding. To comprehend these things the researcher needs to understand them in the sense of the way that people relate to each other. The most common and mundane act requires inference and interpretation. Throughout this book I will be emphasizing the importance of being aware of the socially responsive nature of all behaviour.

Another important component of ethnography is that we must be aware that our own frames of reference may not be the same as those of the people that we study. The behaviour of the aggressive young man in the bar might seem strange to those who do not share this young man's cultural repertoire. This is why I could not impose my own framework of reference upon his behaviour. I would need to see the world how he sees it in order to understand why he gets drunk and becomes aggressive every Friday night.

The list of things that we would need to know about this young man could go on and on. But here we begin to get a hint at what ethnography is about. Ethnography is about locating a particular slice of social action into something larger, into a whole way of life. Any instance of behaviour must be thought about as a person making sense of and finding their place in that world, armed with a range of cultural standards and values, deeply engaged with the minds of others in their society. More than being any prescribed set of methodological procedures, ethnography should be thought of as being defined in terms of the approach that it takes to the way that the social world is constructed. In this book I want to illustrate exactly what this method of examining the social world looks like and how this can help us to understand how people relate to the mass media. We will be thinking about this as the *ethnographic gaze*. This ethnographic gaze involves carrying out something we will call a *reassembled ethnography*. This term refers to the way that, after we have recorded data, or we might say, disassembled it from the flow of everyday life, we must then undertake a corresponding work of reassembly, so that the interesting and relevant details are set back into the flow of experience on the small and large scale. The small scale would be the immediate setting of social interaction and the large scale would be the larger available cultural repertoire. In practice, this would simply mean that we can make observations of how a young drunken aggressive man behaved and talked in different places and at different times, but that we should not take any of these in isolation. We would need to view these instances of behaviour both together and in a broader sense of his culture as a whole. Thus, we would reassemble our data back into the young man's flow of experience. Put simply, this means that we need to have a sensitivity to time, place and occasion.

Doing ethnography

When you come across the term ethnography when someone describes the research they have carried out, it will usually mean that they have spent some time with the usually quite small number of people they studied in the place where these people live. It will probably mean that the data they have collected will include accounts of behaviour or speech that occurred in this place. The ethnographer will have taken this approach as they believe that to understand why a person does something you need to look at it in the context of their lives as a whole. They will have assumed that there is no point simply counting instances of such behaviour, nor is there any point asking people why they behave in a particular way through a questionnaire.

Let us think about this in the context of the drunken young man in the bar. We could count how many young men were drunk on Friday night. We could also find out some information about their background, say, their social class or employment status, as would be the usual procedure in a questionnaire survey. We could then, if we asked enough of the men, be able to make some statements about this kind of behaviour. We might be able say some things about the average age of these drinkers or about what kinds of jobs they tended to do. But would this really tell us much about *why* each of the young men were there, every Friday evening?

Through comparison of the responses to such questions we might be able to say that it is mainly young men from lower socio-economic groups who are drunk and aggressive in bars on Friday nights. Through this we might speculate that there must be something about being from such a social context that leads to such behaviour. But we could not be entirely sure that we were really discovering something about the social world or whether we were imposing our own, seemingly reasonable explanations. This kind of questionnaire survey has the problem that the researcher would have decided what issues or variables would be collected. Therefore the questions asked would be those that the researcher thought were important. They might not be the important ones in the life of the young man. If the researcher came from a very different social world, they might have little knowledge of how the world of the young man hung together. Even if they were from the same background they may not have been aware of the kinds of meanings that comprised this particular way of life as they were taking part in it. As we negotiate our everyday lives we are not generally conscious of the rules, conventions and meanings through which it makes sense to us. As we look at ethnographic research in subsequent chapters we will see the way that researchers have often found things that they would not have been able to predict.

Researchers have tried to get around the problem of pre-formulated questions by using *open-ended* questions which allow the respondent to expand on an issue or make their own comments. Open-ended interviews also have this aim. The idea is that the researcher has some main areas to cover but is prepared to follow the respondent's train of thought.

Another approach, popular with market researchers, has been the use of *focus groups*. A focus group involves getting a group of people to discuss a particular issue. It has the advantage that the participants themselves decide what to talk about. It also has the attraction of allowing people to discuss things among themselves, as in normal social life.

For the ethnographer, however, these approaches are still problematic. This is because the data have been collected in one single environment, such as in an interview with a researcher, or in a focus group where a number of people are given a specific topic to talk about, knowing that they are being recorded or observed. Is what people say and do in these situations really representative of what they do in other situations? Research in social science has shown that people often behave very differently in different contexts and what they say they do may not always turn out to be what they actually do (Lave *et al.* 1977; Clement 1982).

Second, and perhaps more importantly, we cannot assume that people always know the reasons that they do things. When asked why they do things, people often produce a set of common-sense, widely shared 'official reasons' to explain themselves. As we will see in Chapters 1 and 2, one important finding by ethnographers in anthropology and by psychologists, is that people do not generally have conscious access to the reasons why they behave in particular ways. They are not conscious of the cultural tool kit through which the social world is made meaningful to them. This is why ethnographers believe that we need to observe people as they live out their lives. Only in this way can we find out why it makes sense for this particular young man to be getting drunk in a city centre with a group of his friends every Friday night. There is no point asking him to account for his behaviour in one context. We need to gain access to his view of the world and frameworks that make it meaningful to him.

The explanation I have so far offered of ethnography has not been specific in terms of strategies and clearly defined activities. This is because ethnography is by no means something that can be strictly defined in this way. While it is almost synonymous with the discipline of anthropology, many are surprised to find that anthropologists themselves do not seem to know what it is. But what is important is not to try to understand what ethnography is precisely in terms of procedure, but to grasp exactly why, as a mode of thinking about explaining society and social behaviour, it is so useful. The problem is that when someone is just starting out as an ethnographer they need some practical guidelines. These will come right at the end of this book. Before these are considered, it is more important that the idea and philosophy of the ethnographic gaze are fully appreciated. Most of the chapters in this book have this as their central aim. As an anthropology postgraduate I was encouraged to read all of the classic and important ethnographies in order to develop a sense of what ethnography was all about. Now as a Media Studies researcher and teacher I feel that much research could be boosted by an increased awareness of the way that these works approach human behaviour and society.

A person who had just come across ethnography might wonder why, if the methodology is as useful, as I am suggesting here, the most publicized studies of society that we come across in the mass media are large-scale surveys that offer impressive statistics. There are several reasons for this. On the one hand, large-scale social surveys can be useful, if you want to know numbers of things, like how many television sets a person has in their house, or how often people do things, like buying a newspaper, for example. One the other hand, and perhaps more importantly, such surveys are popular because they have the credibility of appearing scientific. While they can often hide the problems of the definitions of what is being counted, statistics have vast appeal and currency in our culture. They are also easy to quote. This is one reason that the survey has dominated communications research in America. For a British researcher visiting a conference in America the extent to which statistical analysis dominates research can seem quite incredible. Ethnographic findings are usually more difficult to summarize in a punchy sound bite.

Another reason that ethnography is not done is that it has generally been thought to require a large amount of time and the full attention of one person. Traditionally anthropologists would go off for years at a time. If I can again return to the example of our drunk in the bar, you will recall that I hinted at a large range of things that we would need to know in order to locate his behaviour in culture. If we knew nothing of this young man's culture at all, then it would indeed take us a long time to gather all the appropriate information. But if a person is able to develop a good ethnographic gaze, then ethnography need not take any longer to undertake in one's own culture than it would to design and carry out a questionnaire-based survey. By the end of this book the reader should have a sense of how to carry out ethnographic research and how this can be applied in the context of the mass media.

If ethnography is like 'hanging out', we might then think that it is therefore not really very rigorous or scientific. Can we trust a person to produce anything other than their own personal view? This would be an important observation. Ethnography does not provide a transparent way of representing the social world. But nor do other research methods. Yet it is ethnography that has tended to suffer most from this criticism. I would argue, however, that when it is done well ethnography can reveal things about the social world that other methodologies cannot. I address these criticisms in Chapter 2.

In social research there is a tension between the feeling of the need to have the credibility of scientific methods and the knowledge that the social world is not like the natural world. But there has nevertheless been a pressure on any research methodology in the social sciences to justify itself in terms of criteria based on the natural sciences. This is why large-scale survey and statistical analysis appear legitimate.

This scientific model, often referred to as *positivism*, means quantified measurements. As in the natural sciences the job of the social scientist is the isolation of variables and the manipulation of these in the experimental context. This is referred to as *quantitative* research because it is basically about counting phenomena. Once the researcher has isolated and counted variables, they can then look for the relationships between them. In this way universal laws can be discovered. We might for example, compose a questionnaire to compare attitudes to television programmes, and then compare these to household income. We select the variables, which in this case would be attitudes and income, collect the responses, and then look for relationships between them. As with research in the natural sciences, this should be done with a distance of objectivity and neutrality.

In social science this need to create a sense of neutrality has led to attempts at standardization of methods of observation and measurement. Scientific objectivity is thought to be established in social surveys where interviewer influence is minimized by the wording of questions and a formulaic delivery. In this way, it is thought, variables can be controlled. In Chapter 5 I will discuss if this is indeed the case. But for such surveys this means that, like research in the natural sciences, there can then be claims to reproducibility and findings can be said to have reliability.

Ethnographers, however, argue that the social world should be studied as it is in its natural state and not in artificial settings or through researchers selecting and isolating variables that they themselves feel are important. Investigating the social world in its natural state is sometimes spoken of as naturalism. In contrast to *quantitative* research, which looks to count or measure phenomenon, this approach is referred to as *qualitative* research. In this approach research should be sensitive to the social world, and come to understand it on its own terms. The aim is not to create scientific principles but to faithfully represent that social world. Basically, the assumption is that social phenomena are fundamentally different from natural phenomena. Human life is characterized by meanings. We do not behave by simple cause and effect mechanisms, which we can isolate from the flow of our lives and the complex web of cultural meanings in which we operate from moment to moment. Because of this, any attempt to isolate variables, for example, by asking pre-formulated questions, will not give insight into behaviours outside of the context of the response to the questionnaire.

However, both open-ended interviews and focus groups, which collect data of a qualitative nature, could be said to be flawed, in the model of naturalism, as they are again an attempt to isolate variables by examining behaviour in one artificial setting. In later chapters we look at phenomena such as beliefs in witchcraft and gang violence in Chicago. We will see clearly that we could not understand these by composing questionnaires or organizing focus groups. This is because in each of these rich settings we find human beings who are acting in a way that is meaningful to them. Interviews and focus groups can both be resources for data, but we need to reassemble this data back into people's lives if it is to be of use. This is why the ethnographer seeks to locate points of behaviour in the larger picture of people's lives. This allows us to see what is going on when we look at someone in Melanesia casting a magic spell or a Chicago gang smashing up a public building.

While I have been creating a distinction between the philosophies of quantitative and qualitative approaches, many researchers will tend to use a combination of the two. They may use a more qualitative approach to begin with so that they can find out what kinds of things are important for the people they wish to research. This will then be followed up by a questionnaire survey. But this qualitative approach has usually taken the form of unstructured interviews rather than ethnography. The unstructured interview would mean asking, say, our bar drinker to tell us about his behaviour, or, say, a soap viewer to tell us why they like the programme. As we shall see throughout the chapters in this book, what people tell us in these situations may have little to do with why they actually behave in the way that they do.

Another term that is often used to mean pretty much the same thing as ethnography is *participant observation*. This term basically speaks for itself. Like ethnography it involves observation of behaviour in natural settings. The difference between the two is that participant observation is not generally thought to include the same sense of the researcher immersing themselves in a culture. Nor does it have the same aim of creating a comprehensive cultural map of the world of the observed. Participant observation means simply that the researcher spends time in a setting of interaction in order to observe what goes on. Participant observation may therefore also be thought to be part of ethnography in that ethnographers might also use other methodologies such as official records. But often the two are used interchangeably.

What is the aim of this book?

The aim of this book is to demonstrate how useful ethnography can be in media studies and to give the reader a sense of what doing ethnography means. The approach I will take will not be to go through all the theoretical justifications for the methodology, although these are discussed along the way. This book takes the approach of looking at the way that specific ethnographies have been done and how this has allowed the researcher to find things out about people's behaviour. It looks at ethnography done in anthropology, in sociology and then how it has been used in media studies. It concludes by looking carefully at how the ethnographic gaze can reasonably be thought of as an excellent way to show how people relate to the mass media. In the final chapters it looks carefully at data from an ethnographic study showing exactly what the ethnographic gaze involves.

The term ethnography is often discussed and used in many academic disciplines, yet too much time is spent worrying about what practical procedures correctly constitute the methodology. This has meant that we have had a tendency to lose sight of the philosophy behind ethnography, which for me is the most important thing. This philosophy means, as I have already begun to indicate, viewing human action and culture in a particular way. We do not, for example, just see the aggressive young man as simply an aggressive young man. We try to locate his behaviour. This is why I choose to start by looking at some of the classic studies in anthropology. These are studies which used ethnography to understand people's behaviour, in cultures which were strange to the investigators, that seemed irrational and which were seen as immoral by their own societies. And this is why I follow this with a look at some of the ideas about culture and human action that I think should provide the basis of the way that we think about the social world, and which should inform our ethnographic gaze. The ethnographic gaze means never seeing behaviour in any one moment as anything other than behaviour in that moment. It means looking for the rules that govern the way that particular instance of social interaction works. It means understanding the frameworks that guide this action for the participants and make it meaningful to them. In other words, we have to think about the way that people talk and behave as being informed by their cultural set of rules and meanings, which are always arbitrary.

Ethnography and the media

In the press and other forums for public debate, we often find the view expressed that people are directly influenced by (mainly the visual) mass media. For example, when children carry out some kind of violent act that we find particularly difficult to deal with, there is usually someone who will blame the mass media. Interestingly, though, the blame is generally focused in the direction of fiction and not on, say, news, or factual, depictions of violence. From the 1920s to today this tendency to think only about the influence of the mass media in terms of easily identifiable negative effects has dominated research.

One thing that the collective research on audiences does show conclusively is that direct causal effects are impossible to demonstrate. We do not simply see something on the screen, like a murder, and then become murderous. Children do not simply see drug taking on television and then immediately go out of the door to find the nearest dealer. Clearly, the way that we are moved to behave is much more complex, as is the way that we watch the visual media. But how can we explain the fact that children may all at some point find themselves involved in the latest popular culture craze such as *Pokémon*? And why is it now that young men flock to gyms in order to have a body like Brad Pitt? In the latter case is it because we now rarely see a man take his clothes off on the screen without him revealing a tanned and toned physique? And does this exist in isolation or along with other changing images of masculinity as it has become increasingly colonized by consumerism?

Many commentators have long pointed the finger at women's beauty and fashion when trying to explain the phenomena of eating disorders. Somehow we are aware that, particularly the visual media, with their now massive output of images of people, places and events, do have an input into our perceptions of what the world and people in it are all about, about what is desirable and about what is right and wrong. This might not be a cause and effect kind of input, but rather something that is simply part of the fabric of our experiences.

Media researchers have struggled to come up with a way to find out what is really happening in this process as a whole (Belton 2000). Many have based their approach on looking at the messages inherent in the media themselves. This follows from the assumption that if people are continually exposed to a particular definition of the world, then they may be encouraged to think about the world in that way since they are deprived of any alternative. Other researchers have taken people into the laboratory in order to wire them up and see how they respond to violence on the screen or to ask them questions designed to get them to reveal attitude changes after seeing something that depicted women negatively. Others have taken a psychoanalytical approach. This involves looking at the unconscious factors that affect the way that we identify with screen characters, for example. Others have used the much more popular method of focus groups and interviews. Depending upon their nature, it is thought, these have the advantage of allowing people to express themselves.

In Part II of this book we will look at some of the ethnographic studies that have been carried out in media studies. While these studies provide fascinating and valuable insights, many of them are still unable to really locate something like television in people's lives as a whole. This is because these studies often still tend to rely on an approach that is more like focus groups or interviews rather than ethnography. These studies do not have what I would think about as an ethnographic gaze since they rely on data gathered in only one context and assume that people can simply transparently reflect upon their behaviour. The ethnographic gaze would mean mapping a phenomenon like *Pokémon* into wider social meanings.

The collective work on audience studies has provided some fascinating insights into the ways that we relate to the media. But very little has been revealed about how the media are now part of the way that we experience the world. By what means can we research how we are affected by the way, for example, that every time we see sex depicted on the television, movies or in advertising, it is beautiful, sensual, perfect? How can we evaluate the impact of being exposed to a vast array of narratives about relationships in the mass media, where there is little time to develop issues and where sex has come to signify love? A couple are thrown together. The couple do not really seem to have had much to say to each other but then they end up in a typical soft focus lovemaking session. They both have beautiful skin tone. To find out the answer to this, can we ask people? Can we expect them to say that they are aware that it has influenced them in a particular way? Many people are generally keen to point out that they see through such absurd representations. But does this mean that such images, therefore, do not influence the way that they then think about the world?

This is where the difficulty has largely been for audience studies. How do we place the voice of the media into people's lives in a broader sense? One way of doing this is through ethnographic research. This methodology can do this because of its two main assumptions. First, we accept that we have to understand human behaviour not by looking at any one moment but by observing it in different contexts and at different times. Second, we have to assume that people may not have access to the reasons why they do things. Societies generally have available official reasons why we do things which people often use but which may not be their actual motivation. But as we shall see, the reasons that people do give are a valuable source of data so long as we understand them in terms of broader cultural representations. Research which does not do this, I would argue, is not truly ethnographic. In the chapters in this book I will draw this point out. However, I would like to offer an illustration of exactly what I mean right now as it really is the central point which runs through the book and which lies at the heart of the ethnographic gaze.

Consider the following comments made by a woman talking about why she thought it was important to buy a newspaper each day.

> Isa: I think it is important for the children. They should know about what is going on in the world ... it's too easy these days for the kids to just get stuck in front of the TV.

In this first chunk of conversation the woman describes newspapers as a crucial site of formal knowledge in contrast to television which is bad for children. We could accept this as being her point of view and therefore as being the simple reason that she likes to buy a newspaper each day. But several minutes later, the conversation had progressed to thinking about why she chose that particular newspaper. The first reason that she gave was that she tended to agree with the newspaper's politics. But when the researcher asked her to say what that politics was and how that differed from the politics of the local rival newspaper, she responded in the following manner:

> Isa: Well, I don't know. One side makes things up about those, then they make up things as well. In the end you don't know who to believe. Most of the time you just know it's all a load of rubbish. That's why I just don't bother reading sometimes

So, on the one hand, she says that newspapers are an important source of knowledge but on the other she says that they are full of lies. If we were carrying out a survey looking for people's opinions on newspapers and why they buy them, which of the two comments would we accept as her true belief? What we consider in this book is that we should not think about research in this way. We should not think about looking for people's real beliefs. This is why it is always important to reassemble our data into the flow of people's lives. This is what I mean by the ethnographic gaze. There is clearly something much more complex and interesting going on in the way that this woman is talking than her simply giving her opinion. It is this that can give us a much more valuable insight into how people relate to newspapers and why they buy them.

What this example indicates is the way that we must never take individual instances of behaviour in isolation. This is exactly the problem created by questionnaires, interviews and focus groups. What this kind of research does is disassemble bits behaviour from the flow of social life. This is necessary in all research as this allows us to make recordings and to focus our investigation. The art of investigation requires that we do this. But this must be followed by a subsequent act of *reassembly*. The comments made by the woman above are disassembled from the flow of her life and the meanings that make it possible for her. To understand them, and the contradiction that seems apparent, we need to reassemble them in her life and this can only be done through ethnography.

We look more closely at the above data in a later chapter. We will find that both these ways of talking about newspapers are fairly typical in the Spanish setting where the research was carried out. In this particular example the speaker bought a newspaper each day partly out of habit and family tradition which helps to inform her political stance. But when asked to talk about why she does in fact buy, she uses two representations of newspapers which are particularly prevalent in Spain. One of these is that newspapers are an indication of superior cultural status and the other is that newspapers are part of the lies and self-interest of officialdom. Both of these representations of newspapers, along with the idea that television is bad for children, are well-worn conversational manoeuvres, and the woman could utter them with some kind of certainty that they would be widely shared – that they were common sense. These ways of thinking about newspapers and television are part of the arbitrary way that Spanish culture provides people with ways of doing things together – shared meanings about the world. When the woman was asked why she behaved in a particular way, she responded, therefore, by producing the common-sense or commonly accepted reasons available for such explanations. The task for the ethnographer is to look for the way that these explanations influence behaviour and what people are really doing.

The only way to find out how such available explanations influence behaviour is to spend time with people talking about news, stories and the press in general and a whole range of other things so that individual comments can be contextualized. In a later chapter we look at how these ways of talking about the press in Spain add up to some particularly striking contradictions which are characteristic of the Spanish press.

I now want to include a second example to help illustrate the nature of the ethnographic gaze regarding media audiences. The following data is taken from a focus group discussion involving 10-year-old children. The data does not result from an ethnographic study. But we can still think about such data with an ethnographic gaze. By doing this we can think of the speakers not as revealing their opinions on the subject of television but as indicating the cultural tool kit that they have for doing this. By looking at the data in this way we are given an indication of just what we need to look at if we are to develop a deeper understanding of how television does fit into their lives.

In the following example we find a 10-year-old girl talking with a group of other children and an adult about what she watches on the television:

> Nikita: My brother, he sort of watches cartoons like Tom and Jerry and stuff like that. I used to like it when I was young but I don't like it now. I've grown out of it because they sort of keep repeating them and you always know who's going to win.

But shortly afterwards the conversation has moved onto scheduling and how this can sometimes be inconvenient.

> Nikita: The best thing is in the mornings when they put on cartoons and they put them on at six in the morning and my mum says, 'Right, you're not watching until you're totally ready for school.'

In the first example Nikita says that she does not watch cartoons. In the second example she talks about enjoying cartoons. Does she then enjoy cartoons? We could accept her first comments as her real opinion. But by understanding these comments more broadly, connected to Nikita's sense of self and connection to broader cultural meanings, we can think about Nikita as using television, in the first instance, to indicate her maturity. In the second comment she is also indicating a sense of being herself as an active person as she struggles with parents to watch the programmes she likes.

The way that Nikita criticizes cartoons in the first instance is in itself fascinating. To dismiss cartoons because you always know who will win is a strange thing. Most of the classic cartoons involving the Road Runner, Tom and Jerry, Tweetie Pie and Sylvester only have basically one storyline. But for Nikita this is what she associates with what a person might say who has grown out of cartoons. In the second case Nikita is talking about the way that one often has to battle with grown-ups to get to watch one's favourite programmes. Here she talks as the cheeky child who has to out-wit the adult. As we will see in Chapter 13, we can further extend our understanding of these comments by looking more carefully at children's talk and by connecting this to broader discourses in society. What we would then need to do is to look at how the person in fact behaves in different settings. This is what the ethnographic gaze should be all about. We need to see people as social actors who, along with talking about the world in order to make sense of it, are also concerned to find and indicate their own place in that world. And the way that people talk, as we have just seen above, is strongly influenced by representations which are available to them in their culture. The job of the ethnographer is to look at how people communicate about the world and what they do in that world, and think about these in terms of the cultures in which these people find themselves.

A further point that these two sets of data raise is that we cannot understand the audience external to the media texts and the production of those texts. If we want to understand the way that Spanish people talk about news stories, we also need to know about the nature of the Spanish press. In Chapters 10 and 11 I will indicate how a knowledge of the history of the Spanish press and its current nature helps us to understand how people relate to it. I will also show that an ethnography of how Spanish people talk about news texts can also be enriched by understanding the way that the journalists compose them. Similarly, understanding how children talk about television can, as well as looking at the way that the children talk, also mean under-standing what the television they watch looks like. And it also means looking for the ways that the society in which they live understands television and children.

Here I would like to introduce a quotation from Kenneth Burke to help us to visu-alize the way that the mass media are not external to people's lives but are part of culture.

> Imagine that you enter a parlour. You come late. When you arrive, others have long pre-ceded you and they are engaged in a heated discussion, a discussion too heated for them to pause and tell you exactly what it is about. In fact, the discussion had already begun long before any of them got there, so that no one present is qualified to retrace for you all the steps that had gone before. You listen for a while, until you decide that you have caught the tenor of the argument; then you put in your oar. Someone answers; you answer him; another comes to your defence; another aligns against you ... The discussion is interminable. The hour grows late, you must depart, with the discussion still vigorously in progress. (Burke 1944/1971: 110–11)

I think that society can be reasonably viewed as just such a conversation. And we can think of the mass media as being a part of that discussion. Ideas and definitions which comprise the conversation can be thought about as culture. The woman talking about newspapers and the girl talking about cartoons can be thought of as participants in that discussion. Both use agreed-upon definitions and established rules. Both are concerned to find and demonstrate their one place in the discussion. Both speak with an intricate sensitivity to fellow interlocutors. Both are involved in the act of engaging with and creating society.

The mass media in their need to speak to people in particular ways to entertain broadly, to draw people in quickly, are a voice of a particular kind in that conversation. In order to understand this voice and the way that people relate to it, we need to comprehend it in the context of that broader discussion, as its imagery and messages are understood by people who are involved in that discussion and importantly as these people are trying to find meaning and a place for themselves in that discussion. This way of looking at society is what lies at the heart of the ethnographic gaze. Throughout this book I hope to demonstrate just what implications this has for the way that we need to investigate the mass media as part of social life.

PART I

Ethnography

Observing people in culture

In this Part I will look at how ethnography has been used in different disciplines and how it emerged as a solution to understanding media audiences. In this part I point out the most important features of ethnographic research.

Chapter 1 looks at the reason that ethnography was used in anthropology, how it was a way of understanding social practices which otherwise seemed bizarre. I show how media studies, like anthropology, also needs to think about behaviour as being understandable in terms of people using culture to think about and act in the world. Chapter 2 spells out how the ethnographer should view culture. Here we take a closer look at the nature of the cultural tool kit that allows people to negotiate social life. It is this that the ethnographer needs to become aware of in order to understand how the world works for the people that they study. The third chapter looks at the use of ethnography in an urban setting by the Chicago School in the early part of the twentieth century. This body of research is largely forgotten now but it allows us to see how important it is to understand behaviour, for which we might already have explanations in our society, in a completely different light. This can be done if we are prepared to look at what this means for the people actually living out those lives. In Chapter 4 I discuss how researchers have looked at media audiences and how ethnography came to be seen as one way to look at how the mass media really fitted into people's lives. In Chapter 5 I assess ethnography against some of the criteria commonly used to evaluate research methodologies.

Ethnography in anthropology

From magic to the media

This chapter looks at the emergence of ethnography as a research approach. One good way to begin to develop an understanding of the spirit of ethnography is to look at how the methodology was developed in anthropology. This allows us to see that ethnography, more than being any specific set of procedures, is a way of thinking about human behaviour. In anthropology the methodology was employed to understand cultural practices which seemed incomprehensible to those from the West who first encountered them. Ethnography was a way of understanding how these behaviours were meaningful to the people in those cultures.

I will show how this way of thinking about and analysing human behaviour can equally be applied to the study, for example, of what people do with television. The reader might initially wonder how the beliefs in magic and sorcery that we will examine in this chapter can be likened to watching television. This will become clear as we progress. I can begin to show the similarity by returning to the image of society as a discussion that we considered at the end of the Introduction. We can think of the belief in magic as being one of the taken-for-granted, commonly accepted ground rules in the discussion in one particular society. When a speaker arrives in the discussion these ground rules will seem self-evident. They will appear to naturally reflect the nature of the world. There will be important speakers in the discussion, like sorcerers, who will be reminding each of the participants of the crucial importance of following certain practices. We can also think of television as being one voice in a different discussion. This voice will draw upon certain commonly held assumptions in that society about the way the world works. And, as with sorcery, the key to understanding how people relate to television is to see it in the context of how people live out their lives with shared meanings.

I suggested in the Introduction that ethnography is very much like 'hanging out' with people in the places that they carry out their affairs. This is certainly one important feature of what has been thought of as ethnography in anthropology. Anthropologists who travelled to study other cultures early in the twentieth century began to realize that something more systematic was needed to help get away from the kind of arrogant ethnocentric assumptions that were being made by many explorers and missionaries. One means of doing this was to actually live with people and observe their way of life rather than just catching a glimpse of the surface. The approach that they came up with at the time was underpinned by a philosophy of non-judgementalism and the acceptance of other ways of doing things as being reasonable if understood in the context that they happen. Put simply, this meant discarding the idea that there was a morally correct method of doing things, or even that there could be superior ways of conducting oneself. This was a considerable step considering the prevailing attitudes of the time which emphasized progress, rationality and truth.

Ethnography in anthropology: primitive beliefs understood in context

When people think of anthropology they generally think of the anthropologist in some exotic location explaining the peculiar yet fascinating ways of the local inhabitants. This is basically a fair representation of what anthropology is. The anthropologist in this case is doing ethnography. But it is the philosophy that underpins this approach that may not be so easy to perceive. To grasp precisely what that entails we need to take a closer look at what that anthropologist is doing. To understand this, it is best to start by thinking about just how they came to be doing that.

The birth of anthropology and considering the view of the primitive

Anthropology started out in Britain as missionaries and travellers began to record their encounters with the populations of the colonies. These populations were viewed as primitive people with bizarre and often disturbing beliefs and customs. There were dark tales of cannibalism, head-hunting, witchcraft and sorcery, scandalous immorality in the form of sexual behaviour and religious practice. There was a big market back home for accounts of these people which would intrigue, astonish and repulse. This market was made up of a more general public and by scholars who wanted to theorize about the nature of humans and society. What both groups had in common was a conviction that the views of their own culture were right and even inevitable. Other ways were inferior and primitive. This was based on the context of a belief in the triumph of rationality, science and systematically acquired knowledge. Those who gathered information about these exotic people became known as ethnographers. There was no methodology associated with this. The term simply described those who catalogued and recorded the beliefs and practices of primitives.

The intellectual environment at the time was one which saw the popularity of evolutionism in biology. On the one hand, intellectuals who studied societies wanted in on the respectability of the natural sciences, with their rigour, objectivity and discovered laws. Theorists such as Comte (1854) wanted to develop a 'science of man' which would be based on these characteristics and to discover the underlying principles of society. On the other hand, archaeological evidence found in Europe suggested that the Europeans were once savages themselves. This fuelled the idea that societies, like organisms in nature, evolved from the primitive and basic to the complex and sophisticated. Around the end of the nineteenth century theorists began to think that gaps in the archaeological evidence could be filled using information about the nature of non-European primitive societies. This was known as the comparative method. Basically it was reckoned that life in savage societies found in the colonies must have been very much like life had been in the barbaric and savage European societies that had become extinct.

The search for evidence of the evolution of societies led anthropology to come into its own. One example of a scholarly work of this period was E.B. Tylor's *Primitive Culture: Researches into the Development of Mythology, Philosophy, Religion, Art and Custom*, published in 1871. This volume compared practices of different societies to Victorian English society. Such authors thought that the aim of such work was to reconstruct the progress made from simple to complex in terms of politics, religion and technology. James Frazer (1922) was another of these classic armchair theorists who used data collected by missionaries and travellers. His aim was to catalogue cultures and compare them. Like Tylor, he looked for common phases, stages and types. The focus was not on any of these cultures in their own right but in terms of comparison to their own Northern European culture. Some theorists became concerned about the nature of the data being collected, that material was only collected which was convenient for comparison, resulting in much being ignored.

Anthropologists working on both sides of the Atlantic at the end of the nineteenth century began to challenge the view of the savage and the view of societies being primitive versions of our own. In the USA, the visionary Franz Boas (1921) rejected the ideas of the evolutionists. He believed that cultures should be studied in their own right. He did not rule out the idea of a general theory of culture but thought that first we must learn to study the life and history of individual cultures.

Boas decided to study one particular culture. He chose the people of the North Pacific, both in North America and in the northern region of Asia. He had observed that there were some similarities between the cultures of the two societies and he set out to find out whether they had previously been in contact. After spending time with people of the two groups he concluded that there had, in the past, been contact between the two cultures. Both the Indians of British Columbia and the East Siberians shared a number of myths, for example, regarding creation involving a great spread of water and a beetle and a spider who produced the land. After plotting how the myth changed slightly in different areas, he came up with the idea of diffusion. By this he meant how cultural traits can be spread to other cultures. He described the way that these traits would then become integrated into the host culture, possibly with some modification, to fit with local cultural requirements. The cultural whole is thus always changing but is always coherent.

One new thing in Boas' approach was its cultural and moral relativism. This meant considering each culture not in terms of how it compares with others but in itself.

In Boas' view we cannot understand a culture by simply looking at how it relates to our own. We need to understand how it came about historically and how it forms a coherent whole. In this way we might develop a sense of how a person in that culture lives out their life. In Chapter 3 we will see that this non-judgementalism and ability to see social behaviour in its own right without comparison are equally important in the context of ethnography in an urban setting. If we want to understand gangland violence, for example, we need to look at it on its own terms. In our own contemporary Western societies discussion about such criminal behaviour is generally undertaken through the value system of the more powerful groups which simply see it as wrong and immoral. Like the early colonial travellers such commentators impose their own perception of the world. In Chapter 4 Thrasher (1927) shows how gangland must be seen as people's response to a particular kind of social situation. It must be understood as a way of life that has become meaningful to a particular group of people. Such a way of thinking about the social world is crucial for the ethnographic gaze. When we look at mass media audiences we need to be mindful of the way that people operate in and through culture. The ethnographer needs to create a picture of the cultural tool kit through which people accomplish everyday life if we are to understand any instance of behaviour.

The students of Boas later developed his theories to include a view of culture as an integrated system. For example, Ruth Benedict in *Patterns of Culture* (1934), studying two groups of American Indians, described how differences in culture can be explained not just through history but also in the way that cultures may involve a particular set of temperaments. These temperaments will influence the kinds of cultural practices that will become assimilated, and how they become modified. This view of other cultures was radically different from that of the nineteenth-century evolutionists.

On the other side of the Atlantic the model for the anthropological fieldwork was being formulated. Boas had no formulated methods. He thought that the anthropologist should use any means to gather information. While he helped to establish anthropology in the universities, he offered no systematic plan by which it should be done. In Britain the Polish anthropologist Bronislaw Malinowski was busily and loudly condemning anthropologists who had compared contemporary cultures to earlier versions of their own, or where they had looked at parts of cultures that were irrational or incongruent. Malinowski urged that societies be studied on their own terms. This did not mean looking only at how they arrived at certain practices and beliefs, but finding out what these meant for the people who held them. In the Introduction to *Argonauts of the Western Pacific* (1922) he said that the job of the anthropologist was to grasp how the native saw the world. The anthropologist should come to see the world through the eyes of the people that they studied. Where writers such as Frazer and Tylor had lumped together the practices of different cultures without reference to context, Malinowski argued that the focus should be on the study and understanding of one society. The emphasis was on the contemporary workings of that society and how its institutions function as a whole.

Malinowski's view of society as a whole, and understanding the world as the person in that society sees it, is exactly the way that we will look at media audiences in later chapters. The idea of seeing the native's view of world can equally be applied to any culture. But what is needed for this is to make human behaviour problematic. This was not an issue for Malinowski as he looked at the belief in magic in the Trobriand Islands. But when we look at a child talking about television in London or New York it is easy to think that what they say and how they think that things work are something natural. But it is important to view this as being just as arbitrary as the world view of the Trobriand Islanders regarding magic.

Malinowski's methodology

Malinowski carried out research in the Western Pacific during the First World War. The research he carried out was very significant, marking a transformation in the notion of ethnography. Like Boas, he thought it crucial to spend a period of residence with the group under study and he emphasized the need to live as one of these people in order to become immersed in their everyday lives. This method became known as 'participant observation'. Malinowski insisted that the anthropologist should learn the language of the subject group, involve themselves in the ordinary and trivial details of everyday life and come to feel what these mean to the people, systematically recording every detail. And only this level of immersion would encourage informants to be trusting and open. Only in this way can the anthropologist hope to develop a sense of everyday meanings.

Where Malinowski differed from Boas was in his firm stance that societies should be thought of and studied as functioning wholes. All practices in that society should be considered in terms of the way they contribute to the functioning of that society and in terms of the way that they help meet the physical and psychological requirements of its members. Under no circumstances should any small detail of behaviour be considered in isolation. Malinowski believed that the evolutionist approaches had made this mistake. There could be no possibility of understanding social phenomena if the ethnographer was only looking for features of the society under examination which would allow some comment upon their own society. Good fieldwork means connecting behaviours to the wider context. That involves looking at the way that society worked and at what practices meant to the inhabitants. Through this process behaviours that might have seemed bizarre will come to be understood as being perfectly comprehensible. And this was the new model for ethnographic fieldwork.

Malinowski's model for fieldwork looked something like this: the anthropologist would arrive in the field. Their first task would be to learn the language. Of course this would take a while. But until they had done this it will be difficult to grasp the meanings of everyday interactions or understand the concepts used to understand the world. This is important as they may be very different to their own. The ethnographer will then develop relationships with informants who will help them to gain access to the events and behaviours taking place. It is important, however, that the ethnographer learns the native language so that they can have first-hand access to what is going on. Informants may tend to give idealized accounts.

In our own culture the reasons we give for a particular behaviour may be an 'official' reason. By this I mean reasons which are widely accepted as the reasons that things happen. These may have little to do with what we actually do or the real reasons that we do things. As Malinowski said, these might be idealized accounts. For example, if someone visited my society for the first time and asked me why I bought a particular pair of jeans I might say that I did so since they look good and reflect my individual taste. A closer look at jeans buying in my culture, however, would reveal something different. It would be found that my proclaimed individual desire was tied up with a complex of images regarding fashion and the use of cultural representations of masculinity, individuality and adventure in related advertising campaigns for the jeans. These representations may themselves relate to current images in film or popular music. But in my culture it is not a legitimate reason to say that I buy jeans because of advertising imagery. We have no vocabulary in our everyday life to express how we assemble our identities is interrelated with the mass media in this way. In fact, in everyday life, and in the fashion industry, it is the rhetoric of individuality that is the very discourse that is often used to market products.

Another example of an official idealized account would be if you were told by one of your friends that their 20-year-old son wanted to travel the world in order to have experiences and find themselves. Such a statement would have to be understood in the context of a Western mythology about travel versus tourism, freedom/non-conformity, identity and self-discovery. The whole of the Western idea of travel can be traced to the same Enlightenment movement which saw the emergence of anthropology.

These two examples help us to see the importance of Malinowski's idea that any behaviour or social phenomenon must be understood in its social context. To understand jeans buying or 'travelling' we must locate it in its social context. Likewise, if I hear a person say that they do not like to watch soap operas because this genre of programming is superficial and undemanding, saying that they prefer documentaries, we must understand these comments in the context of wider cultural meanings. Soap operas are often associated with low intellect and superficial entertainment. In contrast, documentaries are associated with informing and with education. We might find upon further ethnographic study, as did Tulloch (1989), that this person is able to draw on this commonly held distinction between high and low culture in order to present themselves in a particular manner. When they make this distinction to the researcher, they will assume that this is a widely held common-sense distinction that will simply be understood by others.

Malinowski suggested that while the ethnographer was learning the language they should pass the time making maps of the area, plans of the local community, buildings, record material goods, clothing, livestock and food. Once the ethnographer became integrated into the community they would be making detailed notes on everything they observed. At this point they would not make generalizations and it would be crucial not to have a preconceived theory as this might mean that certain details were not recorded.

As regards a study of media audiences, the researcher might not find themselves in a position where they are learning a language and therefore in need of filling in time. But Malinowski's point about mapping is still relevant, although this would be more in the sense of taking notes about early observations on routines and interactions. Sometimes these first observations can be the most interesting as the ethnographer is still unconnected to the people they are studying.

This account of ethnographic procedure is about as specific as it gets in anthropology. In a nutshell, it is the detailed and systematic study of a culture through participation in its everyday occurrences and observation of even the finest detail. This should be done without judgement and the ethnographer should learn to see the world through the eyes of that culture. By adopting this approach any behaviour or social phenomenon will become comprehensible as it is meaningful to that culture's members. And that behaviour or social phenomenon will make sense as we see the way that it relates to other aspects of that society.

It might still be difficult to see how relevant all this is to understanding media audiences. Let us address this by looking at Malinowski's points individually. First, we have the process of the systematic study through participation. Arguably this is the only way that we can understand how people use the mass media. In later chapters we look at cases where researchers have used such an approach to study the mass media. Fishman (1980) followed journalists as they went about news collecting. He found that, rather than working as investigative reporters, the journalists relied on institutions such as the courts and the police. These agencies provided a steady predictable flow of material that could be thought of as newsworthy. Journalists simply did not recognize incidents that fell outside of the institutional processing of these institutions. Fishman uses his observations to explain why certain news events, such as crime waves, may not in fact have any relationship to what is happening on the streets or in current crime statistics. The observations he makes and the conclusions he is able to draw are a result of the methods he used. It is difficult to imagine that the same results could have been produced through a questionnaire survey or through a focus group study. There are two reasons for this: first, the researcher might not have expected these findings and therefore would not have been able to design a questionnaire capable of generating the right insights. Second, the journalists may not have been directly conscious of the way that they carried out their work and the kind of values that they used to assess news.

Next Malinowski recommended that we make observations of the finest details of social life. In Chapter 6 we look at Lull's (1990) investigation of watching television in the home. By spending time with families in their homes Lull was able to challenge the way that we had commonly imagined the act of watching television. He found that people would not watch television passively but would argue with it, deride presenters, criticize scripts. His team found that for many families the television was the principal site of interaction. Rather than being a mode of social isolation, viewing was often a way of sharing. The television was also used as a structuring device for the daily activities. These conclusions were made by recording all the details of conversations, status of family members and other features of daily routines.

The last of Malinowski's points was that of seeing the world through the eyes of that culture. This might not seem relevant here. We might have a tendency to think about the mass media in terms of something that is culture-neutral, that reflects the world as it is. But this is where we need to think about the way that the mass media use the kinds of definitions of love and relationships that we have previously discussed. Representations of relationships which are expressed rapidly through soft lovemaking sessions are not culture-neutral. From Malinowski's point of view we would need to draw out the nature of such representations, and find out how these relate to the way that people in general both think and act. Similarly, the way that the mass media represent masculinity and femininity is not something that simply reflects the natural state of the world. Adverts must draw on particular imagery in order to draw us towards a product. We can all now think of the absurdity and constructedness of the imagery of the macho Marlboro man and other hairy-chested medallion men who appeared in adverts in the 1970s, but we will be less aware of the constructedness of current imagery. But to what extent does this imagery, which now blasts us continually, fit into our everyday sense of the world? To what extent does this fit into the life of the young drunken aggressive man in the bar?

Media researchers, particularly in the 1970s, looked at the way that the news media used certain representations of society, for example, regarding industrial disputes (Glasgow University Media Group 1976). These researchers argued that the news was biased towards official accounts of events and emphasized the harm caused to society, ignoring the actual issues of the dispute. But it is difficult to know how these representations then go on to take their place in people's cultural frameworks of reference unless we spend time with them, unless we can see the world through the eyes of specific people.

Understanding the strange in social context

I would now like to look at two examples of where anthropologists have used ethnography to help us to understand social practices which might seem strange or irrational to the Western cultures by locating them in their broader cultural meanings and practices. The first of these is Malinowski's fascinating study of magic and sorcery in the Trobriand Islands. The second is Herdt's highly challenging look at masculinity in the Sambia. As I have suggested above, ethnography, wherever it is carried out, should take the approach of making everyday life problematic. That means we should never assume that there is anything natural or self-evident in the way that people understand and behave in the world.

Magic in the Trobriand Islands

In his fieldwork in the Trobriand Islands Malinowski came across beliefs in magic. Earlier evolutionists would have viewed such beliefs as primitive and irrational. But, by locating these beliefs in the context of Trobriand culture as a whole, and by trying to understand these beliefs from the point of view of the people he was studying, Malinowski showed that this was not the case.

The Trobrianders lived in small communities on the kind of islands that Western cultures might commonly associate with paradise. The islands lie in Melanesia in the Western Pacific. The islanders lived by fishing and cultivating gardens where the principal produce is yams. They were expert canoe builders which they would use for both fishing and for travel to other islands to trade shells, pottery and baskets. There were many fascinating aspects of Trobriand life that Malinowski explained by showing how they fitted in with the broader Trobriand culture and by showing what these things actually meant to the islanders. One of these things was the belief in magic. This is something that earlier observers had tended to explain as being indicative of irrationality and the primitive mind at work. Malinowski wanted to show how the Trobrianders understood magic.

Malinowski's ethnography

Malinowski spent two years living in the Trobriand Islands. He learned the language, lived with the people and documented everything he saw. In Trobriand life that Malinowski described about half of an islander's time was spent in the gardens. This involves planting, weeding and generally caring for the crops. But when talking about gardening, one of the main topics that the Trobrianders would talk about was magic. Magic was needed or else there could not be a successful yield. In fact, no part of the gardening process could properly happen without the correct spells being cast. While each person tended to the labours needed to maintain their own garden, the magic was taken care of by the garden magician, who next to the chief and sorcerer, was the most important person in the village. The magician would carry out a series of spells and rituals over the garden which would accompany all the labour processes of planting and caring for the crops. All parts of the gardening process, from planting through to cutting, burning and weeding required the correct magical accompaniment. The magician also helped the plants to sprout, grow high and to produce a good harvest. He would also make sure that all of the work was done properly and at the right time.

Earlier colonial travellers had thought about such practices in terms of them being irrational and as being evidence of the thought processes of more primitive peoples. Malinowski tried to understand such practices from the Trobrianders' point of view and in the context of the culture as a whole. On the one hand, Malinowski argued, magic was good for the gardens in terms of the way it regulated and systematized gardening practices. It made the gardeners carry out tasks correctly and at the appropriate time. This account alone would be acceptable if we were looking for a rational model. However, on the other hand, Malinowski observed, magic also wasted a lot of time, hampering labour with all its taboos and rituals. In this sense we might conclude that the whole practice was irrational. We might even assume that the Trobrianders were simply lazy and preferred to rely on magic.

Malinowski was keen to point out that the Trobriand gardeners were not lazy, but worked hard, systematically and purposefully. This included fence maintenance, caring for plants and weeding. There was also competition as to who could produce the greatest yield. Good gardeners were respected and had status. Gardens and produce were often compared and the chief would even declare competitions on years of good harvest. Additionally, it was important for social prestige to give away what was produced, especially to the chief, and by convention to the in-laws. Malinowski was keen to point out that these were not people who lived hand-to-mouth but were producers with highly complex motives of a social nature.

Malinowski emphasized that the Trobrianders were aware that magic alone could not ensure a good harvest, but that magic helped. This is not unlike the way that a football coach might decide that his players should keep wearing the same kit during a winning streak. He knows his team also needs to train hard, be organized and have good players, but he knows that sometimes they have off days. Form is an elusive thing. So we might think about the kit as a rite which helps him to feel that he controls the mysterious forces that seem to affect such things as luck and form. In the Trobriands this is brought out by the magic and ritual carried out on newly built canoes which were used for fishing and for trading. The Trobrianders, Malinowski said, were fine canoe builders. Again, magic and rites accompanied all parts of the canoe building process from the tree felling to cutting and carving and lashing the parts together. These rites chased away wood sprites that might have had a malevolent influence. These were generally invisible although some people did see them. They could cause bad wood, sickness and could even steal food. As in the case of the gardens, the Trobrianders knew that skill and knowledge made the best canoes. But the magic helped to protect them from the dangers of the sea. It helped them to feel in control of aspects of something over which otherwise they had no control. Even the best canoes could sink leaving their occupants to drown. The Trobrianders would have known that a canoe was smashed by a storm but thought that magic could help prevent that happening. In a later study of

Azande witchcraft by Evans-Pritchard (1937), it was argued that people know why things happen, for example, a house might fall over because it has been eaten away by termites, but they will use magic to explain why it happened to a particular house when someone was sitting under it. Likewise, why is it that a person should tread on a sharp stone in a field, when they might have stepped anywhere else in that field? We have all felt that sense of injustice. For the Zande it would be the work of a sorcerer.

As humans we seem to need to have a sense that the world is ordered and that we can understand what is going on. But we inhabit a world that is full of unforeseen things, dangers, misery, and injustices. So it is helpful if we have beliefs about the world that help us to deal with this. Basically, we need what Anthony Giddens once called 'ontological security'. All societies will have a belief system which does this. It will allow the world to make sense. This belief system does not need to actually tell us the truth about the world and need not be consistent. This system might be magic or it might be science. We will use the ideas from these systems to make us feel as if the world is a safer place in which to live.

The development of masculinity in Papua New Guinea

I would now like to look at an ethnographic study carried out by the anthropologist G.H. Herdt (published much more recently than Malinowski's work) in *The Guardians of the Flutes: Idioms of Masculinity* (1987). This particular example is particularly challenging for a Western reader as it deals with a subject that touches on several of our taboo areas, which itself reveals a lot about our own culture. The example therefore reminds us how useless our own frames of reference can be when trying to understand the social behaviour or others. In the Foreword to Herdt's book, LeVine says that this ethnography is one of those that challenges the taken-for-granted assumptions that we hold in our own society about human development. In this way it challenges us to re-evaluate the basic assumptions that we hold regarding what is normal for humans in general.

The Guardians of the Flutes tells us about a culture where boys ingest the semen of their elders. What we in the West would think of as a homosexual practice is thus encouraged. These practices and beliefs were widely known about by those who had worked in New Guinea, and have since been acknowledged in around 30 other societies, but Herdt was the first to carry out an intensive study. From a Western perspective the practices seem abhorrent and unnatural. In our own societies, homosexual practices are by no means widely accepted, although this has changed considerably over the past couple of decades. But, more powerfully, the idea of children being involved in sexual activities goes against our whole ethos of children as innocent and asexual (even though this was challenged long ago as in the writings of Freud). It is hard for the Western reader to see Herdt's book as anything other than a tale of child abuse and an instance of enforced homosexuality.

In the Western model of sexual development the official view seems to be that children should not be exposed to homosexuality as this will lead them to be homosexuals. This is often embodied in the form of legislation. It was such a belief that led the British government to pass a law in the 1980s that prohibited homosexuality being mentioned in schools. But for the Sambia this behaviour was natural, necessary and did not lead to lifelong homosexuality. LeVine suggests that this is a basic challenge to our developmental ideas of gender identity (1987, p. x).

Herdt's study is a particularly good way to look at the idea of ethnography and to visualize how culture lies at the root of even our most fundamental behaviours. This case challenges us to accept that to comprehend phenomena, even sexual behaviour, we need to discard the notion that anything is natural or inevitable. Even if the practices that Herdt studies appear morally wrong, they compel us to ask why they are seen as natural by those who live by them. This applies equally to behaviour with which we are more familiar. Why does the young man in the bar think that being drunk and aggressive every Friday evening is a natural and desirable state of affairs? An ethnographic study might reveal that his society has a set of definitions about masculinity that interact with a sense of lack of self-worth, itself dictated by his culture, which results in his behaviour seeming reasonable to him.

In the Introduction I looked briefly at the example of a woman talking about her decision to buy a newspaper each day. What she said about newspapers and what they meant were contradictory. At one moment she said that newspapers were an important source of information for children to have around the house and then she dismissed all news as lies. But both of these reasons seemed real enough to her as she expressed them to the researcher. They will have this appearance as they are widely held ideas in her culture. Sociologists who have studied news, such as Fishman (1980), whose work we look at in Chapter 7, have demonstrated that news is a social product and that it to some degree is very different from the way we widely perceive it in our society. Yet this woman talks about news as being about informing and high culture. This is even though she later said that she never in fact read the newspaper.

These representations of news are just one part of the repertoire of cultural representations, our cultural tool kit, through which this woman is able to think about the world and find her place in it. Such representations as these are not experienced as arbitrary or just as constructs. They are thought of as natural and simply as the way the world is. In the same way the Sambia, and people in the Western world, have cultural representations which inform us about sexuality.

The Sambia way to become a man

Basically, the Sambia believed that a boy must be orally inseminated to become masculine. But why is this so? Can we say that this is simply irrational? And is such a belief any less rational than the means by which a man can be a man and carry out masculinity in the West? Are we in the West convinced that it is enough just to be biologically male for a person to be masculine? The fact is that we are not. A whole range of behaviours indicate what it is to be masculine. One of these might be drinking heavily in a bar.

Herdt lived with the Sambia for two years, gradually becoming more and more accepted and trusted. The Sambia lived in forested mountains at about 3,500 to 5,500 feet. They were hunters and horticulturalists and cultivated individual or communal gardens where they grew mainly sweet potatoes, still using some traditional stone tools alongside metal ones which had arrived in the 1960s. The Sambia numbered about 2,000 and lived in six groups. At the end of the 1980s there was still no road access to the area due to difficult terrain. The people lived in nuclear families in huts which were always formed in lines for defensive purposes. The hut was built by the man once he married when he left the men's house where he previously lived. In this hut would live the man, his wife and children, although the women would not remain there during menstruation or childbirth. Girls lived with their parents until marriage. The Sambia clans owned tracts of land which was their primary hunting territory. They had little material culture, perhaps, Herdt says, because they were constantly at war and needed to be mobile. Much of male culture was oriented towards warfare.

The women usually tended the gardens while the men hunted in the forest where they themselves could be hunted by forest spirits. The women did not often go there and it was the place where masculine rituals began. Boys began their childhood in the garden activities but later joined the realms of warriorhood in the forest. In the forest the Sambia were attentive to the life-giving forces of fluids. They were aware of the way that cutting fluids from a tree allowed it to be later cut as good fire-wood. The fluid seemed to be the life-force of the tree. Plants and the world around them were alive with these kinds of references.

For a boy to become a man and a warrior he had to undergo two rituals, both of which were closely connected to life-giving fluids. First, the boy started with nose-bleeding. This was to purge the boys of contact with the mothers. It mainly served the purpose of eliminating menstrual blood – a form of pollution that could reduce a man's masculinity and potential as a hunter and a warrior. Even married men carried this out following their wives' menstruation. This was achieved by pushing sharp grass up the nose. It was at first shocking and painful for young boys. When the boys were first bled in this way it would be accompanied by a war cry by the other men. Herdt says that this also helped to purge the boys of bad talk which can be another form of contamination from the women. The elders would often use bleeding as a threat by reminding the boys that it was the necessary treatment for disrespectful talk.

The proof of what could happen if boys did not have nose-bleeds was the women themselves. This was thought to make women bad reasoners. Nose bleeding was also associated with a general toughening up of the male as a warrior and was talked about in terms of becoming familiar with the blood of the gruesome battles in which they would take part.

The second of the fluid rituals was semen ingestion. Semen eating was important for a male to be strong and big. A small weak man would be evidence of infrequent consumption. Acts of weakness and misfortune would be attributed to lack of semen. Like the nose bleeding, this ritual was carried out in special men's camps away from the main village. They would be done in a secret house, usually at night. Just as a tree's sap is its life-force, and menstrual blood was associated with femininity, so semen was thought to give masculinity. Since semen is something that a male is not born with, he must develop through ingestion of semen. Semen was thought to be the male version of breast milk. The semen would generally be taken from older boys who, when married, would cease to be involved in giving semen. Once they were married and had performed coitus they were not to put their penis into the mouth of another male as this would have been dangerous and polluting. A young man would not want to be fellated too often as this would deplete his semen and reduce his masculinity. There were other taboos governing the fellatio. It could not, for example, be carried out by a biological family member.

Herdt emphasized that it is important to be mindful that for the Sambia boy he was not performing a homosexual act, as the younger boy who requires the semen is not yet a man. And, while this giving of semen is a life-giving act in the same way as sexual intercourse, it is not thought of as sex in the same way.

Boys would spend time performing fellatio on a daily basis. The elders would teach the younger boys that semen was absolutely vital and that it should be consumed regularly as biological maleness and the maintenance of masculinity depended upon it. Once they reached puberty then the boys themselves would provide semen for the younger boys. At the same time the boys had to avoid women, in particular, menstrual blood could even be lethal.

From a Western point of view what we might think of as heterosexual behaviour only emerged much later once the male had acquired masculinity. Before this the young men from about the age of seven would spend about ten to fifteen years participating in the homosexual fellatio activities. But after this time all of the Sambia men would become exclusively heterosexual.

All this is challenging for a Western reader. Paedophile behaviour is often high on the media and politic agenda. But just because these practices do not fit in with our model of sexual morality and gender identity development, can we then simply dismiss them within our own model? If they do make sense to people, and form part of wider cultural practices, then we need to understand why this is so. In Western culture it is often the case that masculinity is associated with rituals of aggression and competition. In both British and American culture this might be connected to the amount of alcohol that a person can drink in one session. It might mean vigorously supporting a local football team. It will mean not wearing particular clothes. If a man walked into a local bar wearing a mini-skirt and high heels he might attract the wrath of some of the other drinkers in the bar. This is because this seems to challenge our idea of masculinity. Such things are constructed in cultures in different ways.

As with magic in the Trobriand Islands, we need to understand semen ingestion among Sambia men as it is meaningful in the broader context of cultural beliefs and practices and how it is meaningful to the Sambia themselves. In the picture that Herdt creates we must understand that for the Sambia boy he would simply never be masculine, and therefore a real man, if he did not both make his nose bleed and ingest semen. This process of being a man will have seemed natural and inevitable to the Sambia boy as it formed part of his culture's explanation for what masculinity was all about. These beliefs would gain further credibility as they were tightly interwoven with other ideas about the life-giving properties of liquids and the way of life of a warrior.

The ethnographic gaze in media studies

While in later chapters I will be emphasizing the need to be sensitive to the ethnographic moment, I think that the anthropological research we have looked at in this chapter provides an excellent introduction to the idea of doing ethnography in media research. Imagine that we arrived in America from one of the cultures which the early colonial travellers had come across. We knew nothing of life in America. We were invited to stay in someone's house. When we arrived there were two people sat watching TV. On the screen is a movie. It is a detective thriller. The main characters are very attractive and always wear great clothes. The main male protagonist meets a female. They go for a meal. They have said very little to each other but the scene cuts to show them having sex in a gently lit room. They are sensual and the sex is perfect and abandoned. This seems to defy all of your experiences of real life. Since you have never seen anything like this before, what would you need to know to understand what is going on? How has such a representation of human love come about and why do the viewers accept this?

To understand what all this means we would need, as Malinowski said, to understand things about the institutions in that society. In this case we would need to know things about the film industry and television. We would have to know things about the nature of ideas and mythology about relationships in that culture. We would also have to understand how television imagery connects to other representations in people's lives. Would these kinds of representations of love make people aspire to a particular kind of relationship? Would it mean that their sense of what relationships should be like would be informed by such images? According to Malinowski, we could not simply ask these people about this but would need to study the minutiae of everyday life to see how these people talk about and think about relationships. How do they talk about them and how does this relate to the different discourses in society about relationships? As Malinowski said, we need to find out how reality hangs together for these people. In other words, we must discuss the natives' vision of their world. This would apply to how people relate to the reality portrayed in the news, in fashion magazines, tourist brochures, soap operas, documentaries, etc. Let us now look at this in later chapters.

2 How the ethnographer should view culture

In the last chapter we looked at the way that anthropologists came to understand things that puzzled them in other cultures by looking at how people living in those cultures understood the world. Through ethnography researchers could look at how people behaved in all the different settings that they found themselves in each day. This meant that behaviour that seemed strange or puzzling when viewed in isolation could seem reasonable and natural when located in the broader context. In our own culture, however, we tend to take the explanations that people give for what they do very much for granted. They seem natural, self-evident and not worthy of further examination. Let us consider an example regarding the mass media. I might ask you if you prefer theatre or cinema. You might answer that you prefer theatre. When asked for a reason, you might say that it is because it is more challenging and intellectually demanding than cinema. Yet it might turn out that you hardly ever go to the theatre. In Western culture we make certain distinctions between high and low culture. Theatre is seen as high culture, even though this has not always been the case. Theatre is associated with classics in literature and literature is itself also associated with higher intellectual functions. We find it very difficult, however, to associate main-stream cinema with creativity and intelligence. This is because it is seen as being for a mass audience and is produced on an industrial scale. This sits uneasily with our idea of creativity in Western culture. Interestingly, though, such movies can later become classics depending upon the career of the director. Frank Capra's *It's A Wonderful Life* (1946), now considered a classic, was once a critical and box office failure, as was Orson Welles' *Citizen Kane* (1941), now thought to be a work of genius. In these two cases the idea of the single *auteur* director sits more comfortably with our idea of the individual subjectivity being the origin of creativity. When a person says that they prefer theatre they are drawing on this whole cultural baggage of what can be seen as high culture, the mythology of creativity, and the way that this allows us to think about ourselves. Likewise, a person may pride themselves on the fact that they dislike theatre. In this way they can position themselves against what they see as elite views even if they have no experience of theatre. Bourdieu (1984) in his book *Distinction* emphasizes the fact that we should not consider taste as individual. He was interested in the way that different social groups tend to have different clusters of tastes and cultural judgements. But he was more interested in the way that these different groups will find themselves in different positions to make their tastes appear more worthwhile and valuable. Such tastes can be used to make social distinctions allowing these groups to present themselves as being superior in terms of intellectual judgement. For example, middle-class people will be more likely to associate themselves with higher cultural tastes. This is why they will be keen to criticize the value of watching soaps. They will tend to distance themselves from mass entertainment forms. This will allow them to position themselves in a particular way in society by aligning themselves alongside artistic sensibilities. Of course this will appear natural to people in this society as they will have been socialized in these values.

The explanations given by these people for their behaviour are based on meanings that are not inevitable or natural explanations of the world but are completely arbitrary. Without knowledge of these, it would simply not be possible to live in that society. We would not be able to do and say culturally appropriate things. In each case the person can make such utterances with a confidence that others will share in these meanings. One of the most important steps in ethnography is learning to think about all behaviour as being accomplished through culturally accepted meanings. It is these that we must look for and systematically record. From the above example we can see that it would be possible to look at the cultural framework available to talk about and understand theatre or cinema.

From birth we learn an arbitrary tool kit of interpretations and rules. These are not written rules but largely those that take the form of taken-for-granted shared notions which are generally hidden from the people who live by them. These cultural interpretations appear simply as how things are. These notions will inform how we think of things like marriage, love, mental processes, careers and gender relations. These will interweave with the meanings that are produced by the mass media and the ways that we relate to them.

In this chapter I will look more closely at the nature of the cultural tool kit through which the world becomes meaningful to us. Being mindful of the nature of this tool kit and how it is the organizing basis for the way that humans interact with the world and each other is a crucial part of the ethnographic gaze.

When thinking of the way that people use this cultural tool kit we must be aware, however, that people are not cultural robots. People act with a vivid sensitivity to setting and to other people. We are all concerned to navigate our own place in the social worlds that we live in as we align ourselves alongside different ideas allowing us to indicate the kind of person that we are. Since settings differ and may not always be predictable, we must be able to improvise with our tool kit, picking bits up and dropping others according to the requirements of the moment. Life is not always predictable and culture must be able to deal with this, although culture itself allows us, to some extent, to predict the ways that the people around us will interpret what is going on. If we want to understand behaviour, then we must locate it more broadly within culture and within the life of the person we are observing. Watching a person in any single moment would not allow us to really understand what they were up to.

Cultural frameworks and the ethnographic gaze

The ethnographic gaze means that we approach cultural explanations, including those in our own culture, as never being rational, natural or inevitable. Human behaviour in our own culture, like that in any other, must be thought of as being accomplished by virtue of a cultural tool kit. Basically, much of the order that we see in the world is not inherent in the world. We put it there.

The way that we categorize things that are there in nature is arbitrary and will generally determine how we behave towards such a thing. For example, in one culture something might be categorized as sacred, whereas a different culture might see this same thing as irrelevant. Even the idea of seeing that thing as of religious importance may be completely repugnant to people of another culture. We also organize our lives and worlds through cultural ideas such as marriage, dating, politics, gender. None of these things are inherent in the world but are fundamental to the way that we behave and think about ourselves.

Anthropologists were the first academic group to emphasize this arbitrariness in their empirical approach. The American anthropologist Franz Boas (1921) thought that one way to understand culture was as the way that a group of people cognitively classified the world and their experiences. In other words, the things that we do, how we explain the meaning of the world, and our material culture, can all be thought of as the way a group of humans have come to impose order upon the world so that they can both make sense of it and find their own place in it. This idea influenced Benjamin Whorf (1956) who was interested in the way that the language we have not only allows us to talk about the world but also creates a model of the world. He compared Western languages with Hopi language and observed that Western languages, for example, quantify time in a way that the Hopi language does not. This research suggested that our language categories influence the way that we experience the passing of time. Time is not therefore something that we should think of as being inherent in the world.

Writers like Lakoff and Johnson (1980) have looked at how our concepts structure what we perceive in the world and how this influences the way that we relate to those things. The conceptual system that we have thus defines our realities. Lakoff and Johnson gave many fascinating and amusing examples of this in their volume *Metaphors We Live By*. For example, they show how in Western cultures we have the idea that consciousness is up and that unconsciousness is down. Expressions of this are found in statements such as: 'Wake up', 'He rises early in the morning', 'He fell asleep', 'He dropped off to sleep', 'He's under hypnosis', 'He sank into a coma'. Lakoff and Johnson also show that we have the idea that rational thought is up, whereas emotion is down. For example, the discussion 'fell to the emotional level, but I raised it back up to the rational plane. We put our feelings aside and had a high-level intellectual discussion of the matter. He couldn't rise above his emotions' (ibid., p. 17).

From this and more examples they conclude that the majority of our basic concepts are organized in terms of spatial metaphors. Happy is up, more is up, less is down. Lakoff and Johnson say that these metaphors give away some of the fundamental values of our culture where we value the rational consciousness. The point is that there is too much information out there for the brain to simply process as it goes along. Therefore it is better to have theories and expectations. For our idea of the ethnographic gaze this is important as we must realize that we talk and think about the world through just such a repertoire of cultural concepts. These influence what we will think of as meaningful and how we make sense of things.

The way we impose order is more apparent in how we organize our social worlds. A look at a textbook of anthropology will show an incredible array of customs which organize how we think about marriage, death, sexuality and power. These ways of organizing the social world are shared by others in that society and are assumed to be natural or inevitable. The members of society behave as if such things were real. And anyone in a particular society who did not have this knowledge would be unable to act in an appropriate manner. The questions for anthropology have been: how are these systems organized, and how do they work for people? This is also an appropriate means for us to think, for example, about research in media studies.

Anthropologists and primatologists have considered the way that these shared systems of beliefs emerged. And I think it is important to take a look at this as it helps us to visualize what people are doing when they communicate about things in the world. There are three parts to this. The first is the distinctive human ability to imagine what the world, things in it and people might mean. The second is the question of why this should have been done collectively, and the third is why these collective explanations often seem strange rather than practical when looked at from outside.

On the first point it has been argued that we must see our ability to imagine and to ask questions about the world as something that developed out of the increased sophistication in early social primates. Humphrey (1976) tells us that these social primates inhabited worlds with only a very short temporal horizon. Basically this means that they had very limited abilities for reflection, to think either backwards to the past or forwards into the future. But the ability to reflect more in itself became a selective advantage, helping individuals to survive, as this would allow them to manipulate situations. An illustration of this is that a dog cannot really imagine what you are thinking. And it certainly does not imagine that you will be imagining what it is thinking. Therefore it is not difficult to outsmart a dog and this would mean you have an advantage over that dog in terms of natural selection. This power of imagination would also give you a selective advantage over members of your own species if you could do this a little better than them, and therefore outsmart them. Through developing their powers of imagination early social primates started to open up this window of reflection. This meant that these primates opened up spaces where they could reflect on past interactions and imagine possible ones. They started to imagine narratives in which they could plan and then act. This opened up the ability to worry about what one's relationship to things and other people was all about.

While the ability to manipulate situations would have given the individual a selective advantage, the ability to collectively negotiate the environment, to plan together, would also have brought massive advantages. And this would have been even more powerful if the group shared meanings about what they were doing and why. It is these explanations – the stories that these people told each other about what everything meant, the way they told these stories and the accepted forms of social interaction – that we can think of as culture. Examples of this culture might be the kinds of organizing concepts discussed by Lakoff and Johnson above. Or they might be the kinds of shared meanings that lead to the way a culture thinks about love and sex such as in the Sambia or in Hollywood films.

It would not matter what strange interpretations of the world these cultural systems threw up so long as they were good for giving a sense of sharedness, a sense of having a mutual place in the world. Shared meanings would give these people a better chance of operating together, and this was important in the development of human sociality. It did not matter so much that some of these ways of seeing the world might in fact be basically false, that is unless this was to the extent that they inhibited the survival of the group. The most important fact was that they were good for mutuality. We might note that in Western belief systems some of the ways that we organize the world are strange and ultimately harmful. But they are shared and now seem inevitable and simply part of the way the world is. Science may be one such example, which in the West is invested with much prestige. Such belief may not even be agreed upon, and may exist alongside other contradictory beliefs.

Holland and Quinn (1987) have looked at the way that people are able to hold contradictory beliefs at the same time but that this is not important to us for practical purposes. For example, in the West academic psychologists have come to provide us with models for understanding our ways of thinking and motivations. Holland and Quinn point out that this is despite the fact that neither the people who have taken them on nor the psychologists agree on any single system. But they will tend to use the bits that suit them, when they suit them. Fascinatingly, Kempton (1987) shows how informants simultaneously held two false models of how central heating works. Although the two in fact refuted each other, people would switch between the two in order to provide an overall explanation. It seems that general consistency is not an important factor in the models we have of the world. Kay (1987) says that culture should be thought of as providing bits and pieces that we can use as the moment calls.

In Chapters 12 to 14 we will look at how when people talk about newspapers and television they draw on different contradictory representations. We will see that the ethnographer must be sensitive to this process. People do not have fixed, concrete responses, but use culture with a sensitivity to people and setting. This does not mean that they are free to say absolutely anything. They will rely on a range of commonly accepted representations which are given weight generally in the society in which they live.

One approach in sociology called ethnomethodology (literally, people's methods) pioneered by Harold Garfinkel (1967) has made the finer details of how we use our cultural tool kit, not to be rational, but for practical purposes, its central focus of investigation. Garfinkel famously made his students return to their homes during a vacation and act like complete strangers. He was interested in the ways that parents explained away the inappropriate behaviours as illness or drugs for example. Garfinkel used the experiment to point out how everyday interactions are complex accomplishments, which require mastery of a set of taken-for-granted rules. His point is that culture is not just about things like styles of food, or the way that one particular nationality might be thought of as gesticulating a lot. Culture is also about the tiny rules, for example, that govern how we end a conversation. These rules are what we think of as shared mutual understandings which allow us to negotiate the otherwise chaotic flow of experience. This sharedness is important for understanding culture in that we carry out our lives with an assumption of just what everybody else knows. This sharedness is what gives our cultural tool kit its feeling of being simply what reality is rather than a way of dealing with it. The methodology I am describing in this volume is strongly influenced by ethnomethodology.

Unconscious of our cultural framework

We are generally not conscious of our cultural framework. This means that we cannot necessarily rely on people to be able to offer explanations for why they do things. What they will actually tell us upon asking are the official reasons that are available. This has massive implications for researchers. In sociological research, including media studies, research is still carried out with the assumption that people are simply aware of, and can clearly formulate, the reasons why they do things. This is something that we really need to move away from if we are to make any progress in our understanding of media audiences and of social life in general (Belton 2000).

Using science as an example Polanyi (1958) argues while a society may have an official version, or story, about why things are done in a particular way, how things are actually done may be very different. This is important as it means that getting the native's point of view means not only asking them, as all they will be able to provide us with is the 'official' reason. What we need to do is to investigate how their whole social reality fits together, particularly in terms of the cultural framework that is available in that society for thinking about the things that we are investigating. The example I used in the last chapter was of the young man who gets drunk in a bar with his friends every

Friday night and becomes aggressive. We cannot, in Polanyi's view, simply ask him why this behaviour is meaningful to him. In the cultural framework that he carries, the response to such a question would be something like: because it is a good laugh. But to understand why he is there every week, we would need to understand more things about his society and the ways available for thinking about being masculine and how this relates to alcohol, to bars and to aggression. We might also have to look at advertising imagery and how this can be found in his behaviour.

Polanyi made two important observations. One dealt with the way that we relate to our culture's knowledge about how the world works. The other considered the fact that we generally do not have access to the reasons that we do things. When asked to do so we will use the common-sense reasons provided by our cultural framework. We will not have access to the real reasons that may underpin what we do. I might say for example that I like to watch European art house films rather than Hollywood movies. The reason I might give for this is that they are more artistic and intelligent. In our society this is one way we tend to represent the distinction between these two film genres. Writers in film studies, like Bordwell, Staiger and Thompson (1985) have shown how this distinction will generally reject the incredible amount of creativity required for a Hollywood movie as this is associated with production on an industrial scale. In contrast, art-house film is seen as being closer to the idea of the individual director artist. When people see such films they will tend to expect surrealism, a non-linear narrative, chance happenings, extremes of emotion both sexual and violent, male nudes – evoking an ambience of painting – and references to high art, like literature, music, the theatre or poetry. Writers like Bordwell *et al.* (1985) argue that this genre of film is characterized by conventions just like Hollywood. But these characteristics have become commonly associated with creativity and intelligence. When a person goes to see a Hollywood film, no matter how much artistic talent went into it, it will not be considered intelligent or artistic unless it has some of the art-house conventions. Recent examples might be *American Beauty* (2000) and *Traffic* (2001). Recently in Hollywood the studios have realized that this can be a marketing hook for audiences who gain pleasure from thinking that they have an eye for talent. In Polanyi's model people are not aware of the reasons that they make such a distinction, which is in fact historically and culturally based.

This does not mean that we should not think that people who pride themselves on having an eye for cinematic creativity are deceiving themselves. The point is that it is important that we think about what people do, say, and create in terms of their method of accomplishing everyday life, of finding meaning in the world and in themselves. We should also remember that people always talk with a delicate responsiveness to what they think that other people know and believe. The person who talks about preferring art-house cinema will assume that the listener shares in the kinds of distinctions that this utterance draws upon and therefore in the way that this will allow them to be received as a person with a sophisticated aesthetic eye.

Is science more rational than witchcraft?

Polanyi wanted to show how these cultural frameworks managed to appear to be natural to the people that use them. To do this he made a comparison of science and witchcraft showing that the way that people relate to them is very much the same, even though we might think about witchcraft as irrational. His basic point was that belief systems form a framework which will allow everything to appear to be naturally explained by it even if for an outsider it seems obvious that certain phenomena actually offer a serious challenge to it. Polanyi argued that this is true both for science and for witchcraft.

Polanyi drew on the anthropologist Evans-Pritchard's (1934) comparison of Zande – an African society – reasoning using witchcraft compared to his own using science. Evans-Pritchard described the way that the Zande used an oracle to answer questions, for example, to solve a dispute or to establish guilt. The oracle involved giving a poison called *benge* to a chicken along with the casting of various spells and carrying out appropriate rites. It would be decided that to get an answer to a particular question, for example, that if a man was guilty, then the chicken would die. Evans-Pritchard was fascinated by that fact that belief in the oracle was maintained in the face of evidence the European would see as starkly illustrating its inadequacy. Even where the oracle was not successful, this would be explained through reference to procedure or to other magic.

The Zande thought that *benge* was not a poison but a sacred substance that worked alongside the ritual address. If asked whether the poison would work without the accompanying spells the Zande could not imagine why anyone would want to do such a thing. Evans-Pritchard argued that the Zande cannot stand outside their individual beliefs as these form part of a whole interpretative framework which has magic at its heart.

We might have a tendency to think that such beliefs in oracles and magic are of a different nature to our own view of the world which is based on science. Evans-Pritchard suggested, however, that there are many similarities. For a start we must think about the way that individuals come to accept such interpretative frameworks. The Zande would explain rainfall in terms of witchcraft whereas the Westerner would talk in terms of meteorological causes. For Evans-Pritchard this has nothing to do with superior intelligence. Westerners have little actual knowledge of these physical processes. Certainly most of us do not hold these beliefs through any kind of observations of our own. Rather, we simply accept the established view in our society. It is an idea that existed in our culture long before we were born into it.

I have no idea how electricity stays in the wall or if it is there at all. I have no idea how calculations relate to a bridge staying up. If everyone in my society believed that it depended upon magic spells I would have believed them. This is not to say that science does not bring some powerful analytical capacities. It is to say rather that the way most people relate to science is much the same as the way people relate to witch-craft. Polanyi argues that how we relate to science must be understood not as being because we know how it works but because of the way that our society talks about it. In *Science, Faith and Society* Polanyi says of the person who learns science:

> At every stage of his progress towards this end he is urged on by the belief that certain things as yet beyond his knowledge and even understanding are on the whole true and valuable, so that it is worth spending his most intensive efforts on mastering them. (1946, p. 45)

Polanyi was specifically interested in how a system of beliefs like science maintains itself in much the same way as a belief system which embraces witchcraft and sorcery. He cites this comment from Evans-Pritchard: 'They reason excellently in the idiom of their beliefs, but they cannot reason outside, or against, their beliefs because they have no other idiom in which to express their thoughts' (1946, p. 288, cited from Evans-Pritchard, 1934, p. 338). Evans-Pritchard is referring to Zande belief but Polanyi says that this could equally be applied to any interpretative framework like science, psychoanalysis or Marxism. He sets out to provide a systematic breakdown of the way that belief systems are able to be maintained in the face of evidence that should invalidate them.

Circularity

Any idea in a belief system will be explained and validated by reference to another idea in that system. And this second idea will itself be explained by reference to yet another idea in the system. And objections to the belief system are not met all at once but individually. There does not have to be consistency among the responses so long as each objection is explained away. And once a belief system has been applied to lots of instances, it gains power. Polanyi compares this circularity to a dictionary where the meaning of a word is given by the meaning of another word. Happy might mean contentment or pleased. And in its turn pleased might be given to mean happy. Reference and legitimation come from within the system. We might think, for example, about a framework like psychoanalysis which when a patient claims to reject all agreement with the diagnosis, that patient might be said to be either in denial or to be projecting the problem onto the analyst.

Explaining away things

All belief systems have convenient tools to explain away that which is not convenient. As we have just seen, the Zande can explain away failure of the oracle by procedure or by counter-magic. In science there are 'anomalies' which appear which should not be seen as serious challenges to a theory. Polanyi, himself a scientist, gives examples of theories which were maintained for many years in the face of anomalies and so-called natural errors due to method. A belief system basically will not listen to anything which falls outside its framework and will therefore deny these things legitimacy. New ideas will not be given respectability by experts and will probably be ignored.

Polanyi does think that science can eventually give up its theories in the face of overwhelming anomalies and he does think that it can have excellent descriptive power, but he questions the way that we think of science as being a neutral activity involving the gathering of evidence to establish laws. Basically, he suggests it is select-ive and can be highly closed as an interpretative framework.

Polanyi's points are extremely valuable for the way we can think about people's cultural tool kits in the context of the idea of ethnography reassembling social action to the flow of everyday life. When we encounter people talking or explaining them-selves we can think about them as using a set of ideas which have become established in their society. These ideas will seem self-evidently true and inevitable. They may not have any direct connection to whether such ideas are fundamentally worthwhile, or true. But they will appear as such to them by virtue of them being widely accepted in that society. Data that we look at in the last three chapters of this book reveal people making sense of the world in terms of taken-for-granted shared ideas about why things are the way they are and what motivates us to behave as we do.

Cultural frameworks and media studies

Before we continue, let us just take a look at how the ideas we have considered so far can help us to understand the way that a person might relate to the mass media. In the last chapter I raised the problem of how we might think of the way that the represen-tation of love and sex in Hollywood movies might be adopted by the people who watch them. Such representations are not like our everyday lives. When any man takes off his clothes in contemporary movies he will be suntanned, toned and hair-less. We do not stop to wonder how the protagonist had the time to do this. Harrison Ford in *What Lies Beneath* (2000) is an ageing physics professor yet he has an incred-ible body. John Torturro in *The Luzin Defence* (2000) is a socially incompetent and eccentric chess genius who would surely have smelled of urine, but he looks terrific without his clothes on. In *Captain Correlli's Mandolin* (2001) the Greek fisherman peasant hasn't a hair on his body and could model underwear.

When these people fall in love it is indicated through sex, even if they have hardly spoken to their heroine. The film *Pearl Harbor* (2001) contains some classic examples. There is one hilarious scene where one of the male heroes has sex with the heroine. The scene takes place in a store for parachutes. But the parachutes are silken and are blown by a gentle and soothing breeze. The lighting is fairytale moonbeam, which saturates everything. The expressions on their faces indicate meditative bliss. Lust is absent. There is no awkwardness. They do not even seem to be aware of each other. And their bodies are perfect of course. The couple seem to have no relationship and have said basically nothing to each other. Yet as movie-goers we accept that the soft sex stands for love.

In the last chapter I suggested that these depictions of love might seem strange to someone who has never seen such a film before. If we think carefully, it is peculiar that even those who are familiar with them accept them so readily. Bordwell *et al.* (1985) have hypothesized about the fact that audiences have become schooled in being able to follow movies in a way that means that we do not find such representations strange. If we asked someone if they expected love and sex to be like these representations, they would most likely say that they would not. But to what extent do these images become part of the framework by which we understand sex and love? Some of the key psychologists in child development such as G.H. Mead (1934) spoke of the way that we assemble our sense of who we are and of how to behave by reference to people around us. They are the main source of our cultural framework. More recently developmentalists have tended to ignore the role of the mass media. Raymond Williams once pointed out that never before have people watched so many people acting out fictions. Do these fictional representations of love and sex leave us without resources for contemplating things like commitment? We may be now schooled in such film representations, but does this mean that we just apply them as a framework for understanding movie worlds or do we use them in some way as a frame of reference in our own lives? And to what extent are we able to see these representations as arbitrary rather than as natural?

In the previous chapter we looked at an ethnographic study of how men in the Sambia of Papua New Guinea believe that they should become a man and carry out relationships. The way that they did this, the ideas that underpinned the process, would seem strange to Westerners. What the anthropologist Herdt did was reveal the cultural tool kit that was used by the Sambia to inform them about how the world worked, how they could become a man and how they should relate to women. In our own societies we also have a cultural framework which informs how we perform being a man or woman and how we do relationships. If we are to understand how these movie depictions of sexual behaviour and love work, we must locate them in the everyday lives of individuals. We should not think of them as being natural or unnatural but as part of the cultural framework that a particular group of people use to make collective sense of the world. They are no more or less strange than those beliefs held by the Sambia.

Cinema is not the only site of mass media representations of sex, gender and relationships. The advertising industry uses these as their main source of ways to draw in audiences. Put simply, when you only have a maximum of two minutes to make people identify with the narrative into which you have located your product, these are things that apply to most people. Let me give an example from a mobile telephone advertisement which uses a particular representation of young women and sexuality. The advert begins by showing two young woman dancing in a night club. The night club does not look real at all. It looks like a place out of a glossy magazine, but evokes a rave party. It is full of super-fashionable 'happening people'. The camera cuts quickly, showing highly sexualized clothing, revealing a lot of skin and glamourized sweat. The girls are 'crazy', uninhibited and having 'fun'. Everything happens in slow motion, giving the impression of space and atemporality. It is immortalized and epic – this isn't just a moment, it is a way of life. This is a technique generally used in pop videos to give the band a larger-than-life feel. One of the girls meets a beautiful guy with whom she dances very closely. She immediately finds out his star sign and uses her mobile phone to do an Internet search to match with her own sign – which amazingly works instantaneously! He is Gemini and the match is a good one. But as she looks up she finds he has an equally beautiful identical twin brother. Still in slow epic motion she nods raunchily at her friend and the scene is over. The advert draws on a particular image of the confident woman that is no more arbitrary than that used to represent the Marlboro man in the 1970s. This young woman is confident, knows what she wants, and is having fun. As was the fashion at this time, she showed this through things such as overt assertiveness – in the West a cultural representation, or metonym, for confidence – and by being in control of her body. In the advert this is clearly indicated by her lack of concern about the fact that there were two guys. In the early years of the twenty-first century the mass media has trafficked heavily in images of female confidence. These are indicated by 'fun', aggressive sexuality, tattoos and body piercing.

As part of our cultural tool kits we have representations of what it means to be a man or a woman and how we are to interrelate in order to have relationships. These representations take on a natural appearance for people in that society at that particular time. Theorists like Polanyi (1958) would argue that these people would not have access to the fact that such representations were bound to that culture at that particular time. They would generally perceive these as natural.

People in the West do often comment that they find the mass media representation of the world exaggerated or absurd. But in Polanyi's terms we might expect them to be able to perceive *certain* aspects of mass media representations as absurd. But these will only be certain agreed upon representations. This might be illustrated by comparison to the way that everyone might criticize weather broadcasts for always being wrong but still generally accept both the fact that they should be done and the scientific premises that underpin them. We generally get pleasure from the shared knowledge that certain representations in the mass media are absurd, for example, that long-lost brothers continually appear in soap operas. But generally people will be unaware just how arbitrary the more general representations or models of the world are and how this motivates them to behave.

An ethnographic study would look for the way that people's behaviour in different contexts related to this media imagery. If we asked a young woman who resembled the imagery of the advertisement, who had several tattoos, if she was affected by such representations she would most likely say that she was not. Her tattoos would be an expression of her identity, she might say. An ethnographic study might therefore broaden out to think about what other resources this young woman draws on to think about identity, as did Herdt in his study of the Sambia.

This depiction of the way that people in a society share their cultural frameworks as they interact with each other and through the mass media can be thought of in terms of Kenneth Burke's depiction of society that I looked at in the introductory chapter. He evoked the image of speaker joining a discussion in a parlour. The speaker listens to the topics of conversations, gets the hang of what is being said and then puts in their oar's worth. The discussion was going on before the speaker entered the room and continues after they have left. There will be certain dominating themes in the discussion and the speaker must learn the rules of participation. The example of representations in the mass media that I have given above, however, suggest that one voice can be very powerful. And if the voice of the advertiser, for example, can be very powerful, what are the consequences of this? I now want to look at the ideas of discourses and hegemony. These can help us to think about the way that in society certain definitions of how the world works can be very influential.

Discourses and hegemony

Related to this idea of people having a cultural tool kit which they use to comprehend the flow of life, writers like Foucault (1966, 1969) have looked at how we talk and think about things is influenced by the discourses that we have for doing so. By discourses Foucault means a kind of cultural model. These cultural models appear natural and objective even though they are models. One example of this in society might be the way we generally think about crime and prisons. While most people who find their way into prison in the Western world are from the lower or marginalized classes, we still officially think about these people simply as law-breakers, criminals and against the common interest. For Foucault this could be explained as being a discourse promoted by the dominant groups in order to protect their interest. For Foucault power could be had not by coercion but by being in a position to define just what is knowledge. In Britain governments have frequently blamed society's ills not on corporate greed or capitalism but on poor people who abuse state benefits systems, on immigrants and criminals.

To illustrate this we can use the example of a talk show which has crime as its topic for discussion. The show will present two sides of the argument. One of the positions will be that criminals in prison should be there to be punished and should have a hard time. This would prevent further criminal activity and would send out a warning to other criminals – the idea of prison as a deterrent. The other position will be the view that prison should be about rehabilitation. Here criminals learn new skills which will allow them to change their life and learn the error of their ways. In the talk show ex-cons and victims speak about the pluses of each point of view. The show is presented as a debate and as giving the two sides of the argument. However, at no point is the nature of who goes to prison and how this is affected by poverty and inequality raised. Those who go to prison will more than likely be from the lower social classes and will be over-represented by black people. Areas of industrial decline where people become marginalized from participation in the values of mainstream society are breeding grounds for future offenders. Yet this discourse is generally itself marginalized and is seldom found in official sources.

Newpapers and television news generally emphasize crime as conflict against the values of the wider society rather than as something that is caused by it. Antonio Gramsci (1971) described the process whereby knowledge is controlled in this way as the dominant group having *hegemony* of knowledge. In other words, what people generally accept as common knowledge is controlled by the dominant group. This is why Foucault thought that cultural control could be maintained through discursive practices. He thought that people have difficulty thinking beyond a particular discursive framework. This framework can become the basis upon which we evaluate things. In some ways, then, discourses can be thought of as policing the way that we can think about things. These dominant forms of knowledge control us because they define the knowledge and discourse which we have available for talking and thinking and therefore knowing about things. These discourses therefore have an influence on how we behave and the way that we think about ourselves. Of course, there is never complete hegemony and there are always competing discourses, but the important point here is to realize that our tool kit for understanding the world, ourselves and the people in it may tend to support particular interests.

In the section on science and magic we looked at the way that people have belief systems which may not allow certain things even to be visible to them. We might think about social discourses in the same way. This could apply to the way that people are able to think about things like crime or gender and relationships.

The idea of discourse is therefore important in terms of how we should think about the way that we will find people talking in specific settings when we are carrying out research. If we found a group of people talking about the importance of television in terms of its role as informing people in society, can we assume that this is really how people assess the programmes that they watch? Or does this tell us more about the official discourse in society available for talking about television? As we look at some examples of media research in later chapters I will show how on occasions we can clearly see such a process taking place. In such an instance we must take an ethnographic gaze and assume that people are using a cultural tool kit in context. What we do not have, as Polanyi warned, is people having access to what their real motivations are. This idea of people talking in context also needs drawing out.

Speech genres

I would like to draw out the idea of people talking in contexts a little more. In the ethnographic gaze we need to be aware of the way that all behaviour is relevant to setting. Wertsch (1991) in *Voices of the Mind* argued that we have particular sets of speech styles or ways of talking that are acceptable in different settings. He gives the example of how children have to learn to use a particular kind of formal impersonal way of talking in the classroom. From the very beginnings of a child's school career such speech is sanctioned by teachers. He points out how children from lower socio-economic backgrounds have more difficulty producing accounts in this genre. The point here is that people must be understood as talking in a way that is specific to a context. Usually this is one criticism made of, say, focus groups or interviews when they are used to investigate media audiences. The argument goes that these are not natural settings. But if we follow Foucault and Wertsch's view, then people only have discourses available through culture that can be used in settings. Therefore where is the 'natural' or 'real' setting? Ethnography has been heralded as being unhampered by this problem of context as it gives a much broader picture of people's lives and how they talk in different settings. This realization can also empower focus group and interview approaches if we view the data that is produced through the ethnographic gaze. That is, if we assume that what such methodologies produce is not data which tell us what people actually think about something in terms of their true opinion or belief – anthropologists have warned us that people cannot reveal this. We must assume that what we have is people using particular cultural discourses in a particular setting. While this means that we will not be able to make conclusions about what people 'believe', we can develop a sense of some of the discourses which suffuse society, and which shape the way that people can talk and think about things.

Improvising with a tool kit

We have looked at the way that we have a tool kit for understanding the world, which ethnography can allow us to examine. But it is the flexibility or 'more or less' of this knowledge which is of crucial importance. Bourdieu, in his description of 'habitus' (1977) attempted to formulate how we possess these cultural models with which we have an ability to improvise. He called this tool kit our set of regulated improvisations. He said that these mean that our behaviour will be governed pretty much by this tool kit, but that we will be free to improvise depending upon how we perceive the situation, which itself will be governed pretty much by our tool kit.

The kind of system of knowledge I have in mind here is distinct from that posited by the cognitive school in psychology (e.g. Schank and Abelson 1977; Mandler 1984). This view tended to create an image of humans as cultural robots. They wanted to provide a description of the cognitive models or schemata through which we organize and understand the world and our experiences. All human thinking and action was described as being organized by its own cultural model. Mandler's ambition was to describe exactly how different schemata or models which motivated various bits of our behaviour were hierarchically and structurally interrelated. The view of our cultural tool kit that we are considering here suggests that the idea of models must be balanced against that of setting. That is, the actual action going on in any setting must be seen as having a great influence in its own right. The point here is that humans act primarily towards others rather than to the system of knowledge, although this system of knowledge will provide regulated notions about the world and people through which these interactions will become meaningful and show the way that they will be performed. As Polanyi (1958) argued, people will not see their cultural tool kit as a system of interpretation but rather as objective knowledge. It will provide a common-sense world which feels objective due to the consensus of witnessing others around us sharing in its meanings.

Culture and media studies

It would be easy to think that all this attention to culture and human knowledge about the world was not relevant to research in media studies. In the chapters that follow we will see the importance of seeing our data as people in Western culture making meaning using a cultural tool kit. Some of the ethnographic studies we look at do not, which, I will argue, may be a limitation. As media audience researchers like Radway (1988) have suggested, we simply need a way whereby we can connect the mass media not just to concrete demographic features, like gender, but to people's lives as a whole.

Think about young children growing up. They may spend a lot of time in front of television. What they watch and enjoy may increasingly be informed by their race, gender and social class. It will also be increasingly defined by the way that parents might be seen to prohibit certain kinds of programmes, leading to them seeming desirable. The children may then go to school where they will realize that other children watch similar programmes. Knowing the right programmes can be important in terms of status for children. The children begin to realize that what we watch and like says something about who we are. This may be something like *Pokémon* which peaked in about 2000. Children must know about the characters and then own the merchandise. Children learn to feel part of things and also feel individual by what they own and what they know. Being at the forefront of a latest craze brings kudos.

But all these things must be understood in the context of what it means to be a child in this particular culture. Perhaps children liked *Pokémon* because it was not under-stood by most adults. This is important in a culture where children are generally thought of as passive and innocent. This must be also thought of in terms of television programming which markets itself to children as 'the latest thing'.

In terms of researching this, could we ask these children why they liked *Pokémon* and expect them to be able to solve the whole problem for us? We certainly need to ask the children, but we should be aware of what the children say in the context of what we have discussed in this chapter. We must be aware of the way that we tend to see things in our own culture as being much more transparent. For example, we tend to see consumerism as inevitable. Yet how we have looked at culture in this chapter tells us that we need to understand things like *Pokémon* as part of our material culture, and think about how these form part of the way that the world works for people.

3 Ethnography in the city

The Chicago School

In this chapter I look at the way that a group of social researchers at the University of Chicago in the early decades of the twentieth century, working initially in a joint Anthropology and Sociology department, came to feel that ethnography was the best way to understand life in the city. Carrying out ethnographic fieldwork in an exotic setting can seem a naturally appropriate place to use ethnography as cultural practices can seem immediately strange, therefore calling for a method which allows us to understand them from the native's point of view. But the use of such a methodology in our own contemporary society might seem less useful. This is not the case. On the one hand, we are not used to seeing behaviour in our own societies as anthropologically strange. Therefore we tend to be unaware of the way that it is arbitrary and constructed through a particular framework of cultural representations. On the contrary, we tend to rely on the existing official common-sense explanations. For example, we generally think about a young man who is drunk and aggressive in a bar as anti-social and brutish. We tend not to think about the meanings that allow such behaviour to make sense to him.

On the other hand, the explanations for social phenomenon can be likened to those produced by the early colonial travellers to describe the behaviour of people in exotic cultures. Such explanations are constructed through a frame of reference which is alien to that used by the people in that setting. At the root of the Chicago philosophy was the idea of understanding urban social problems in terms of the native's own point of view. This was underpinned by a model of human behaviour which could sit comfortably alongside that of Malinowski. Phenomena such as drug use, crime and violence should be viewed as the behaviour of malevolent people, but should be understood in terms of how certain people find their way in, and make sense of, the world in which they find themselves.

Most of the work by the Chicago School was carried out before 1940 and the methodology that was pioneered has not been widely used in subsequent research. This has been partly due to the popularity of Cultural Studies, which has tended to be highly based on textual analysis, and the American tendency towards statistical analysis. Because of this the urban ethnography carried out by the Chicago School has been largely forgotten. For our own purposes these studies have an important message for the way that we can learn to treat media use as anthropologically strange and as something that takes place in both an immediate context and a broader cultural setting.

In the 1920s American sociology started to debate the relative merits of the two main research strands, the case study and statistics, which were the two dominant approaches to investigating the social world. Herbert Blumer (1969), working at the University of Chicago at this time, disliked statistics and positivism. He held the view that social life must be understood as being meaningful to individuals and that these meanings emerged in and through social interaction. This view is very much like that taken in the anthropological studies that we looked at in Chapter 2. Like the belief in magic, behaviour in the inner city should not be thought of simply as evidence of barbaric, primitive or evil people, but as the behaviour of people who find themselves in a particular place making sense of their lives through a particular cultural tool kit. Blumer wanted social research to move away from general theorizing and historical work. He valued close observation of people as they lived out their lives. This approach was to be the basis of the philosophy which underpinned research carried out at the school.

The Chicago School, drawing on the social survey movement aimed at social reform, came to dominate American sociology until the 1940s. During this time a unique group emerged which drew on a range of disciplines to look at specific urban problems in the United States at that time. This was the first time that research had been carried out in this way in a university department. The Chicago School was funded by philanthropic foundations which supported the need to address problems in the city caused by industrial growth, urbanization and capitalism.

The Chicago School did use survey-style approaches and statistical analysis of social phenomenon but led the way in qualitative research. It brought together theory and research practice with a commitment to empirical work. The Chicago School was influenced by the ideas of the anthropologist Franz Boas and by a school of thought called 'pragmatism' by G.H. Mead and John Dewey. These theorists had believed that experience was the basis of all knowledge and that we cannot know anything outside our own experience. What we can know of the world is filtered by what has already happened to us and the existing meanings held in our community.

Also important in the School's philosophy was G.H. Mead's (1934) view that there is a close relationship between environment and mind. He believed that humans define their environment in terms of their needs and change it as these are met. So both the environment and the way that we think both develop and change over time. Blumer (1969) argued that the individual self should thus be seen as something that emerges through a process of interacting with a particular environment. These ideas underpinned the Chicago School's notion of looking for the way that people responded to and created their own worlds of meaning within particular circumstances in the city. Immediately we can see that this approach means that we have to understand the native's point of view. We have to find out how the things that people do and experience in their lives are meaningful to them. We cannot understand behaviour external to the environment in which people live and what this means to them. This may sound obvious but it is a long way from the view that in our societies we generally approach and explain social behaviour. And much research of a quantitative nature overlooks these processes.

The first of the Chicago studies were *The Polish Peasant in Europe and America* (Thomas and Znaniecki 1918–20) and the race relations study *The Negro in Chicago* (Chicago Commission on Race Relations 1922). Both these works combined empirical research with generalizing and theory, but crucially they were both based on observation of everyday life. These were followed by a series of studies which looked at the urban community and city life. The aim was to understand what life was like for those living in Chicago. What was the urban experience? The head of the School, Robert E. Park, in the Preface to Anderson's study of homelessness, *The Hobo*, said 'The old familiar problems of our communal life – poverty, crime, and vice – assume new and strange forms under the conditions of modern urban existence' (1961, p. xxiii). He mused that, 'If it is true that man made the city, it is quite true that the city is now making man' (ibid., p. xxiii). For Park the task of the Chicago School was to find out what was going on in that city. What kinds of people was the city making? The emphasis was on how people adapted and survived. He said that in the city, 'new and unusual personal types flourish and new and unsuspected problems have arisen' (ibid., p. xxiv). This is a view which focuses on problems as a response to the city as people coping, surviving and trying to make meaning out of their situation. This radical approach to understanding social life involved a reformulation of the idea of social problems. Rather than looking to blame the individuals who are the problem, we try to understand how it is that they come to live the lives that they do. Only then, possibly, might we know what needs changing to make the situation better.

Of this anthropological style approach to research Park (Park and Burgess 1925) commented that how we had viewed exotic cultures should be applied to more familiar but in fact equally exotic ones. Park thought that urban life was more complicated but that what people were doing was the same in both instances. Therefore he argued that the very methods which anthropologists like Boas had used on the culture and practices of the North American Indians would be just as appropriate for the study of the beliefs, customs, social practices, and world views of the inhabitants of a Chicago slum.

Park made the point, which was fundamental to the work of anthropologists, that human nature, while being based on a rough set of human traits, is basically a product of the human environment in which each of us finds ourselves. Therefore, he concluded, all communities or places in which we live will tend to produce certain kinds of social values, opinions, language and personal traits. This is a fundamentally political view that does not hold people individually responsible for crime or other 'anti-social' activities, but sees their behaviour as a response to a setting and to a particular set of meanings. From this we can understand why many of the projects carried out at the Chicago School were chosen. Many of the projects involved social problems or communities seen as problematic by the wider society. The School took the approach of understanding these as people simply making sense of, and finding a place in, a particular environment.

One reason that Thomas and Znaniecki (1918–20) chose the Poles as the first study at the School was because of their behaviour, which was thought to be very difficult to understand. This was particularly in terms of their acceptance of authority which often seemed extreme either in their acceptance or rejection.

The Polish Peasant was a landmark study in that it was the first to engage with the social world in such a close empirical manner. Previously, sociology had been characterized by library work and theory. The Chicago School stressed the importance of concrete, detailed observations of social behaviour. This was also accompanied by theory on the way that people's identities were formed in cultures. The authors talked about deviance as culturally patterned behaviour. It was not about people being lost or without norms. Deviance could be made sense of in terms of people behaving in the contexts, the worlds, in which they found themselves.

The methodology used in these early studies was not what we might immediately think of as ethnography or participant observation but was more of a documentary method. Thomas wrote of the importance of all kinds of sources of information such as letters, newspapers, records of court trials, sermons, pamphlets by political parties, the records of local social groups. In short, anything which reflected the life of the people he was studying could be a useful source of data.

Thomas had originally looked at documents on Polish folklore but found that they dealt with things like craftwork and agriculture, which is generally the kind of thing that we in the West still think of as indigenous or ethnic culture. Much of the material he ended up using were letters written by Poles who had moved to the United States. He advertised in a newspaper and paid for letters that people sent to him. He had been inspired to take this approach after finding a letter from a Polish girl to her father in some rubbish in the street which he felt was a rich source of data regarding attitudes and experiences of a new life in the United States. Later he would get letters from families who had made exchanges over a period of time. He also used written life-history accounts.

The Chicago School is best known for some of the monographs published in the 1920s. These studies were *The Hobo, The Gang, The Slum, The Taxi-Dance Hall*. All of these were urban studies and provided a foundation for studies of deviance, criminal behaviour and social problems. The emphasis was on understanding the social forces that produce these phenomena. Like Malinowski, they sought to understand people's behaviour as part of a whole. These studies moved on from *The Polish Peasant* by going into the worlds and lives of those who were studied. This approach still used personal documents and interviews but was based on observation – although the studies tended not to be clear about precisely how the research was planned and carried out, and much of what is known about this has been dug out of archives from the school.

The idea of spending time in the real-life setting was partly influenced by Park's past as a journalist where investigating issues and talking to sources had taken him into the heart of city life. He felt that this kind of intimacy would take the researcher closer to people producing meanings and would overcome the remoteness of many sociologists working on social problems. Park thought that there was no point studying life in a lab. He thought all that this would show was the obvious. Here is the idea of ethnography being able to reveal things that we do not expect.

Nel Anderson's study of homeless men, *The Hobo,* saw him go around in the kinds of environments where the people he was to study spent their time. He did not identify himself as a researcher and mainly wrote down what he saw and heard. Interviews took the form of conversations. The term participant observation had not been coined then but this is basically what he did. Anderson seemed to find the role comfortable, probably because he had come from a background where his father had been a hobo and had travelled much with him and his family before they became settled.

Anderson emphasized that the study was of a separate urban world of Chicago. But his study was not just about observation. He, like the other studies at the time, drew on records of social agencies. He would also use historical documents and life histories and even statistical materials. The point was to create a map of the world in which the homeless man lived along with subjective experiences of the people living in that world.

Landesco looked at Chicago crime in *Organised Crime in Chicago* (1929). The study began by analysing crime reporting in the press. The names of those involved were noted and newspaper archive material was used along with police bulletins and probation records and the police bureau of identification, to create a picture of the different groups operating. This allowed some kind of life histories to be constructed. These were filled out with three and a half years of contact with gang leaders. The point was to enter these other worlds, map them out and show what it meant for the people who were living in them. And as in Anderson's case of living with homeless men Landesco's own background made it easier, having grown up in an immigrant community on Chicago's West Side where he had experience of many of the criminal groups.

In our contemporary society it would seem strange to think in terms of crime as meaningful to the participants. This would seem to be forgiving them somehow, or at least sympathizing with them. In a way, the work of the Chicago School did sympathize with their subjects. But this did not mean that they thought that the things that they did were acceptable. The point was that phenomena such as gang violence seems reasonable (if still a terrible thing) if you understand how for some people this is a response to their environment. It is only in this way that we can have any hope of being able to know what we must change in order to stop this kind of behaviour.

Some of the Chicago research was heavily dependent upon life history. Clifford Shaw, who worked in the Chicago School before moving to the Institute of Juvenile

Research, collected over two hundred life histories of young offenders. His most well-known study was a case history of one boy published in *The Jack-Roller: A Delinquent Boy's Own Story* (1931). This involved Shaw getting the boy to write his own story. Shaw provided the framework in terms of key events he had gathered from various official records and the boy Stanley was to fill in the details as to what happened and how he experienced these events. Initially he only produced a short account but later after a period in prison he produced around 50 000 words, which was done mainly through lengthy recorded interviews. Shaw would check details with other sources such as police records, medical and psychological reports. Discrepancies could then be taken back to Stanley for his response. Shaw thought that the life history gave insight into how Stanley experienced his life and responded to events. They showed how the agencies in Stanley's life, such as institutions and other offenders, had affected him.

I now want to look at two of the Chicago studies in more depth. I want to present these in much the same way as I presented the case studies in Chapter 1 where I looked at ethnography in anthropology. As with the studies of magic and of Sambia notions of masculinity, these Chicago studies look at phenomena that could be thought of as puzzles for the outsider that can be solved by considering how things are meaningful in their social and cultural context. The two studies I want to look at consider gang fighting and deviance through the use of drugs. Both might be thought of as social problems and both might be considered as simply strange behaviour to the outsider. Both kinds of behaviour are often misunderstood, as is evident through policy which takes the stance of stamping them out through punishment rather than comprehending how they are simply people responding to a particular environment.

It is important for us to look closely at these studies as much of what the Chicago School studied might seem quite simply explained through existing cultural frameworks. Drug abuse is the activity of weak squalid deviants and gang violence is carried out by mindless or vicious thugs. These behaviours seem to fall outside of what many think of as normal society. On the one hand, these studies remind us to think more carefully about any behaviour that we find in our own societies. They show that the cultural frameworks that people use in our own society are equally as arbitrary as those in exotic cultures. They also give us a model of the way that we might approach the study of mass media audiences. To what extent, for example, might we find discourse about such phenomena in film and television? How might this discourse then frame the way that people think about or explain what they are doing? Nigel Rapport once said that we could think about the way that people talked and thought about their worlds as being like a city map. The roads on this map could be thought of as the guiding principles of any cultural framework. To what extent, then, if we look at the way that someone talks about what they do, can we find landmarks on this city map that are present in particular kinds of mass media representations? And to what extent do these representations get taken on or transformed?

Inner city gang culture as people getting on with their lives

F.M. Thrasher (1927, abridged version 1963) *The Gang: A Study of 1,313 gangs in Chicago.* Chicago and London: University of Chicago Press.

Thrasher carried out a study of gangs in Chicago but he says little about how he collected his data. All he really gives away is that it took seven years. He began by using data from organizations that came into contact with gangs such as youth clubs, courts and schools. Then he moved onto interviewing hundreds of boys in schools. This was typical of the Chicago method: a search of public documents, interviews, observation and life history. He then went on to spend time with the different gangs. He did this in a covert manner, meaning that they did not know that he was a researcher.

Thrasher's book is fascinating. As with most of the volumes from this period it sometimes comes across as a bit antiquated and precious in its comments but it is non-judgemental. And it tells about the fascinating world of gangs with raids, slashings, deaths and comradeship. Its aim is to reveal what life is like for gang members and how it is meaningful to them. In the name of social reform it calls out for the reader to view gang members not just as deviants or as a social problem which needs to be dealt with – a disease which infects an otherwise healthy society. His vision rejects the view that if such phenomena were simply eradicated, then the wider society will be protected and safe. Gangs are a response to environment. They are about people who have no access to the wider social world who try to live, feel worthwhile, and better themselves.

The gang

The origin of the gang was usually the street for a range of about two blocks. The kids would have played together and would have known each other all of their lives. They may have gone to different schools, but this would not affect gang membership. The gangs generally grew out of the group of children who played together. These groups would compete with other groups for space to play and for other privileges. Natural leaders would emerge from the need to organize play activities. The gang could start from two or three boys and then other pairs or threes would join in. These may later have formed a club or other interest group and started rivalries with other gangs, which would bring pleasure and enhance solidarity. These gangs might make allegiances with other gangs for various purposes. All this negotiation would bring about a sense of comradeship.

The gangs would always be in a state of flux. Members would develop new interests or move away. Members could have been removed by the police, even resulting in the break-up of that gang. They may simply have ceased to get along. Thrasher gives the example of one boy who joined an enemy gang after moving house simply because he did not want to have so far to walk. But marriage was the main cause of gang break-up in his study. Membership, therefore, was an adolescent phenomenon. The gangs may even be comprised of sub-gangs of different age-groups, ranging from Senior, Junior, Midget and even to Pee Wee (p. xlii, in Introduction by J.F. Short 1963).

Thrasher found that many of the gangs were formed by mixed nationalities, although of the 1,300 he only found 25 that were mixed in terms of black and white. About 60 per cent, however, were not mixed. He found that there were only five or six gangs comprised only of girls. Girls did enter gangs, were adopted, or protected, by them but largely it was a male activity. Thrasher gives two reasons for this. First, social models of behaviour for girls are basically contrary to gang-type activities. Second, girls are much more closely supervised by parents and more closely tied in to the family.

Gang membership compensates for lack of status in life

The main theme of the book is that the boys who formed gangs in Chicago did so to generate a sense of worth, belonging, status and purpose. Boys from the slum neighbourhoods of the city had no opportunity to enter the same kinds of status networks as boys from more middle-class areas. Therefore these boys sought prestige elsewhere. Since there were a lot of people about in the same situation, Thrasher says, everyone opted for the same solution. Young people did not want to let themselves be at the bottom of the social hierarchy. They simply create their own world where they can be part of the status hierarchy. Instead of valuing academic achievement they will value characteristics such as toughness, excitement, streetwise credibility. 'The gang adopts the patterns which have prestige in its own social environment, selecting those which appeal to it and setting them up to be followed by its own members in so far as the group controls them' (1963, p. 180).

Thrasher found that gangs offer a range of benefits for the young men. They control boys, give them a sense of belonging, self worth and purpose, all in a context of excitement. He says:

> The failure of the normally directing and controlling customs and institutions to function efficiently in the boy's experience is indicated by disintegration of family life, inefficiency of schools, formalism and externality of religion, corruption and indifference in local politics, low wages and monotony in occupational activities, unemployment, and lack of opportunity for wholesome recreation. (ibid., p. 33)

Basically, then, the gang offers escapism and fills a gap which the wider society leaves vacant. Thrasher sees that gang, therefore, as symptom of problems in the wider social framework. It can be thought of as what happens when young men create their own society, with its own rules and values where nothing is provided by the wider society in which they can really participate.

Thrasher found that for boys and young men from the slum area, contacts with people from the wider community outside of the gang or even the immediate immigrant community would usually be disheartening and even humiliating. The gang member would know little about these worlds and only see them in terms of them potentially suppressing his usual activities. Thrasher suggests that most knowledge and awareness that the middle-class boy takes for granted is foreign to the gang boy. It is what he refers to as 'lack of cultural communion with the world at large' (ibid., p. 181). These boys are denied access to wider social meanings. The boys are also poorly equipped to enter the middle-class jobs market. They lack interpersonal skills and the confidence in communication that the middle-class boys have.

Thrasher says that the boys will encounter demoralizing social patterns wherever they go. This involves both their experiences in the official institutions and also treatment by older gangs who may force them to give over money or carry out illegal activities for them. Thrasher concludes that for the gang boy the world will be defined basically through the moral, cultural and economic disorder of which the gangland is itself a product. Gang behaviour therefore can be seen as inseparable from the patterns which exist in the immediate environment.

The boys live in a world free from conventional forms of control and direction. The gang therefore takes over, and is even necessary as a response to the enemies which the boy will encounter each day, such as other gangs and authority. This necessitates an effort to act as a unit. This leads to structure, the development of a code of behaviour and methods of control. Living by the gang morality will itself bring a sense of belonging and integrity. The idea of honour, for example, was very important in the gangs. Revealing the identity of a co-offender in the gang would never happen. Often gangs would raise money to pay the fines of the caught member. Members may undergo severe hardships to help another member. Disloyalty could be punished by ostracism, violence, death or threats to family members.

Identity through conflict

Thrasher said that gangs only became tightly bound, having their own consciousness, rather than transitory, with the appearance of conflict. And conflict – having to fight for territory – helped to give the gang members a greater sense of belonging and group identity. Some delinquent activities seemed to be adopted mainly for the purpose of interdependence. These activities require cooperation and inter-dependence. Conflicts with other gangs or with authority are particularly important for this process of creating unity.

Thrasher felt that it was not surprising that gangs fight. On the one hand, aggression is a status symbol. A gang with a reputation for immediate violence will attract respect. On the other hand fighting is the only way the gangs can resolve anything, as much of what they defend is illegal. And it has to fight to maintain its privileges, its territory, on which it may be involved in liquor running of the older gangs. It must also fight just to maintain its status and thus give the members of the gang a sense of worth. The original cause of a feud may even be forgotten, but be lost in the need for revenge and the need to take back lost ground, although most relationships seem to go in cycles of conflict, peace, accommodation. Gangs may join with others for the purposes of defending larger territories and on the basic of shared grievances.

Excitement

One important feature of gang life is that it is exciting. It involves truancy from school to hang out in the hide out. It involves illicit or forbidden activities such as gambling. It involves pursuit and being chased, conflict, comradeship, standing by these people by not squealing, thus having principles and a moral code. Thrasher describes gangs who started young with a gang hideaway in an old barn where they would take food and pitch pennies. Then they would gamble more money, steal food and annoy the police who pursued them. Sometimes other gangs would try to run them off just for fun and they would have to defend their territory.

The gang world tended to encourage a life that is different from the world of work. The boys from the slum areas will only be able to get very dull routine jobs with no status. Often by quite a young age they are used to hanging out and gaining from petty crime, and they are already familiar with the status of being part of the gang.

Crime and excitement

Thrasher's data revealed an intriguing way of thinking about crime and vandalism. He says that some crime is about sport and must be thought of in this way. For example, stealing, which is one of the main activities of a young gang, is as much to do with the sport ethic as it is with material gain. He also points out that theft is a perfectly natural activity for the gang member. There is no sense that it is either wrong or immoral just as in the same way a middle-class youth would not think of his own achievements, opportunities and privilege as either wrong or immoral.

The younger gangs would have an awareness of the criminal underworld which was controlled by the older gangs. They will see lawbreaking everywhere they look. They can easily learn the necessary skills, find out where to buy guns. There is also an economic environment of poverty that leads to a ready market for stolen goods that otherwise would be out of reach of many families.

Theft might take the form of robbing fruit peddlers by distracting them. This might be to make money, eat or just for fun. This may involve robbing wholesalers. One gang Thrasher spent time with would spend days studying shops for a planned raid at the weekend. Younger boys would steal from drunken men. Carrying out such crimes in another gang's territory may provoke retaliation which itself would bring further excitement and an increased sense of group cohesion. Sometimes the thefts would be accompanied by destruction. Just the act of vandalism made the boys feel liberated, excited and doing their own thing. No one could tell them what they should do. Vandalism may even take place just to provoke a chase, to demonstrate that they could get away with it or some other skill. Thrasher talks about gang members feeling themselves to be above the petty rules of a society to which they felt superior. Interestingly, he describes the world of the gang as one rich in romantic imagination where the slum environment become a battlefield and where enemies are assigned special roles.

Thrasher did not think that gangs in themselves caused crime. They may have influenced members but primarily they were a response to a particular social environment. Therefore if we were able to integrate the gang boys into the wider society, the gang would not be necessary. Thrasher thought that the blame lay with institutions which failed to take into consideration the life experiences of the boys. He found, however, that despite poverty some of the Jewish areas had less gangs, suggesting that greater organization of recreation and the tighter-knit family communities could have an important effect on behaviour. Thrasher concludes that while gangs are a problem in that they are associated with all sorts of criminal behaviour, and are seen as a puzzle by the authorities, why they exist is basically quite simple and how they develop is quite predictable.

Thrasher's study of gangs is not unlike Malinowski's study of magic, in that it allows us to comprehend a behaviour or aspect of life that may seem peculiar to the outsider as something that makes complete sense to the person who lives within that culture. Both magic and gang membership, when understood in context, can be seen to be a result of people making sense of the world in which they find themselves, using the cultural definitions which they find around them. Therefore if we wanted to understand how people watch television, we would need to understand this as part of a way of life. What would one of Thrasher's gang members do with television and how would its images and representations of the world fit in with their wider experience of life? To do this could we ask them to fill in a questionnaire? Could we interview them, or get a group of them to sit around and discuss the relevant issues? These methods would all yield interesting and probably useful data but we would need to know how these people went about their lives, what they thought the world was like, and what cultural framework they generally brought to bear upon the world. Only this information would allow us to think about what would happen when they watch television. Hodge and Tripp (1986) suggest that it is very likely that people will interpret and take on television through a framework that they use to interpret their lives in general. An ethnography of how young people watch television should be a part of an ethnography about how they live their lives in general. Such a study should reveal the frames of reference through which the world generally makes sense to them.

Social deviance as something that is constructed by the wider society

H.S. Becker (1963) *Outsiders: Studies in the Sociology of Deviance.*
London: Collier-Macmillan Ltd

Outsiders is a fascinating and amusing study of marijuana users. The book is a study of the idea of deviance in society. Marijuana use is approached in a way that is very much like that taken by Thrasher to explore gang life. The gang member could only be thought of as deviant if we try to explain such behaviour through the values of the wider society. Therefore we need to look at exactly what meaning such behaviour has for the participants.

The concept of deviancy

Becker starts the book by saying that there are two kinds of rules: formal rules, enforced by law and the police, and informal laws, enforced by sanction. Becker was particularly interested in the informal rules which govern membership of a group. He wanted to understand the way that people who do not follow these rules and are therefore pushed outside the group are dealt with. He wanted to understand the process by which people become labelled as deviants.

Becker points out how the conventional questions asked about deviants are: why do they do it and how can such behaviour be prevented? The first of these questions is usually thought about in terms of some characteristic of the deviant such as weakness or malevolence. The answer to the second is usually that such behaviour can be stopped either by force or by somehow showing the deviants the error of their ways. Deviancy is often thought about as some sort of disease that should be stopped before it contaminates the wider society. At the least, it is seen as possibly destabilizing.

Based on his research Becker questions the assumption that there is something deviant about behaviour that is not in accord with accepted rules. Conventional wisdom sees the act of deviance as being something to do with the person who is the deviant. Such assumptions simply accept the values of the group who perceive the act of deviancy. Becker's basic point is that deviance is created by society. Deviancy is not an intrinsic quality, a kind of behaviour or a kind of a person but is simply a label used by other people. Deviance is therefore a kind of transaction between a social group and someone who is seen to break its rules. In this way it is a political act. Becker also points out that we cannot assume that those labelled as deviant will form a homogeneous category. All that people labelled as deviant have in common is that they share the label.

We can see that all this fits in with the basic Chicago School view that we cannot judge people but should understand their behaviour as being part of a social environment and as them making meanings within it. Deviancy is a label that the wider society may apply to gang violence, organized crime, homelessness and drug taking. Yet according to the perspective taken by the Chicago School these phenomena are ways in which people live as they make sense of their environments in the city. To view such behaviours simply as deviant is to view them through a set of evaluations that are not applicable to those worlds.

Becker was interested in the way that people could become seen as deviants. He wanted to understand how people could be labelled as such and how once they had acquired a trait that put them into that category, then they would remain there. This may be because they had once broken into a house to steal from it, or even because they were a black person, which would allow them, even if they were a middle-class professional, to be associated with a group associated with acts of deviancy such as crime.

Becker argued that once someone moves into the category of the deviant it will follow that their behaviour will generally become more like that thought of as appropriate for a deviant. Much of their behaviour will be interpreted as being evidence for this. They will be excluded from membership of non-deviant groups. Thus such a label produces a self-fulfilling prophecy. Labels of deviancy may give the individual little recourse other than to perform other acts that are thought of as deviant. A drug addict is labelled as deviant and as a wrongdoer. This puts them in an outsider position where they will probably have to turn to crime to support their habit. They will associate with other outsiders and inhabit a marginalized environment.

Marijuana users enjoying deviancy

Becker offers marijuana users as an example of deviance. Marijuana use was interesting as it allows people to feel deviant. Becker said that initially people's use of the drug was based on curiosity, but that later on behaviour is transformed into something else. More regular use produces definite patterns of action. But this will depend upon people's ability to interpret a rather ambiguous physical experience as something pleasurable. To an extent, the attraction of the deviancy label may be important in taking this step since the drug is widely known as a symbol of counter-culture. However, Becker's study was not as interested in this kind of use, but rather those people who were routine and perhaps even secretive users.

Learning to become a user

Becker wanted to develop a description of the stages that people went through in their use of marijuana. He said that to investigate this he used a method of analytic induction, meaning that he would look at cases and attempt to develop a theory. Any case which did not substantiate the theory/hypothesis would lead to a revision.

The research involved interviews with fifty users. Becker was himself a musician in a dance band where the drug was extensively used. This allowed him to learn about the drug's use from the point of view of a participant observer. We might think about

Becker's research as typically ethnographic. He immersed himself in the setting and was able to solve his anthropological puzzle which was why people become regular marijuana users.

Becker starts by looking at the way that people learned to smoke marijuana, which involved a technique different from that of smoking ordinary cigarettes. An important part of this was that the user had to learn how to perceive the effects. Even when early users used the correct smoking technique, they sometimes were not able to get high. Becker says that this would have been due to a problem of interpretation. It is not enough simply to feel effects of marijuana as these may not initially be experienced as being an indication of being high by the novice user. Usually, however, even though they did not feel high, novices would maintain faith that this would eventually happen as they had seen the effects of the drug on other people. Later, once the user was more experienced, early failure to get high would be explained in terms of lack of smoking technique. But the novice would persist as they had heard interpretations of being high like having rubber legs, cold feet and suffering from an intense hunger. They will be keen to participate in this and will learn to apply the things that they have heard to their own experiences. Becker says that it is only when this can be accomplished that the novice can be high.

Once the novice is able to recognize the symptoms of being high, they must then learn how to enjoy them. Becker points out that the effects are not something that people are generally able to automatically feel as pleasurable. The user will feel dizzy, confused and thirsty, and these experiences are unlikely to feel immediately pleasurable. But if the user is to continue marijuana use, they must decide that they are. These initial experiences may even be frightening. Many of the users in Becker's interviews said that this had been the case, as they found that they could not follow a conversation and felt disorientated. This redefinition of these things as pleasurable has to happen through interaction with experienced users who continually refer to such experiences as pleasurable. As the user continues, they will continue to learn a repertoire of the drug's effects. Once this is fairly wide and stable they can get high with ease. Basically, Becker is suggesting that on our own we would be unlikely to get a taste for the drug.

In Becker's approach so far we can see the ethnographic gaze that we talked about in previous chapters. Becker has not assumed that he can simply ask people why they like marijuana. He has taken the approach of looking at what people say about the drug and then checking this against how they behave. People might say that they like the drug as it makes them feel good. However, this does not correspond immediately to why they initially became involved in its use.

Becoming a deviant

Becker asks why people would want to use marijuana. There are heavy legal penalties, so use can be dangerous, and discovery may lead to others perceiving the user as a drug addict, irresponsible or even as a law-breaker. Families could respond with ostracism. Typically the user will be seen as being on a slippery slope to complete dependence on the drug and possible other harder drugs. Becker found that all of the people in his study kept their use secret as they feared the consequences of being found out by their family or others with whom they had relationships. This tended to be more of a worry to the novice. More experienced users were more comfortable with the fact that no one would find out. Some said they had to modify their behaviour due to concerns that their parents, wife or other family members would find out.

Becker says that notions of morality surrounding drug use also have to be overcome. For one thing there is the idea that marijuana is one step on the slippery slope to becoming a junkie. Becker says that the novice will at some point previous to being a user have held this conventional view. As the novice becomes more familiar with users they will come to see that this may not be the case. They will then come across other rationalizations that counter those of the wider community, such as the legal use of more harmful drugs like alcohol and the belief that the drug is in fact beneficial. New users also regulate their use to show themselves that they are definitely in control of it.

Becker's study is both amusing and informing. It allows us an insight into the way that people take up and come to enjoy marijuana. His observations also have broader implications for understanding the way that people in society come to find things in general as pleasurable. In earlier chapters I gave similar examples, for example, regarding why a person might say that they dislike Hollywood films but like art-house cinema. The latter is seen as authentic, the former, no matter how amazing a creation, can never be seen as a serious act of creativity. The person who says that they like art-house or world cinema will be aware of the way that, in their society, an appreciation of lesser-known cinema can appear an indication of intelligence and the ability to recognize creativity. Like marijuana use, it allows the speaker to mark themselves as different to the wider society. Art-house cinema-goers can sit and watch such movies knowing that they are few and that they, uniquely, have the aesthetic eye. They will have discovered this knowledge by experiencing the way that cinema, creativity and intelligence are represented in society. Becker would have wanted to look at the ways that these cinema-goers expressed their pleasure and aesthetic eye in social contexts.

I was once in an art-house cinema in Madrid to watch an afternoon of Gary Cooper films. I overheard a conversation at the next table where two men and two women in their thirties sat cross-legged, smoking cinematically, discussing films. My attention was particularly drawn when one of the men blew out his smoke thoughtfully and commented that he found it difficult to talk about real movies in his native Spanish saying that English and French were much more appropriate. This person's behaviour can be thought of as drawing on a range of discourses about elite knowledge, language, and art. Like the gang members and the marijuana smokers, it can be thought about in terms of a person making sense of their lives and expressing their place in the world using the framework available to them. Importantly, we can see that the person is using this framework in a way that is responsive to the people around him. He is not a cultural robot. I have never before heard someone say they preferred to speak in the appropriate language to discuss a foreign film. Yet the framework to which it belongs is immediately recognizable. Likewise his companions nodded in agreement.

The Chicago School and media studies

The reason for revisiting the approach used by the Chicago School is that these studies show how ethnography is suitable for research in the urban setting. It shows how we can make behaviour and social phenomenon that we normally take for granted appear arbitrary and constructed as we reveal the rules, strategies and cultural frameworks which people use to find their way in the world.

This means that we must look beyond isolated instances of social action, and we must move beyond the idea of simply being able to ask people to reveal the reasons for their behaviour to us. Thrasher helped us to understand vandalism in terms of the sport motif. Therefore the behaviour of the gang members can be seen as being connected to wider social discourses. Something becomes understandable if it is seen in context. We can think in the same way if we want to understand how people relate to television or movies. What social discourses inform the way that people interpret what they see when they watch a soap opera? How do the representations of the world offered up in these become part of the way that people live out their lives? How do these become part of their tool kit for understanding the world and their place in it? We need to think about this in terms of more general cultural frameworks through which we can demonstrate self, agency, power, and counter-culture.

4 Research approaches to the mass media

It is not unusual to hear the view expressed that the mass media have a powerful effect on people. It is this very view that saw the emergence of censorship in most Western countries in the first decade of the twentieth century, and underpinned European policy regarding television towards the end of that century. In each case the fear was that the media could influence what people think and what people do. In the latter case the European Commission feared that Hollywood imports would lead to the dilution of European cultures with cheap low quality programming.

Politicians frequently blame television for episodes of violence in society. In Britain in 1993 two young boys killed a three-year-old child basically by stoning him to death. The idea of the child murderer was a difficult one to swallow, but the easy answer came in the form of the video nasty. While sections of the quality press did speculate about the influence of poverty and social deprivation, the majority of the British news media and the Prime Minister at the time were more interested in the view that it was the fact that the children had possibly seen the film *Child's Play*, which contained scenes resembling those acted out by the killers. This idea that film was somehow to blame for crime is something as old as cinema itself. Some of the earliest studies into audiences took the starting point of looking for the effects of films on young offenders (Jowett 1976).

Much theorizing has gone on in academic writing about the effects of the mass media. However, very little actual audience research has been done. Audience responses are generally provided by the academic who is presumably able to rise above the way that the audience will read a particular television programme or movie. This may not be wholly problematic. An academic who has spent their career analysing films and their ideological content may indeed be tuned to see details that others might not. But without looking at what audiences are doing, we might argue, this can be nothing more than speculation. This seems especially the case if we return to our anthropological view of culture and our ethnographic gaze. Imagine if Malinowski had done no detailed ethnographic research. The accounts he produced of Trobriand beliefs in magic would have been no more sophisticated than those of the colonial traveller/explorers or missionaries who saw such beliefs purely in comparison to the beliefs held in their own cultures. In the previous chapter on the Chicago School we saw how it was important to see life in gangland in terms of the experiences and meanings of those who inhabit that world. Some film theorists might suggest that they live in the cultures about which they write and that therefore they are qualified to speculate about how people in that culture might be influenced by movies, or at least be in a position to decode the dominant message in the movie. No doubt they can speculate. But we have to ask whether the insights offered by the Chicago School about gangland could have been generated by the speculations of an academic who would have had a very different cultural framework. Some of the studies that we look at in later chapters point forcefully to the value of the observation of the finer details of social interaction.

In the rest of this chapter I want to look at some of the different approaches that have been taken to media audiences, some of them empirical and some not. In the 1980s, particularly in British Cultural Studies, there was a turn to audience research that is often referred to as the 'ethnographic turn'. A look at the different research approaches allows us to understand why this emerged. But we will see that while this research was pioneering, and revealed some fascinating features of the way that people relate to the mass media, it often lacked both the methodological approach that characterized ethnography in both anthropology and the participant observation of the Chicago School. Most importantly it lacked the approach to culture that lies at the heart of ethnography.

Histories of research into media effects usually take the form of a narrative which describes a progression from primitive to sophisticated. However, as Curran *et al.* (1982) suggest this narrative is artificial and different research paradigms can be found at different times. The narrative usually starts with the 'hypodermic' or 'magic bullet' model which assumed that people were directly affected, i.e. their views and behaviour could be changed in a causal way by the mainly visual media. It then usually moves on to more sophisticated views like the 'uses and gratifications' approach and Marxist views which suggested that effects were more difficult to pin down. In this latter approach it was thought that it was more useful to look at the way that the news media set the agenda for what people think of as being important in society.

For our purposes it is important to look generally at the different research approaches to media effects, although it is the case that such approaches were never quite as clearly contrasted as is often made out. This will allow us to see why ethnography can offer something special to the study of media audiences. We will see why Cultural Studies decided to look more closely at the audience in the ethnographic turn of the 1980s and we will look at why these studies were not, in some ways, very ethnographic at all.

Early film research

Most early media effects research was generated through fears of the negative influence of movies. One interesting early piece of research was carried out by Peterson and Thurstone in 1933 looking at how films influenced children's knowledge of ethnic groups. The study found that children who had no personal contact with certain ethnic groups had strong ideas of the characteristics that defined them. Although there were no control groups, and therefore it was difficult to be certain of the source of these stereotypes, the findings did seem to suggest that films could be powerful in informing where people had no other source of information.

Two other studies about the same time were much more sophisticated methodologically, coming from the Chicago School which, as we saw in the previous chapter, was pioneering the use of qualitative research in an urban setting. The studies were published in two separate volumes by Blumer (1933) and Blumer and Hauser (1933). In the first volume researchers collected data from several thousand young people who talked about their experiences of films and also about their lives in general. The data included autobiographies, reports on conversations about film, observations of children at play and in cinemas. The volume reports that film was a resource for many things, including fashion, behaviour and aspirations. The second volume looked specifically at how people in prison talked about film. Again, this used interviews and life histories, which were also corroborated by other official documents. This study also found that films offered a range of images through which people compared themselves and through which they thought about what was possible or desirable in the world.

Blumer refused to make any firm conclusions about any cause and effect relationship between film and behaviour. However, he did suggest that there could be problems where films presented romanticized images of criminal activities, even where in the end the criminal activity was punished. But most of all Blumer emphasized that film was received by audience members in the context of their social background and individual life histories.

Some aspects of this research can be criticized as the researchers had a tendency to simply accept what respondents told them. For example, Blumer and Hauser said: 'Seventy-one per cent of the sample of 252 delinquent girls acknowledged that motion pictures make them want to have fine clothes, automobiles, wealth, servants, etc.' (1933, p. 97). The researchers give examples of the comments of some of these respondents, for example, whom they describe as

> White, 16, sexual delinquent – In seeing movies you get a desire to have pretty clothes, automobiles, and several other things that make one happy. If you have no relatives to get these things for you, usually you get in trouble trying to get them yourself. (ibid., p. 96)

The authors do not seem to consider that what these young people may be doing is simply reproducing a cultural representation of how films affect people. In our society it is a long accepted discourse that this is one method that the media uses to affect audiences. In terms of the arguments we looked at in Chapter 2 on the ethnographic way of looking at culture, we might view such statements as one cultural way of talking about the media and its effects.

At other times, however, the authors did express the view that in order to be certain about such statements we need to look at data from a range of sources. We cannot take people's statements alone but need to triangulate, i.e. use data from a range of sources.

Political economy

One of the most influential ways of thinking about media effects has been through what is called the political economy approach. This approach is not so much a look at how the audience themselves are affected but is an analysis of the nature and origins of the programmes, films or magazines which audiences interact with. This approach has limitations as it has little to say about what audiences actually do. But it has the value of explaining things like the processes which lead to the production and emission of a television programme in terms of patterns of ownership.

The starting point for accounts of the political economy approach to the mass media is usually the work of Theodor Adorno, a German Marxist who had fled Europe during World War II to live in America. Having witnessed the way that people seemed to be manipulated by the mass media in Nazi Germany Adorno was equally concerned by what he saw in America where he thought that people were being turned into passive receptacles of consumerism.

Adorno (1941, 1991) felt that mass communications in America offered a diet of everything that was undemanding, superficial and mind-numbing. He argued that the mass media were being used to manipulate the masses and create a culture where consumerism was seen as a natural way to self-fulfilment and happiness and where awareness of the nature of inequalities in society was increasingly absent. Adorno was very critical of the new wave of jazz music at that time, dismissing it as being formulaic, highly repetitive and completely predictable. He thought that this could be explained as being in the interests of media corporations only concerned to sell as much as possible in order to increase profits. Thus, rather than innovation and creativity, which he thought characterized classical music, corporations were only interested in the formula that would sell. This argument is very much like one frequently heard at the beginning of the twenty-first century as a criticism of pop music, which is often thought of as being dominated by manufactured acts dreamt up by record companies.

Adorno thought that this tendency towards the formulaic at the expense of creativity and innovation would lead to a loss of intellectual stimulation in the name of consumerism. The masses, who were being encouraged to buy into this one-dimensional world, would become numbed to the real nature of the capitalist world.

Adorno's view has been challenged both for its misunderstanding of the origins of much of the music he criticized and for its elitist and dismissive view of the working classes, a point made strongly by the American structural functionalists (Shils 1971). Adorno, in fact, later modified his dismissive view of the working classes and talked more about what he called the 'culture industry' rather than mass culture which seemed to present 'the masses' as basically stupid. This view of the passive audience was later challenged in British Cultural Studies. Much emphasis was placed on the way that audiences were active and critical. But Adorno's main point was an extremely important one. Even if we are active as consumers, our capacity to be critical may be limited if all the music, television and newspapers to which we have access come from one particular source which has the main aim of making as much money as possible.

The work of Adorno and the Frankfurt School to which he belonged have inspired a generation of media analysts. Works on the political economy of communications have taken the form of examining the structure of media ownership and analysing the media texts themselves, showing how they generally reflect the interests of capitalism. One of the best-known political economy writers is Noam Chomsky. In the book *Manufacturing Consent* (1994), co-authored by Edward Herman, he argues that the American media offer a partial view of the world which supports the government and the interests of capital. The authors argue that the American media are owned and controlled in a fashion that links them into the ownership of other large corporations and capital interests in general. To demonstrate their arguments the authors give examples of the way that certain international conflicts, where America has an interest, may not even make it into the news if this might reflect on the country badly, or if this clashes with corporate interests. Reporting on Third World countries tends to favour US interests in supporting or destabilizing a regime. Where peasants stand against a government supported by America they are described as communist guerrillas whereas US-backed and US-funded military action in oppressive regimes is talked about in terms of the fight against communism. The authors argue that the news media use the term terrorism to report on what are basically a handful of acts of violence against American interests while they ignore the many people who are killed in systematic acts of violence which are supported by the government.

In Britain during the 1970s the Glasgow Media Group took a political economy approach to the British news media. They looked at the miners' strike, demonstrating how reporting failed to explain issues and reasons for the strike clearly. Reasons for the strike were always taken from an 'expert' or 'official' source. Any non-officials appearing in the news would be members of the public who were concerned about the effects of the strike. Likewise, Golding and Middleton (1982) studied agenda setting in the way that the news media blamed certain social groups for the state of the economy. They examined the way that those who 'cheat' welfare benefits are described as 'scroungers' who appeared as one of the major enemies of the national good and of the ordinary decent person. These studies offered thought-provoking accounts of how the media may limit the information that audiences are given, thus encouraging certain ways of viewing events. But we are given no sense as to what the audiences make of what they receive. In one sense, the work of Adorno removes the necessity for this to be done as people are dominated by the ideology of the dominant classes. Only the free-floating intellectual is able to perceive the true nature of the content of the mass media.

Some of the Marxists moved away from the traditional emphasis of looking at how external social and economic factors determined ideology to focus more on textual analysis. These writers drew on structuralism, semiotics and psychoanalytical theory. These studies (e.g. Williamson 1978; Myers 1988) examined the way that the dominant ideology is not so much imposed upon audiences through biased and selective reporting but influences them through it being part of everyday life. For example, these writers looked at advertising. They offered analyses of the way that products are used to signify personality traits and lifestyles – a mobile phone is used to indicate the world of the independent confident young female, sexually assertive and sporting tattoos. We are therefore encouraged to think about ourselves, our aims and the world, in terms of consumer products. Consumption is presented as the natural state of affairs. The dominant ideology is thus maintained by being attached to the everyday.

These studies were also influenced by a mode of analysis that was applied to the study of the way that films influence people. This approach, dominating the film journal *Screen*, particularly in the 1970s, drew on French film theorists such as Metz (1975). Contributing writers, like Mulvey (1975), Wollen (1982) and McCabe (1976), were interested in the way that the world was constituted by films. This writing was heavily influenced by Lacan (1977) who had been interested in the constitution of the human subject through language. This was translated to the study of film in order to think about how films constructed the gaze of the spectator. It asked how films place us in their imaginary worlds and what effect this has on the way that we then see the worlds we inhabit in everyday life. For example, Laura Mulvey (1975) argued that since, in films, the protagonist is generally male, it is his gaze that defines the way the world is viewed. This male viewer will take on the male protagonist as his ideal self as he watches the film. This will, therefore, influence the view of the world that the spectator will take. Mulvey felt that this would be problematic for the female viewer who would have no choice other than to identify either with the view of the male protagonist or the female romantic interest, who would be passive and eroticized. The reason that men liked women to be presented in this way was because their subconscious recalled the moment when they felt that their mothers had been castrated. This would have lead them, through anxiety, to exaggerate emphasis placed on aspects of the mother that were obviously different such as her breasts and legs. Therefore the women that appear in movies are generally fetishized. This can only serve to further legitimize women's subordinate positions in society.

One criticism of this approach to the way that either advertisements or cinema influences people is that it is the theorist who provides the reading. These studies give us little sense of what the audiences themselves are thinking. As we shall see shortly this criticism was to influence a generation of research. One study that was particularly critical of Mulvey will be looked at in Chapter 10.

Functionalist approaches

In post-war America researchers challenged the pessimism of the hypodermic model from the view that this had concentrated too much on the message rather than effects. Merton (1946) focused on propaganda, saying that while it was clear that it used stereotypes and rhetorical styles to evoke national images no one had looked on how people were in fact affected by this. The effects had been described by the unaffected analyst. Later Katz and Lazarsfeld (1956) undertook small group research to argue that people were not directly injected by the mass media message as reception involved personal environment and the opinions of those around us. Other functionalist approaches (Riley and Riley 1959) considered the way that the media functioned for the good of society, offering a view of media as a democratic instrument. There was some quite subtle and quality research done around this time involving large-scale surveys looking at behaviours and attitudes of children and the way that television fitted into their lives. For example, the study by Schramm *et al.* (1961) *Television in the Lives of our Children*, indicates in its title that the medium should be studied in terms of reception in context. These studies tended to reject the idea of media effects that could be easily measured, emphasizing the importance and complexity of reception by very different children. Children are given credence for having the ability to process what they watch. But in the USA after the 1950s the pressure for research into media effects was growing (Wartella and Reeves 1985), particularly with the growing concern with the relationship between television and violence. Research with more sophisticated and complex findings was not much use to politicians who wanted simple quotable results.

Lab studies

This call for the demonstration of what effects televisions had encouraged psychologists to become involved. While this drew on the use of what claimed to be scientific methods shrouded in concepts like hypothesis and null hypothesis, such studies generally based their whole premise on certain cultural representations. For example, Singer and Singer (1981) carried out experiments which looked at the way that television limits imagination. Such research often harks back to idealized forms of stimulation like reading. Starker (1991) has argued that all forms of media, even literature, have attracted such concerns about limiting imagination in their time. Singer in his

Introduction even reminisces fondly about the lyrics from classical musicals by Gilbert and Sullivan which in his own youth had stimulated his own imagination into lands of mystery and fantasy. This is based on a very narrow view of what imagination means, and it tends to get mixed up with elitist notions of what is healthy to think about and what should be forbidden knowledge for children.

The experimental approach involved measuring immediate physiological or emotional responses to television. Singer concluded that children sat in front of the television blankly absorbed by its seductive colours and styles, even though they admitted that actual experiments seemed to show nothing conclusive.

One criticism of lab studies is that they are carried out in an artificial context. Can we take how people behave in a laboratory as evidence for how they would behave in everyday life situations? And are immediate responses a good means of measuring the way that people relate to the media which, after all, forms a much more regular part of people's lives?

Liberal-pluralist approaches

Usually referred to as the 'uses and gratifications' approach, liberal-pluralist approaches were the first since some of the early American studies to think it worthwhile to take a look at what people actually did with television. This approach tended to see a much greater degree of harmony between the media and society. It came from an assumption that the media tended to represent the views of audiences who otherwise would withdraw their support. McQuail *et al.* (1972) looked at the different reasons people gave for watching programmes. They looked at what people said about game shows, finding that audiences referred to different kinds of pleasures, including education, excitement and the social interaction that shared viewing facilitates. These categories were extended when they looked at soap opera to include things like emotional release, companionship, escapism, emotional moments, and empathy of life situation. These studies claimed to challenge the view that most television viewers were only interested in simple entertainment pleasures. They also found that these different gratifications could be fulfilled by different genres. The point was that we needed to be aware that people have different reasons for watching television, and therefore the kind of effect that it had on them would certainly depend upon this.

Lazarsfeld *et al.* (1944) looked at the way that voting behaviour was influenced by the media. They concluded that, by and large, people stayed with the same views. The media message either reaffirmed their existing views or was rejected. Katz and Lazersfeld (1956) looked at the influence of the media on how women thought about a range of opinions and also concluded that pre-existing opinions were most important.

These studies were important, as they were a reminder that we need to be more careful when making sweeping generalizations about audiences uniformly sitting blankly in front of the screen waiting to be pleasured. They were certainly popular at that time as the idea of democracy seemed safe (Barrat 1986). But the problem with such studies is that they involve asking people what they think of television and how they respond to it. This in itself is an important source of data. But from this data alone we cannot be certain whether this corresponds to what these people actually do. And we are still left with little idea of how people take on what they see into their overall lives as effects are given a rather narrow definition. Simply put, these studies tend to present the findings in a way that makes them difficult to locate in terms of social context.

Another criticism which has been levelled at these studies points out that the programmes watched will still tend to contain certain dominant ideological messages about the world which will encourage a certain world view, even if viewers have particular reasons for watching.

Cultural studies

In the 1980s there was a wave of media research in Britain that turned its attention to the audiences themselves. Much of this had its origins in the Birmingham Centre for Contemporary Cultural Studies (CCCS). This emphasis on the audience has been termed 'the ethnographic turn'. In this section I will look at how and why the CCCS considered it important to return to the audience.

The director of the Birmingham School, Stuart Hall, had become concerned with the political economy approach which tended to look at media ownership and at the nature of texts that were produced in relation to this – texts that were suffused with dominant ideology which made capitalism and inequality seem natural, inevitable and even appropriate. He thought that such a level of analysis was important in the first instance but still thought that on its own it was too simplistic. He and the members of the CCCS asked what happened to these dominant ways of viewing the world once they were received by audiences. The Birmingham School moved away from the idea of economic determinism which saw the ideas in society as simply reflecting the interests of the economically powerful and being imposed from above. They drew upon the writings of Althusser (1984), who thought that society was already suffused with such ideas which had become part of the taken-for-granted way that people see the world. These ideas underpin the practices of institutions, such as education, in society.

Hall was also influenced by Gramsci's (1971) idea of *hegemony*. Hegemony refers to the way that a group works to infuse its ideas into society to give them the appearance of being natural and inevitable. Society is always a site of ideological struggle for hegemonic control. This control is achieved by being able to influence the ideas that people have in their heads about how society works and what is believed to be right and wrong in that society. For example, in Western capitalist societies this might mean the ideas that legitimate massive inequalities, social problems and exploitation in the name of a minority of people remaining rich and powerful. These things are accepted by most people and are considered as both natural and inevitable. Such ideas are not imposed by coercion but form part of everyday life and are seen to form the consensus. It would be an interesting project, Gramsci suggested, to actually examine the aspects of society that help to keep certain ideologies dominant and look at how this works on people. This was exactly the project taken up by cultural studies. The mass media were one important organization that spread the dominant ideology.

There was also a dissatisfaction in the CCCS with textual analysis where the writer gave an authoritative analysis of, say, a film or television programme showing how it was suffused with dominant ideology which they felt they were able to freely identify and analyse for what it was. This would allow them to deduce what the reading of a more general audience would be. Members of the CCCS, therefore, proposed to actually find out what audiences did with these dominant messages, although much of British Cultural Studies does in fact still deal with the implied reader, which tends to give the text its own intentionality as if the text existed with a meaning external to those given to it by people.

The ethnographic turn

One of the most influential and groundbreaking of these audience studies was done by David Morley. Morley (1980) took issue particularly with the work that was appearing in the journal *Screen* in the 1970s which he considered had just such a tendency to let the analyst provide the reading of the text on behalf of a generalized audience.

Drawing on Hall (1980), Morley (1980) argued that texts are polysemic. Simply put, by this he meant that texts are open to interpretation. Different people will read a television programme, for example, in different ways depending upon who they are and the cultural baggage that they bring with them to the viewing. This sounds a simple enough assertion but was one that had never really been looked at thoroughly by media researchers.

In keeping with the general ethos of the Birmingham School Morley also thought that there was a need to relate these different readings to the socio-economic structure of society. In other words, we should be able to say how people with different backgrounds read a television programme and say how this fits into general ideas in society. In this way we should be able, as Gramsci suggested would be desirable, to map out how certain dominant ideological messages are both placed in society and how these are then taken on by different kinds of people.

Morley brought people from different socio-economic and cultural groups into his department to talk about the British magazine and current affairs television programme *Nationwide*. He divided them into focus groups by their different characteristics and asked them to discuss different aspects of the programme. He found that the different groups interpreted, or (the term he used) decoded, the programme in different ways. He emphasized that this interpretation is 'not simply a question of the different psychologies of individuals but is also a question of differences between individuals involved in different sub-cultures, with different socio-economic backgrounds' (1992, p. 80). He said that texts like *Nationwide* are read according to two different factors. One is the structure of the text which invites a certain kind of reading and the other is the cultural background of the viewer. It is the interaction of the two which will lead to the meaning of the text for the viewer. So the idea was to look at both: on the one hand, the text itself and, on the other, how the audience interpret that text.

Rather than assuming a passive approach to viewing Morley emphasized the active role of interpretation. This interpretation depended upon the extent to which the messages the media give us are similar to or different from our own existing views, which we will have developed through our own experiences and from those around us.

Morley said that the important thing about a magazine/current affairs programmes like *Nationwide* is that it speaks about ordinary people in the world and claims to deal with the relevant concerns that they have about life and society. He said that these items 'tend to constitute what we might think of as a set of "base-line" assumptions about life in contemporary Britain and about what are the "sensible" attitudes for us to take towards various "social problems" ' (1992, p. 82). These will not be openly spelled out for the viewer but are nevertheless present and are the basis upon which issues are approached. Morley said that we should think of the events dealt with in the programme as being 'encoded' in a particular way to offer a particular reading. But the text can then always be decoded in a range of ways by the audience. An example of the different decoding that Morley found were that a group of managers who had quite right-wing views found *Nationwide* to be left-wing. They thought that the programme was far too favourable, for example, to unions. A group of students found the programme sensationalist and offering a poor level of information about events. A group of black students completely rejected everything about the programme. It said nothing about their lives or concerns. They rejected any representations of their own lives offered by the programme. A group of working-class apprentices who were largely Conservative in their ideology thought the programme was a little too formal or middle class but saw it essentially as just doing its job of reporting on the world as it was.

Morley said that his study revealed that people read television programmes in different ways. Some of these are 'dominant' which is fairly close to the reading which would be offered by the programme. This would be characterized by the apprentices who shared the programme's view of the world. The opposite of this would be an 'oppositional' reading, like that of the further education students who rejected the world offered by the programme. And in between these would be a 'negotiated' reading.

Morley's work is important as it inspired a new wave of audience studies. In the United States Janice Radway carried out a similar kind of audience study based on a psychoanalytical approach but inspired mainly by the wave of audience studies originating from the CCCS. This study was published as *Reading the Romance* in 1984. Radway was interested in the way that women read romantic novels. She wanted to challenge the prevalent assumption of the passive audience, the passive housewife with an ever-duller mind soaked in the mindless, uncritical and predictable world of romance fiction which offered nothing more than stereotyped views of masculine and feminine roles. Radway, like Morley, was critical of existing work, which quite conveniently provided the reading on behalf of the audience. She emphasized the importance of working *with* the audience. Radway was also influenced by anthropology and the symbolic interactionism of Blumer (1969).

Radway started by asking what a literary text is evidence of. What can we assume of its readers? Radway was part of a movement within American literature studies which wanted to challenge an assumption in American scholarship that American culture could be found in its greatest works of art, that for example, the great American novels would reveal something characteristic of American people as a whole. The challenge was that most people did not read the classics and therefore that the emphasis should be on what they did read. Radway went into the homes of women who read romantic fiction, spent time with them and talked to them about romantic fiction. What she found was that romance readers used their books to find time for themselves away from their domestic duties. Also, far from reinforcing stereotypes, the books offered images of heroes and heroines that would not be in opposition to feminism. Readers would not buy books if they thought that they contained subordinate women characters. This led Radway to conclude that the women readers of romantic fiction were not passive but active and demanding. The publishers of these books had to respond to the changing demands of the women if they were to continue to command readership loyalty. Through working with the audience Radway helped to challenge assumptions about the way that romance books were used in the lives of their readers.

These volumes by Morley and Radway were influential in stimulating a tradition in audience research often referred to as the 'ethnographic turn'. Media researchers realized the importance of looking at reception in the context of what people brought to the texts with them. Some of these studies will be looked at more closely in the next chapter.

Audiences as people living in culture

The main characteristic of these audience studies was that they emphasized the active audience in order to challenge the intellectual tradition which had provided the reading on their behalf. Later, however, these same researchers became concerned about this model of the active audience. They began to feel that the way that the media were produced for people and the way that people might have been influenced by the nature of its content had been left behind in favour of an emphasis on demand. Morley himself criticized the wave of research that he himself had inspired: 'that in recent years the question of media power as a political issue has tended to slip off the research agenda of this burgeoning field of "demand-side" research' (1992, p. 18). Morley became concerned that such studies had tended to over-emphasize the ability of audiences to construct their own meanings from what they experienced through the mass media. This is reflected in Fiske's (1984) celebration of a 'semiotic democracy'. Observing the way that people could be guaranteed to make their own, often challenging, interpretations of tabloid newspapers, Fiske had felt that it was impossible, therefore, to simply impose views of the world upon readers.

These very same researchers also became concerned with how these studies had been happy to study people as audiences in ways which were disconnected from their everyday lives. Ang (1990) was concerned with how such studies had looked at audience groups based on, say, social class or race. In this way these people become characterized as being static audience members who carry with them an unchanging set of readings of the media. Ang argued that:

> The perspective of the ethnography of audiences has led to a boom in isolated studies of the ways in which this or that audience group actively produces specific meanings and pleasures out of this or that text, genre or medium. (1990, p. 243)

Ang suggested that we needed to look at reception as 'an integral part of popular cultural practices that articulate both "subjective" and "objective", both "micro" and "macro" processes' (ibid., p. 224). This looked very much like a call for the kind of approach that we have already found in anthropology and the Chicago School. In these approaches any single aspect of culture or behaviour is understood as part of a much broader web of cultural meanings.

Radway (1988) herself argued that research needed to get away from thinking about reception in an isolated way, or of audiences as something that are external to the rest of people's lives. Rather than considering an audience member, she suggested, research had to think about people in terms of 'the active producing cultural worker who fashions narratives, stories, objects and practices from myriad bits and pieces of prior cultural production' (1988, p. 362). Radway said that rather than looking for set demographic characteristics of audience members, we need to think of them as 'nomadic subjects'. This term was intended to capture the way that people use culture in a creative fashion in order to make sense of the world and place themselves in different settings.

Research which has attempted to discover how people are part of different and shifting discourse communities – Radway's 'nomadic subjects' – has been sparse in audience studies. Frazer (1992) in 'Teenage girls reading *Jackie*', and Dahlgren (1992) in 'Viewer's plural sense-making of TV news' have suggested that we should look at the way that people talk in different contexts. Dahlgren, drawing on Goffman (1974), distinguished between 'official' and 'public' discourse. He noticed that people used a different style of speech and different content to talk about the news when they talked with him and when they talked in public places. Dahlgren's observation is important, although he is content with the idea of there being only two discourses and still does not connect these to the wider culture. But what I think this illustrates is the need to be much more open to the different ways that people speak at different times and the discourses that they use to do this.

The social psychologists Bruner and Weisser (1991) once described the way that we interact with culture as the 'navigation of self'. We are always trying out the ideas and representations that we see around us as we try to make sense of the world and, perhaps more importantly, as we find our place in that world. In Chapter 2 I suggested that cultures might be thought of as a kind of tool kit for dealing with and organizing the chaos of experience. This tool kit is made up of a framework of notions which help us to live in and manage the world together. Like witchcraft and science these will be accepted as common-sense world-views. But they may also be models of how things work which may serve a particular interest. And when asked to reflect upon their opinions of something, or give the reasons that they behave in a particular way, people will do little more than produce official common-sense explanations which the cultural framework offers to do such explaining. Together, these points suggest that we need to have a much more flexible view of the way that people talk in any context and of the way that they are influenced by things such as the mass media.

Another feature of our cultural tool kit is that the parts of our models need not be consistent. One of the wonderful things about the ideas that are available to us about how things work is that we can use them as needs be. Polanyi (1958) described the way than both witchcraft and science work by allowing us to explain things away rather than directly answer questions. Taking this view of human action on board – one which emphasizes people improvising with culture and a quality of performance – the idea of static audience groups seems a very limited one. This is what we might think of as a disassembled ethnography. These are the kind of moments in people's lives that need to be reconnected to the ongoing flow of people's everyday life if we are to gain any insight into what is actually going on. The ethnographic gaze is one which realizes that this subsequent act of reassembly is necessary. Practically, this would mean examining the nature of the texts, such as a television programme, or a genre of novel, in the way that Radway and Morley did. But then rather than getting people to respond to these texts in a particular setting we need to find out how people talk about them in different settings, and how they relate to some of the themes of the programme in their lives in general. One thing that simply asking them to discuss the programme will illustrate is the kind of models available in a society for the assessment of programmes in such settings.

What Dahlgren (1992) found was that people have official and public discourse for assessing newspapers. Here he was tapping into something that is highly characteristic of human culture and of the way that people talk about things. Such an observation sows the seeds of an ethnographic gaze. These ways of talking can be thought of as the discourse available for talking about newspapers. And it is in here somewhere that people are motivated to act. Morley also has touched on this point when he said:

> Even if it could be seriously argued that my results misrepresent the actual viewing behaviour of these men, it would remain a social fact of considerable interest that these were the particular accounts of their behaviour that these viewers felt constrained to give. (1986, p. 52)

Previously he had said that such studies had given an insight into people's attitudes to, say, television. But what he is suggesting here is much more interesting as he is giving a sense that what his data shows is people using their cultural tool kit. In the ethnographic gaze the approach is to look for the way that people use and live through this tool kit.

In the introductory chapter we thought about the idea of a society, or a public, as being like a conversation taking place in a parlour. In this model the interlocutors in the conversation should not be thought of as having fixed positions. The discussion moves on as people align themselves with some and against others. The conversation had already started before any of them arrived and there were already some taken-for-granted ways of participating, although the conversation will, and does, change. When people talk about something like a television programme they are very much like the interlocutants in this parlour.

In the chapters that follow I will be looking at a range of studies that have been offered as ethnographies and will assess the degree to which they allow us to see people living through culture in this way – whether they have an ethnographic gaze. In the final three chapters I will be looking at some ethnographic data that clearly illustrate the power of this kind of approach to audiences.

5 How good is ethnography compared to other methodologies?

In this chapter we look at ethnography in terms of the way it stands up as a research methodology. In social research there are a number of accepted concepts that are generally used to assess how well a methodology works. These concepts allow us to think about whether the research that we have done actually represents the world out there accurately in the way that we are claiming that it does. We will look at claims that ethnography makes to do this, as compared to other methodologies. Additionally, in anthropology, there has been some self-criticism as regards ethnography which took place particularly in the last few decades of the twentieth century. All ethnographers should be aware of these criticisms and the ways that anthropologists have suggested that they can be addressed. We will take a look at these later in the chapter.

Validity

Validity is a concept used to think about whether or not your data show what you think they show. If in a questionnaire you ask how many televisions a person has in their house and they said that they had two, you would probably assume that there is a high chance that the answer is valid. You have asked a simple question and got a simple answer. The validity of the answer would depend on whether we trust the person to tell us the truth. And we might ask why would anyone want to lie about the number of televisions that they had in their house, unless they had just robbed a warehouse and had rather more there than they would like to admit?

Social surveys based on questionnaires or question–answer interviews rely on the fact that people will tend to tell the truth. It is rarely questioned whether or not people do tell the truth. In something like a national census we might be more certain about the answers being valid due to the threat of legal action, although we have no other way of checking, unless we have other survey data with which to compare the results. However, if we are dealing with, say, questions about what electrical equipment someone has in their home, we might not think it important to concern ourselves as to whether they are lying about such a thing.

The issue of whether our respondents are telling the truth becomes more complex when the questions we ask are about things that people may be more reluctant to share. This is often the problem with questions about sexual behaviour, income and political preferences, for example. People often seem unwilling to be open about such issues. Even though the respondent might not know the interviewer, or the person who will analyse the questionnaires, they may either feel that such things are private, or may be unwilling to be thought of in a particular way. Once I was asked by some students to fill out a questionnaire which asked me to list my top five television pro- grammes. Initially, when I thought about it, I really had no idea which were in fact my favourites. I tried to think what I most often watched. It turned out that this was sports programmes. One other that I really enjoyed was *Cheaters,* an American programme that investigates and challenges people who cheat on their partner. Yet I felt awkward putting this down. I did not feel that these correctly reflected who I was. Particularly, in the case of *Cheaters,* would the students realize that I did watch the programme partly because it was so absurd with presenter Tommy Grand in the role of a guiding angel? In the end I wrote down the football programmes along with some intellectual comedy programmes.

Another problem of asking about people's tastes and attitudes is that people may like to think about themselves in a particular way that they prefer to present as their public self. For example, a person might like to think about, or at least talk about themselves, as someone who does not like soap opera. They might say that they see such programmes as stupefying. They might say that they prefer to occupy them- selves with more lofty pastimes. Yet when we observe these people we might find that they watch quite a lot of soaps. In my own ethnographic studies I have found that it is very difficult to accept what people say about exactly what they do. It is not the case that they are lying, rather, we have to think about how people talk in a slightly differ- ent way. The earliest anthropologists, like Malinowski, warned that simply asking people what they are doing is no way to find out what they are in fact doing and why, although it is important to ask them. As we shall see in later chapters, this in itself is an important source of data.

Additionally, we cannot assume that people have access to the reasons why they do something or what they believe about something. As we saw in Chapter 2, cultures generally provide us with official reasons for doing things. These do not necessarily have to have very much to do with how people actually go about their business. These are practical explanations and are good for practical purposes. Polanyi (1958) and Malinowski (1922) warned that people do not have access to the reasons that they do things, even though in our culture we feel that we always do act with purpose and rea- son. In Chapter 1 we looked at Malinowski's assertion that we cannot just ask people, for example, why they believe in magic. Could you really articulate why you believed in science? There are official reasons that we have available for providing such explan- ations, but these may have little to do with why in fact we end up believing in things.

Questionnaires, it could be argued, are poor on validity. We have no way of check- ing what we are told. Questionnaires, if we wanted to be really negative, are acts of faith. Also, validity might be poor if we base our observations on a little known activity.

The early travellers who wrote about the practices of exotic cultures saw instances of what they thought were grotesque sexual and religious practices. But these observers were simply making conclusions based on their own preconceptions. Thus we might challenge the validity of their observations in that they were not studying what they thought they were studying.

Data generated through questionnaire surveys can be criticized on the grounds of validity on the basis of the way that a framework is created which is then applied to the world in order to measure what is happening in that world. Anyone who has tried to construct a questionnaire or fit observations into a 'data collection instrument', i.e. categories that can then be put into a statistical database, will know how much fudging and arbitrariness this involves.

Emile Durkheim's classic study of suicide (1952), where he correlated suicide rates to social change, was criticized for making just this kind of mistake. By correlating different sets of official statistics obtained from different countries, he concluded that suicide is influenced by rapid social change. Critics claimed that such statistics are themselves social constructs. Different societies have different values and different legal systems that will influence the way that deaths become recorded as suicides. Catholic countries, for example, have low incidences of suicide as deaths are more likely to be recorded as being accidental because suicide is deemed heinous. This approach of looking for patterns which seem relevant in the context of the researcher's cultural viewpoint can be reasonably compared to the view of the colonial travellers who saw magic as evidence of a primitive mind. This is because the reality is approached to see if it fits a preconceived theory. Durkheim concluded that suicide correlated with social change. But, then, this is what he was looking for. What if suicide rates also correlated with ownership of goldfish? Durkheim would not have thought about checking this because he was using a set of preconceived ideas. Thrasher's (1927) example of the sport motif in vandalism and theft in gangland, that we looked at in the Chapter 3 on the Chicago School, is something that could not be discovered by questionnaires, as it is not something that people who had not experienced gang life could anticipate.

The power of ethnography lies right here. Ethnography allows the researcher to be much more certain about the validity of their data. I will know which programmes you watch because I will have been watching with you. I will be able to develop a sense of why you watch this by observing other preferences in your life. Let us say I might find that a person is keen to point out that they watch documentary-style programmes. I might find that generally they like to consider themselves as being informed, sophisticated and educated. Although they have told me that they dislike game shows or candid camera-style shows, complaining throughout as to their absurd nature it could be the case that they do take some pleasure from them. Ethnography allows me to look at this person's life more broadly, how they act and talk about a range of things such as films, politics or social problems. It will allow me to look at the discourses in their culture that are available for assessing television and how these allow us to think about ourselves. Ethnography would allow me to examine what discourses are used to talk about different television genres.

The way that ethnography can look at things from different angles is sometimes called *triangulation*. This will allow me to locate the way you talk about television programmes and yourself into your life more broadly. It will allow me observe how you use your particular cultural tool kit to make sense of the world. We can be more certain about the validity of our observations if we make them from different perspectives. Questionnaire-based surveys could also be said to use triangulation if they also use some participant observation to enrich their data.

Representativeness

Looking at whether a piece of research is representative means considering the extent to which your data are representative of a population. A social survey might carry out questionnaire based interviews of 100 people in a city. These people will be randomly stopped by the researchers in the street. The research might then claim to be representative of all people in the city which has two million inhabitants. This could be challenged if the research was carried out at 4 p.m. in the afternoon and this happened to be a time when many people would be working. In this case it might not be a fair indication of the people in general who live in the city. It would be more accurate to say that the research was representative of the population of the city who did not work. Of course, this could be checked by asking the question as to whether the person was currently in employment. But you get the idea. If we want to make statements about a population then the people we ask must be representative of that population. If that population had a proportion of 52 per cent women, then if we asked mainly men, our results would not be representative of the population.

The attempt to make a piece of research representative is done by sampling. Sampling is the way in which a piece of research goes about making sure that its respondents match the characteristics of the population that it wishes to represent. We might do a *random sample* if we want to find out about people in general. This would mean asking anyone. It could mean sticking pins in a list of names in a telephone directory. Or it could be done by *strategic random sampling* which might involve choosing every tenth name on a list.

But if we want to find out about young people's television preferences, then there would be little point asking people randomly on the street. We will have to ask people under a certain age. This is often referred to as a *targeted sample*. This might mean that we would stop young people and ask them their age before continuing with the questionnaire. We might also want to make sure that we have the right proportion of males and females that represent our population as a whole. This is often called *quota sampling.*

Whether a sample is thought to be representative may also be due to its size. If I asked 20 people about their television preferences, this would not be thought to be representative of the population of several million, even if the sample was proportionally composed of the same kind of people as the population as a whole. There are no rules to how many people are representative but to represent a population of several million we might at least want to ask several hundred people, although several thousand would make the results more representative.

Ethnography is often criticized for not being representative in that it tends to involve relatively small detailed samples. Some of the ethnographic studies I have taken part in have involved the detailed focus on around 40 people. What such a study reveals is the fine details about everyday lives, motives and behaviours. If you came across a questionnaire survey carried out by a government agency which claimed to have asked 40 people, you would think that quite ridiculous.

However, these small samples do allow us to achieve two things. First, the kinds of finer details that ethnography reveals do tell us things about the nature of the way that people live more generally. Anthropologists help us to think about the way that beliefs in a society are located and legitimized by a whole cluster of beliefs which sum up to a cultural perspective on how the world works. These beliefs may be science or witchcraft but individuals in a culture accept them because they are part of that belief system, not because they have worked out their worth or truth value for themselves. The sociologist Irving Goffman (1969) looked at small examples yet his ideas about how individuals act out roles and present themselves in different ways in different contexts can be thought of as a principle that would apply more generally.

Social psychologists such as Jerome Bruner (1990) and Werstch (1991) have argued for the use of ethnography as a method for studying situated action as it happens naturally. Drawing on the idea of psychologists such as Vygotsky (1978) they consider it a mistake to study humans in artificial settings. Humans are social beings and we acquire knowledge through social interaction to use in social interaction. They therefore realize that human action is fundamentally social and contextual. Therefore a methodology is required that can capture this. Any other approach will not provide data that are at all representative of the way that people really behave. Of course we might think that if the questionnaire only had the aim of investigating people's use of public transport, then surely we can just ask them. We do not need to go through the trouble of following people in natural settings. And in such cases of fact gathering, this might be the case.

Second, the smaller samples used in ethnography do help us to understand real instances of social phenomenon. In Part II we look at a number of ethnographic studies of the mass media. Most of them use quite small samples yet all reveal facts about the way that people behave.

We might also ask, what is the point in saying that your study is representative if it is very low on validity? We could carry out a questionnaire on two thousand people who proportionally match the complex composition of a much larger population. But if we then either assume that the attitudes they claim are exactly true without checking them, where does this take us? Further, if we are imposing a model of what we assume that social world we are investigating is like, are we really investigating anything? The ethnographic studies that we look at in this volume, while they might leave us with the question of representativeness, all beg the question as to how else the information they reveal could have been discovered.

Reliability

This is another area where ethnography has had a bad press. Basically, reliability means that the research must be repeatable. A piece of research could be said to be reliable if a different group of people could come along, using the same methodology, and produce the same findings. For research involving surveys this is crucial. Survey planners go to immense effort to design questionnaires which mean that the same things are asked of everyone. They then train their interviewers to make sure that they ask the same questions in the same way of each respondent.

In ethnography the actual process that is undertaken is not systematic, nor planned. Ethnographers basically just wander around and see what happens. Worse, the ethnographic report is essentially the subjective view of the individual ethnographer, what they thought to include, and what they thought was relevant. Ethnographers who have visited areas which had already been studied have been known to say how impressed they were with the existing ethnographic reports. However, others have found reports misleading and selective of the details they have reported – particularly where the writer was looking to support a theory. Many anthropologists have had a very easy time in terms of reliability as they have been the only person who has had the opportunity to study a particular culture. Who, then, could criticize their findings? This idea of a single person, or even several people, doing ethnography has become a problem for anthropology. To some degree the debate on this problem has been overdone. And other research methodologies, in fact, are no less open to the criticisms that were raised. Simply put, the criticisms implied that ethnographers should be aware of what they bring with them to the research in terms of opinions, beliefs, personal biases, etc., and how this will affect what they look for and find. This is basically concealed in the large-scale survey by the additional layers of being systematic with questionnaire composition and ordering. This tends to hide the fact that the questions themselves and the very topic of the survey are a result of massive assumptions and preconceptions of what the world out there is like.

The main criticism of ethnography is that it is all about the interpretation of the individual ethnographer. The ethnographer can only offer an interpretation of what they see and hear. This is where anthropology has been in debate over the nature of what it does. This point takes us back to the idea of validity. If all we can ever do is record our own interpretations of what we observe, then can we say that these are valid representations of the social world?

Transparency

The discussion within anthropology about ethnography as a methodology has basically centred on the idea of transparency. Can the ethnographer simply reproduce what is going on in the world transparently through their research and in the texts that they write? The answer to this is absolutely not. But it is important to realize that this is a problem for all research. And, like all research, this can be less of a problem if we do the research well.

Anthropologists have become concerned to remind us that, whatever the data we produce, we must be aware that they are always a product of the research process. These views, which have tended to come particularly from American anthropologists, and which were motivated partly after the publication of the diaries of Malinowski, have challenged the authority of the anthropologist to discuss how other people live and think. Writers like Clifford and Marcus (1986) and Said (1979) called for anthropologists to look closely at the phenomenon of the white male going to an exoticized primitive world to bring back true accounts of the thought processes and cultures of the other. In Clifford and Marcus' volume *Writing Culture*, a collection of anthropologists looked at the way that the ethnographer always enters the field with a huge cultural baggage, producing reports in a particular cultural context with its academic conventions. Anthropology, therefore, should be understood as being a form of writing and not as a transparent reproduction of a particular culture.

One area that was looked at was the way that we select details from the social worlds that we study in order to create a picture of a world that is coherent to us. In a way anthropology could be thought of as creating, rather than recording, cultural realities. Asad (1986) suggested that it may be impossible to translate the concepts and categories of other cultures into Western concepts without some kind of distortion. In a sense, we might think about very alien beliefs having to be domesticated in a way that can be understood and dealt with by the Western audience. This could be true even of the middle-class educated ethnographer working in an urban setting. This seemed to be one reason that Park, while he was head of the Chicago School, was keen that his researchers were drawn from the areas where they studied. Tyler said that without the gaze of the ethnographer there is 'only a disconnected array of chance happenings' (1986, p. 138). It is the ethnographer who gives them the shape that allows them to be read as a coherent social world. What these writers are suggesting is that we can never access neutral facts through research. Research always constructs a reality and this reality is therefore always historically and culturally situated. But this goes for all research, not just for ethnography. There is no neutral position from where we can make our observations.

Taking this view to its limit, anthropology looked pretty much like any other form of life. It is a product of a particular time and place, just as the belief in magic in the Trobriands was a product of a different setting. In such a case how could we accept that anthropologists had anything authoritative to say if they themselves are convinced that all knowledge should be understood as being historically and culturally situated?

One solution anthropologists have found to this problem of the power of the ethnographer has been to make ethnographic texts multi-vocal. This means that the anthropologist should be only one voice in the ethnography. The voices of the people who comprise the ethnography should also be present. One classic example of such a practice was *Lakota Belief and Ritual* (Jahner et al. 1991), a volume about Native American culture, which was a collection of accounts by different voices, including the ethnographer and the indigenous people themselves. The idea is that none of the voices are given a privileged status. This, it was thought, might help to moderate the fact that the ethnographer can only offer one version. This view, however, easily disappears down a relativistic black hole. If the ethnographer's view is only one version, equal to any other, then if I ask my local shopkeeper for their interpretation of Lakota culture, does that deserve the same status? The problem with relativism is that the end point is that we take the position that we can make no assertions about the world that are better or worse than any others.

Clifford Geertz (1973) has said that while we should not take the arrogant stance of the traditional anthropologists, we should not become self-obsessed. Should we assume, then, that we can never say or know anything about another people? Geertz says that ethnography may be a kind of writing, a kind of telling stories, but this does not necessarily mean that ethnographies are therefore false. Therefore, examining how these texts are constructed does not spoil them but enhances our appreciation of them: the way we research them and how we put them together may improve.

Another way that anthropologists approached the problem of ethnography being affected by the qualities of the ethnographer was to write themselves into the ethnography. The idea was to be 'reflexive'. This meant that the researcher would become aware of what it was that they brought to the research with them in terms of cultural baggage, concepts and personal characteristics. These would be made explicit in the written report. The idea was that the reader would be able to identify the voice of the author. We would have to say therefore if we were, say, a middle-class female from a private school background. We would also have to say how we ourselves responded as we collected the data and how people responded to us. This was supposed to mean that the author ceased to be invisible as they had been in the classic ethnographies of Malinowski. The author ceased to be all-knowing and would drop the pretence of objective, unmotivated observation. In some cases this was taken up usefully although in others there were bizarre attempts at mini-life histories, as if it were possible for us to write down, in the introduction to a piece of research, everything about ourselves that might influence the way that we see things.

It is important that we do not think that just because, as researchers, we have our own cultural baggage that will influence what we see and record, that we therefore cannot know anything, or tell anything, about the world out there. It is important even to use this baggage as a resource in itself, by recording our first impressions and our own reactions.

Ethnography is by no means a transparent way of representing the social world. In fact, there is no pre-existing neutral social world out there to discover. We might argue that ethnography only creates texts that say more about the culture of the observer. But I think that we can develop a trained eye and do it well. In the next Part we look at studies which reveal things about the way that people watch television, buy records, use the Internet. Of course, these studies are all the result of interpretation. But, then, people live out real lives and it is not unreasonable to think that we can find things out about these lives. Reflexivity is important but not the end. We can never say that we have been reflexive enough as this seems to involve some sort of life-long therapy where we end up being able to say exactly what affects what we look for in the world and how we will interpret that thing. As Clifford Geertz (1973) once said, it is important not to throw the baby out with the bath water.

Michael Carrithers (1992) suggests that it is useful to think about the capacities used by the anthropologists as being the same as those used to engage with everyday life. He argues that it is true that anthropological knowledge is partly of an everyday kind. But he believes that it is also somewhere on the scale of the kind of scientific knowledge which has produced the computer I am writing on. Perhaps because ethnography has this quality, it is the best way to investigate human societies.

Ethnography is an excellent means of examining the finer details of everyday life, partly due to the way it is sensitive to how humans actually behave and partly because the ethnographer can learn to be a good researcher. Because ethnography is like everyday knowledge, it is able to deal with the ambiguity and flux in social life, which other methodologies have to conceal or ignore. But because it is like scientific knowledge, this can be done in a systematic and rigorous way. Writers like Hacking (1983), Ziman (1978) and Polanyi (1958) have suggested that the myth of disembodied knowledge that we call science, in fact, inhibits our ability to understand the processes of finding out about the world. Carrithers argues that we need to 'remove the sense of metaphysical absoluteness which we unthinkingly attach to science' (1992, p. 154). In other words, we have to accept that all knowledge is embedded in the social world. It is always relative to a community of knowers. In this way there is no reason that ethnography should necessarily be criticized above other methodologies which simply make the problematic claim of being free-floating and independent from the social world.

PART II

Ethnographic research in media studies

In this Part we will look at six different studies. All except one refer to themselves as ethnographic. The other would fall into the category of the 'ethnographic turn' in audience studies. These examples have been chosen as they offer excellent examples of what ethnography can accomplish. They give a sense of the way that research problems can be identified and investigated.

6 Popular music

P. Willis (1990) *Common Culture*. Milton Keynes: Open University Press

Willis worked in the Birmingham School of Cultural Studies and was the only real ethnographer at the school. He is perhaps best known for his earlier study *Learning to Labour* which looked at the way that working-class boys, knowing that they would not succeed in the education system, developed their own culture which rejected school-like behaviour such as obedience and docility. Influenced by the Chicago School and symbolic interactionism, Willis studied how the everyday life of 'the lads' revealed how people make sense of the world and define themselves in a way that is responsive to the definitions of the dominant culture.

In *Common Culture* Willis turned his attention to the way that young people interact with the wider culture. In this case he was interested in the way that young people used the mass media. As in *Learning to Labour* he considered how young people, rather than simply being passive recipients of the dominant culture, made their own definitions to get by and find some sense of their own identities. While Willis remained one of the few researchers to remain more faithful to the Chicago model of ethnographic research, it is important to recognize that this book emerged as part of a general turn towards consumption of the mass media with a view to showing negotiated, rather than passive, interactions.

The basic theme of the book is that young people are highly creative with the images and commodities that they come across in the mass media – material which is after all produced with the aim of making money from young people. Generally we might fall into the comfortable trap of assuming that these young people simply follow fashions as dictated by mass communications, in terms of the clothes they wear, the music they listen to and in terms of what they consider as worthwhile and desirable. But Willis argues that if we look more closely at what young people actually do with the culture available through the mass media, we find something very different and much more active.

The main premise of the book is that the idea of creativity needs to be reassessed. In our society we tend to associate this with elite notions of high art and genius. Yet, Willis argues, people are continually involved in acts of creativity in everyday life as they manipulate the cultural resources around them for their own purposes and develop a sense of self. His aim was to show how the way that young people encounter and use these resources 'infuses' their everyday world with meaning.

Willis used data which he describes as 'a loose and general form of ethnography' (1990, p. 7). By this he seems to mean something roughly along the lines of that used by the Chicago School. This involves life histories, statistical profiles and mainly recorded group discussion. The study involved groups of young people from all over England, mainly from working-class areas, but involving a range of ethnic groups. These were contacted through youth groups, colleges and mother and toddler groups. Willis said that the study focused on young people as it is here that we find the most attention to indicating identity self-consciously by using the cultural resources available. Willis admitted that sometimes the study sacrificed depth for an emphasis on looking for broader illustrations of young people using popular culture. This seems to mean that his ethnography did not look closely at individual life histories, nor did it explore popular culture in the context of other resources in a young person's life.

Commodities and images

Music

Youth research, Willis suggests, shows how much young people, for several generations, have seen music as their main cultural interest. But, he argues, this hides the diversity of what youths in different contexts do with this music. He says that there is also the assumption that making music is creative while consumption of music is passive. This, he argues, is by no means so clear. This is because the two are bridged by symbolic creativity. By this he means that consumption takes place depending on how young people perceive the music and how it relates more broadly to the music scene. The young people in his study made judgements about music on an informed basis, often with a knowledge of historical sources and inspiration in the music.

In terms of the purchase of music the young people were very interested in the music of the 1950s, 1960s, and 1970s and the club scene that went along with these. While record companies are able to cash in on this by re-releasing records, it would be wrong to see these revivals purely as record company strategies. Young people scour second-hand record shops for music. They enjoy particular music scenes. Willis notes that there is a whole dance scene out there, which while being able to be taped by record companies, also forms a small cultural microcosm of DJs, clubs and clothing styles. The youth who participate are creative in the assembly and use of the aspects of this world that they enjoy.

Willis looked at the rise of home-taping as a way to get round the difficulties of purchasing music in times of unemployment and high prices. The young people in his study had large collections of taped music, but also had taped concerts, dances and other musical events. They also had many tapes made up from the radio, both from the charts and from pirate radio. The youth also taped copies of their own selections of records to distribute among friends. There was also a sort of hierarchy of taste as some were keener collectors who often guided others in what was good listening. Being able to talk about music was in itself a currency. Sharing tastes could be an expression of affiliation. Some of the respondents would mix dance records together – joining tracks together seamlessly or even juxtaposing songs.

The young people in his study talked about music as communicating to them, not necessarily through the words but through the style of delivery. This may be a vocal style or dance or visual presentation. Music can, in this way, convey different emotions – boredom, anger, sadness, energy. Youngsters who liked dance and house music, some of who were rarely without their Walkman, said that they felt that the music itself evoked a particular message in its aesthetic. Dance music can evoke an urban disillusionment and power at the same time. This aesthetic can be experienced at dance parties and at gigs. Being there dancing with others is about feeling and living that aesthetic. And the young people emphasized the way that they learned and appropriated dance styles that they encountered. Willis says that the young people spoke of the all-night or all-day dance parties where they would dance for ten hours without stopping. There would be no alcohol consumed. Many could only afford the admission fee and bus fare home. There had been a policy of club owners renting out their venues for one-off events to make ends meet. This meant that DJs had been able to put on more specialized days or evenings catering to a range of different tastes.

Some of the young Afro-Caribbean youths said that they put a lot of time into practising their dance routines and working out in order to improve their dancing. Again Willis emphasizes that the moves that the youths learn are themselves part of an aesthetic to which they can engage or contribute. And for these youths the level of dancing that they had reached was seen as an achievement. They saw their dance as part of a culture of dance, an aesthetic movement. Willis suggests that with unemployment dancing gave the youths a sense of power and energy and resolution to the emptiness of unemployment.

Clothing and fashion

Willis points out that creativity in fashion is officially the domain of an elite tradition in fashion design, where a few individuals are credited with vision and aesthetic prowess. Magazines and television celebrate these individuals as gurus of style and paint this image of the consumer on the street waiting for these inspirational ideas to filter down to the street level. Willis argues that these fashion designers have much less influence on what people wear than such representations suggest.

Clothes and fashion have long been important features of the way that young people have expressed collective and individual identities. But the young people in Willis' study did not simply buy clothes passively through the definitions of the fashion industry. Rather, they brought clothes with their own aesthetic in mind, often combining clothes and images to create particular images. For example, they might combine clothes from army surplus stores, second-hand shops, or sports shops. He says: 'They make their own sense of what is commercially available, make their own aesthetic judgements, and sometimes reject the normative definitions and categories of "fashion" promoted by the clothing industry' (ibid., p. 85).

The working-class people in the study could not generally afford to buy clothes in a way that would simply allow them to mimic the fashion images provided by the industry. Willis points out that the clothing styles of many youth subcultures have not been directly instigated by the fashion industry but have emerged from creativity in working-class youth and have been a way they have been able to win their own cultural space. An example of this is the British retro-1950s fashion in the 1980s. This was not imposed by the fashion industry but arose particularly in the student and music culture in Manchester at the time. Contemporary rap fashion has become colonized by the fashion industry but originally developed around the club scene. Willis' data suggest that young working-class people saw clothes as very important in that they reflected their identity and self. And they could not rely on high street fashion due to limited financial resources. Much of what they wore came from markets and second-hand shops.

Creativity in society

Willis' central conclusion from these findings is that the young people in his study were not simply passive consumers of mass media imagery and commodities. He bases this on the fact that he felt that these young people were highly creative. Creativity, he argues, is a concept that is very much misunderstood in our society because it is associated with 'high art'. This elitist view hides the fact that people need to be creative in their everyday lives. He sees the way that people choose to dress, listen to music, watch and discuss television, etc. as important creative activities.

Willis said that his aim was not to invert the elitism of art definitions but to show how people use the images and representations around them actively in living cultures. He argues that this symbolic creativity is very important these days as young people have no sense of future in terms of employment, and the powerlessness that this brings and problems for self-definition when much of our culture's models for this involves having a job. Most of society's traditional resources for developing a sense of belonging to society, security and meaning have basically disappeared or no longer appear as valuable to young people.

Willis also points to the fact that many of the jobs that he found young people were doing were very mundane and therefore were low on satisfaction and fulfilment. Such jobs appear especially meaningless in the context of the wider world image of popular culture which emphasizes fun, excitement and beauty. Willis argues that these young people live on the periphery of the social mainstream with all its promise of belonging and rewards.

Thus, Willis argues that his ethnographic data show that this creativity and symbolic activity are taken up by popular culture and the commodities and images that it offers. These are supplied to the market for profit, of course, but they are used creatively by people. He argues that these commodities and images are used by people to create meanings, identity and belonging. They are, he says a 'catalyst' (ibid., p. 18). Consumerism, therefore, should be understood as an active rather than a passive process.

Young people do not just take the artefacts and images of consumerism at face value. Even though capitalism recognizes and exploits this to make more money, people do things with, and act creatively on these products in ways that no marketing department thought of.

Willis has been criticized for his view of young people being so in control of consumer culture. McGuigan (1992) argues that Willis has romanticized the creativity of the youngsters. After all the materials of their creativity are made for them by large corporations. And if all their culture is produced by one or two mega-corporations, then what does this say for creativity? In the book we get a clear sense that Willis is looking for symbolic creativity and therefore finds it in all places. The extracts from discussions and interviews that appear in the book support the view that young people are being creative in the way they consume commodities. But in terms of the criteria we looked at in earlier chapters where we looked at ethnography and the idea of culture in anthropology, we found that one thing that anthropologists were clear about is the way that we may have official reasons for why we do things but we may not have access to why we really do that thing. Anyone who has lived with a 'rebellious teenager' will be aware of the way that they do seem to be in some ways creative with consumer commodities and use them to find and indicate a space for themselves. They may follow music which is slightly outside of the mainstream commercial popular culture. And the teenager may say that they have orange hair because it reflects who they are, that they are different. But these are all very commonplace signifiers of difference and all the images that they use can be seen in magazines and band fanzines.

Willis may be right that there is not a direct relationship in terms of a dominant culture supplying images and commodities and that this industry mines 'street culture'. But his ethnography seems too intent on finding resistance. This can be understood, on the one hand, in terms of Willis' history of looking for the way that working-class people, marginalized from the wider society, make their own meanings. Additionally, in the 1980s, this book emerged at a time of an 'ethnographic turn' in media audience studies which tended to show audience uses and resistance to dominant values, stimulated partly by Morley's work on the *Nationwide* audience. While such works made the important point of showing that readings of the mass media were negotiated by audiences, I think we were left uncertain as to how these dominant messages then took place in the broader way that these people went on to see the world.

Generally, in assessing Willis' ethnography, we have to be critical of the fact that he seems to have simply looked for a particular phenomenon. The data he presents are chosen to support his idea of symbolic creativity. By his own admission the study may lack depth. We are given instances of symbolic creativity without looking more closely at how the commodities fitted into individual lives and how these fitted into culture as a whole. Willis seems to think that he has evidence that young people are creative in the way that they respond to advertisements and that ad companies have to be mindful of their aesthetic tastes. Yet these are multinational companies who mine culture for particular romanticized images to grasp the attention of viewers. While young people might be critical of them on an aesthetic level, how do these images contribute towards the broader frameworks of reference that they have available? In the first decade of the twenty-first century one of the first things that young British men might do upon reaching the required legal age of 18 is join their nearest gym. They are familiar with particular images of masculinity. The *Pokémon* craze was waning by early 2001, but to what extent can we see this in terms of young people being able to produce their own cultural space – *Pokémon* was special in that it excluded adults – or to what extent was it simply a corporate success story for Nintendo? I think that this illustrates the fact that Willis' study might have been more genuinely informative had it focused on one instance of a commodity used by young people. He could then have considered production, design, promotion and done extensive work on the way that young people used the commodity. He could have looked at other representations in society that made this particular commodity make sense to consumers.

7 Watching television in the home

J. Lull (1990) *Inside Family Viewing: Ethnographic Research on Television Audiences.* **London: Routledge and New York: Comedia**

This piece of research was an attempt to find out what people actually do when they watch television. We generally think about this process as being passive. Watching television is thought to be done blankly, without any effort on the part of the viewer. Lull thought, however, that it was surely of crucial importance that television is generally watched in company within the family. He was interested to see how this worked and how it affected both viewing and family interactions. So Lull decided that the only way to study this was to go into family homes and take a look at what people do in front of the television set. Lull was concerned to move away from speculation about audiences' responses. He thought that empirical work could temper 'the often pretentious and opaque writing associated with cultural studies, [and] the frequent imposition of privileged interpretations of texts' (1990, p. 16).

Lull used ethnography as he thought that we simply could not get anywhere by asking people about viewing. On the one hand, he argued this point on the basis of existing observations of television viewing habits. For example, studies by the likes of Collet and Lamb (1986) had put cameras into people's homes and found that people would do many other things while watching TV, like ironing, chatting, mimicking, eating, etc. Such studies suggested that viewing should never be thought of as taking place in a vacuum.

Lull concluded that the way to investigate this process was through participant observation and in-depth interviewing. He states: 'The intent of the ethnography of mass communication is to allow the researcher to grasp as completely as possible with minimal disturbance the "native's perspective" on relevant communicative and sociocultural matters indigenous to him or her' (ibid., p. 31). This is interesting as we can clearly see that Lull is considering television viewing as something that is to be understood in a cultural setting – using Malinowski's maxim of seeing the world from the native's point of view.

The study involved more than 200 families from a range of occupational and socio-economic groups who were studied during a three-year period. The families were contacted initially through various agencies and lists. Acceptance rates were about 30 per cent, therefore we have to take into account that there may have been particular characteristics that already defined the sample. Families were observed from between two and seven days and from afternoon until bedtime. Interviews were carried out on the final day. Family members were then asked to read and comment on written reports. The families had been only told that the researchers had a general interest in family life. They were told of the actual research topic at the end of data collection. Researchers would take some notes while present and then reconstruct events once at home. While present in homes researchers would participate in the normal day of the family, eating with them, carrying out domestic activities, playing with children and watching television. Their main aim was to look for roles and relationships as regards the media. They looked for power relationships and types of talk.

Lull argued that the presence of the researcher did not have to be such a bad thing. He observed that families might carry out an exercise for him formally but then carry on discussing it informally afterwards, while he was there giving different responses – such as in the task of choose a viewing schedule. Families did report that where researchers were present for longer there was no disruption to normal viewing habits.

For Lull another important reason for using ethnography was the anthropological way that he thought about the process of watching television with other people. This approach to audiences drew on ethnomethodology, which we looked at in Chapter 2. The important thing to remember about this approach is that it takes as its object of study the everyday interactions of people in minute detail. It looks at the moment-by-moment subtleties that we take for granted but which if we look at them more closely can be seen as requiring a great deal of knowledge and are therefore massive accomplishments. For example, just the ability to open a conversation and to know how to take turns in it are complex achievements and reveal rules which we must negotiate to carry out even the most basic of social interactions. In this sense we can think about the way that people share and talk about television as involving a repertoire of social knowledge and conventions which are available for study. Lull concluded that through ethnography we could therefore examine the way that mass media enter the world of the family.

Communication facilitation

Lull's data showed that television is often used as a companion for household jobs and other activities. It creates a social atmosphere. He says that it is also used to punctuate family meals, which may be timed in accordance with particular programmes. Conversations and interaction in the family are also often structured around viewing patterns. Television could therefore be described as having the role of a behaviour regulator.

Lull found that television programmes were used as sources of conversation. Family members would debate plots and characters, evaluating them on many levels. Families would often spend much of the duration of the programme debating and chatting. The television would only be used deliberately as a sole focus of attention when guests were present to fill awkward silences and to create common ground. The degree of attention given to any programme fluctuated depending upon the flow of conversation.

Television was also shown to create a sense of a shared experience. This could be in the form of laughing together or in predicting the outcome of a soap opera or a film. Also it could be used as an avoidance technique. It removes the need for more intensive forms of communication and interaction that might otherwise be necessary where there was no other outlet for attention.

Social learning

Lull drew the conclusion from his data that people used television as a resource for knowledge about the world. This was both through news and current affairs and through drama and soap opera. He thought that particularly, it seemed, soap operas were used as a source of suggestions for the way that social and family life ought to be carried out. Behaviour seen in soaps would be imitated by audiences. However, Lull offers no support or specific examples of this influence. How do soap stories become understood by viewers? In what ways do they draw them into their lives? Even if Lull found that people assessed soaps as they watched them, we need further evidence of how they might draw on that imagery in their lives. One of the problems for Lull in this respect is that only a short time was spent with each family and all the observation was carried out in the home. In this way it would have been difficult to know more about individual lives.

Lull found that parents encouraged children to watch certain programmes for educational experiences. This was done very much in the context of what the parents valued in terms of their own view of the world. Lull concluded therefore that television can be involved in the way that the parents' value system is transmitted to the child.

People also seemed to use television to collect knowledge. Certain household members would take on the position of being opinion leaders or knowers. Such people would take a pride in gathering valuable information with which they could inform their friends or family and, Lull says, assert themselves as good members of society. In this way we might think about television programmes as becoming the basis of discussions as they allow viewers then to have the status of being informed. Lull does not go on to consider the implication of this in terms of the way that television may therefore have a massive influence over what people think is valuable knowledge.

Competence/dominance

Lull argued that watching television also allowed individuals to express competence in different ways. For example, many parents were highly attentive to the ways that they regulated what children were able to watch. This was a way of demonstrating good parenting.

Also individuals would criticize and evaluate programmes, allowing them to show that they knew how bad the programme was, that they were cleverer than the television. This may also involve looking for faults in the plot. They would also evaluate characters and their behaviour. This in turn would give a sense of the evaluation of self, by aligning oneself alongside or against particular ways of behaving, or of a particular type of programme. This would allow them to imply that they would behave in a similar way in that set of circumstances. Additionally the roles acted out by television characters may reflect those carried out by viewers. This may demonstrate role competence. Lull speculates that the need to express competence may lead to viewers imitating behaviour, in which case they will be likely to anticipate the subsequent moral assessment by other viewers.

Television viewing in an ethnographic context

Lull concludes that this ethnographic study is revealing as it shows the importance of thinking about the way that television is used by families to interact. It is true that generally television viewing is thought of as entirely passive. In Lull's case it seems as much a tool for the maintenance of interpersonal relations as a means of entertainment. Therefore Lull feels that such a study addresses the problem that most media effects research overlooks: the fact that television is part of people's lives in complex basically social ways that are part of the process by which they make their lives meaningful.

Lull's study is revealing. However, we do have the problem that his researchers spent little time with families. Perhaps the problem is that he includes little data to demonstrate the positions he takes, for example, regarding the way that people are influenced by the morality and roles shown in soap operas. Lull gives us little idea of exactly what does and doesn't influence people and how images are taken on. We are offered far too broad a vision of an audience member. It might have been better to illustrate one group using one subject.

Furthermore, Lull's researchers spent relatively little time with each family. Silverstone *et al.* (1991) said that they gave up on an attempt to do participant observation with families as they realized that one week would simply not be long enough. To generate a deeper understanding of the way that families interacted with the world portrayed by television, the researchers would have needed to have spent much longer periods of time immersed in the everyday activities of those families, both as a collective unit and as individuals.

8 News gathering

M. Fishman (1980) *Manufacturing the News.* **Austin and London: University of Texas Press**

Fishman's ethnography of news production is a fascinating look at how the world that we encounter in the news media is put together in a particular way that is closely aligned with the world of official institutions. This is not due to any crude bias or control by these institutions but to a range of basic practical concerns.

Fishman begins his text with an example of the way that a crime wave is reported in New York. This raises a particular problem which his ethnography helps to solve. Fishman was working in a New York newsroom during a major crime wave in late 1976. The news media were reporting particularly on crimes against the elderly. This was accompanied by public outcry for harsher justice and more policing, which was subsequently promised by the mayor. Fishman began to suspect that the news media were contributing to or even creating the impression of a crime wave. He mentions how one reporter realized at one point that the police figures actually showed a decrease in crimes against the elderly but decided to ignore these. The reporter had to write the story as planned since it fitted in with the current theme. In fact, many of the journalists Fishman spoke with doubted the reality of the crime wave but still wrote about it. He concluded that he needed to understand the system in which this phenomenon happened.

Fishman began to think about phenomena like crime waves as organizing concepts which allow different events to be put together in a way that makes them appear naturally newsworthy. He looked at the way that the assignment editor at a TV newsroom sifted through all the day's sources from agencies, newspapers, and police releases, looking for good stories that could fit in with the theme. Reporters would be sent out to cover events which could be related.

But why, Fishman asked, do these crime waves happen at all if they have nothing to do with police figures? On the one hand, there were the actual ingredients of the particular crime wave. But on the other he found that the explanation why things like crime waves happen is the way that news gathering is so tightly aligned with official organizations. Journalists are not out on the street finding out what is happening but rely on official sources which gather and process the world in particular ways. Let us look at these and then we can return to the specifics of this case to complete our understanding of the crime wave.

An ethnography of news gathering

Fishman argues that within research into news there has been a tendency to look at gatekeeping by editors and at the way that journalists write stories with an angle. But these studies have tended to take for granted that there were objective facts out there to be collected, ignored or distorted. The basic focus was on selection in news. Fishman came to realize that how the world is made into news should be the topic of investigation. Basically, news takes the form that it does due to the methods that newsworkers use. If they used different methods, then the world of news as experienced by the public would look very different. To those who might be accustomed to thinking about the news as being something which transparently reflects the real world 'out there', this might sound quite strange.

Fishman's approach was not to look at news texts in order to see how they were put together, as had been the most popular way of thinking about the construction of news. He worked with journalists to watch them collecting events which then became news stories. He broke his research down into four stages. First, he looked at how journalists detect likely news events. Second, how these are interpreted as being relevant and important. Third, how do they attribute qualities of facticity to these events? And, fourth, how these are then translated into stories.

The way Fishman went about investigating news gathering was through participant observation at one newspaper. He spent seven months working as a novice reporter. This was a position that he took for the purpose of the research. This was followed by five months accompanying reporters on their daily activities. This allowed him, he felt, adequate access into the practices and assumptions of the newsgatherer.

Finding news

Journalists have to provide a steady supply of news for their newspaper. They cannot hope to supply this by simply hanging around and waiting for something to happen spontaneously in front of them. They need to have a predictable supply of news stories. To do this journalists generally have beats. For the past one hundred years this has been the accepted way of organizing news collection. Reporters routinely visit or contact a number of locations to which they are allocated. Two typical beat locations will be police stations and law courts. These places produce events that may be thought of as newsworthy and have a staple list of characters who may be newsworthy.

Fishman found that all of the beat reporters in his study had to meet a quota of stories. None of them ever failed to meet this. The editors simply had to be able to rely on a certain quantity of material from these beats. Therefore it was not possible for nothing to happen. And these stories had to be delivered by a certain time each day. This was not a problem, however, as each of the beat locations themselves had a predictable cycle of meetings and agendas of activities and reports to help the reporter. Basically, events are predictable as these places are bureaucratically organized.

For example, a reporter may arrive at a police office one morning and pick up the file detailing the previous evening's arrests. These might immediately allow the reporter to produce a story, for example, of a particularly brutal attack. The reporter will then look through the coroner's file for the previous day's deaths and through traffic accident reports. The reporter will also chat with any of the people who work at these locations who may inform them of anything else. The reporter will then go to the court house. From a list of the day's hearings they will choose if any seem potentially interesting. Once the reporter had chosen which they would use, they might ring up the police to find more information.

The beat will be organized around the bureaucratic workings of the beat locations. The reporter will be steered away from any organization relevant to crime that is not bureaucratically organized. Therefore the reporter would have no interaction with anything that was not official. And the reporter will be led to the official activities of these official organizations as these practices will produce files and reports which are accessible. The reporter would not simply hang around as this is not sufficiently productive. The reporter basically uses the work already done by someone else.

Fishman said that if a journalist needed to know additional information they would immediately telephone a bureaucratic source that would have events routinely recorded. For fire information the fire station would be called along with insurance agencies. Journalists therefore, Fishman argued, view society as bureaucratically organized. And this provides the reliable and predictable flow of events required to fulfil the day's quota.

Organizing the world into news

Fishman found that reporters also see the world through the way that these bureaucratic organizations deal with them and categorize them. He called these phase structures, for example, the structures of any criminal procedure such as arrest, hearing, sentencing. Phase structures refers to the way an organization divides up the flow of information they have to deal with into phases which are easy to manage for administrative purposes. Examples of this might be the way hospitals reduce patients to sets of symptoms or the way teachers and schools deal with students in terms of defined learning/ability categories. These phases become the reality of each case. Therefore we might think about these bureaucratic accounts as being idealizations. Simply put, bureaucracies cannot deal with the world in any other way. Fishman draws on Goffman (1961) who looked at the way that the case histories of patients in mental health institutions tend to record only issues that were relevant to the particular agency and therefore, he argues, are not a fair representation of the patient's actual life history.

Each of the phase structures provides a potential news event. Therefore we might say that the reporter uses these to interpret events. The reporter will not attend to parts of the process that go on in between or are not recorded in the same way by the organizations. For example, a criminal case for the journalist would involve arrest, hearing and sentencing. For the individual accused the case would be much more complex involving social context, reasons, a traumatic arrest and initial detention, their relationship with their legal representative. The journalist will not attend to the individual oral histories but to the events depicted in the official phase structures.

Fishman gives an example of being at one board meeting for the Sheriff's department budget. A woman stood up and recounted what she felt was a mistreatment by her by some of the sheriff's deputies. This was completely ignored by the journalists who were there to report on the budget changes. The woman represented no organization nor formal group.

News values and respectability

When reporters get information, much of it has been generated by other people. How do they ensure that this is factual? Basically, Fishman found that reporters treat bureaucratic accounts as factual. These accounts are themselves records. While they may involve stereotypes, they are nevertheless official records. No other accounts would be taken as fundamentally factual. Fishman gives an example of a coroner's report read by a reporter who takes the death of man on a bus mentioned in the report as a fact. Yet the report is based on several layers of accounts. At the start are the accounts of the passengers on the bus. Then there are the accounts of the police about these. Then there is the account produced by the coroner's clerk who summarizes the police reports. Yet this is accepted without need to interview original witnesses. The police would have inferred the man's address by looking at an ID card he was carrying. And this the reporter can take as a fact – another person's inferences who works in a bureaucratic organization. But the reporter cannot make their own inferences. Fishman says that in the American media there is very little reporting of information which is not from official bureaucratic sources. Journalists will rarely doubt official sources but will always doubt non-bureaucratic accounts.

Basically, to be a legitimate source, the person must be in a legitimate position to be seen as a knower. And legitimate knowers, for reporters, are officials of bureaucratic organizations. A soldier may be asked their own feelings but not about the nature of events. On the one hand agency officials can be seen as having access to the right information but on the other, and more importantly, they are socially authorized knowers.

Fishman concludes that news is ideological. Basically, this is because what is news will depend heavily on official sources and definitions. The bureaucratic vision of the world may be all that the reader sees when they read the news. The news reflects the idealizations of the bureaucratic world. These idealizations may miss many aspects of each case simply because they are not relevant or convenient to the structures and organization. And this process of giving bureaucratic organizations credibility and putting them at the centre of news itself helps to legitimize these organizations.

So we can begin to turn these ethnographic findings back to our understanding of our crime wave. Immediately we can dispel any expectation that what journalists report on should necessarily have much to do with what is happening out there 'on the street'. The origins of the crime wave will be bureaucratic organizations. So how did the crime wave start? Fishman said that one newspaper reporter had been working on some feature articles on crime against the elderly where he was being helped by a recently formed unit of the police which dealt specifically with crime against the elderly. So the story has its basis in an official organization. To fill out this report on the new unit the journalist used two crimes that he found on the wire service received from the police station, regarding crimes against the elderly which took place on the same day. At the time an editor also thought it would be good to do a series of features on this topic. The reporter followed up with a story about the new unit being understaffed and overwhelmed. By this time the theme had been taken up by other newspapers. The police unit also gave the reporter a specific example of the way that a young offender was being released too quickly. A state legislator read the article and contacted several news organizations stressing his concern. With all the publicity the youth absconded which itself became big news. The mayor then gave his press conference to air his plans to fight the new social problem. Once the police had been mobilized to treat such crimes as special cases, more were available for the attention of the journalists. To understand the crime wave, we have to understand the way that journalists do not go out onto the streets to find out about such events but are closely aligned to organizations.

Fishman's ethnography allows us to completely rethink the way that we might view news. His ethnography does not tell us a lot about individual journalists and nothing about audiences, but by looking at how journalists carry out their everyday activities and looking carefully at the way that they respond to the different things that they come across during their daily routines, Fishman allows us to think about news as something that is a social construct. Audiences read about crime waves and then behave in a particular way as a response. Fishman says that they might avoid certain areas or decide to live in a particular place. This is because we have a particular framework for thinking about the nature of news. As Fishman's ethnography shows, this has little relationship to what news actually is. But like science and witchcraft, news is commonly thought of as being something that is natural and neutral.

Why we watch soaps

J. Tulloch (1989) 'Approaching the audience: the elderly', in Sieter, E., Borchers, H., Kreutzner, G. and Wrath, E.-M. (eds) *Remote Control: Television, Audiences and Cultural Power.* London and New York: Routledge

Tulloch uses ethnography to shed light on several interesting aspects of the way that we watch soap operas. His approach was to spend time with elderly people watching television both in their own homes and in a residential home. He also used letters which people wrote to soap operas to gain access to what they thought about them. Tulloch helps to complete the picture by also providing interviews with producers.

There is often a snobbery about soap viewing and a dismissive attitude to those who watch them. Soaps are thought to have shallow repetitive plots and be particularly unstimulating viewing. Tulloch's observations challenge these assumptions.

Some aspects of this research are what we might more conventionally consider ethnographic while others rely on one-off interviews. One thing that Tulloch does show through detailed consideration of people's viewing is that it is very difficult to think about a homogeneous audience. When we think about the elderly audience or the young audience this hides a wealth of details and subtleties.

Letters from the elderly

Tulloch looked at letters written to the Australian soap opera *A Country Practice*. Such programmes receive many letters from elderly people. The example letters stress enjoyment of the show but also tend to wander, mentioning why the show was liked in the context of family situations and personal memories. This, Tulloch suggests, is because, unlike younger people, the elderly do not have the facility of chatting about a soap to friends and work colleagues. They may also find themselves in situations where they are watching television alone. One letter he cites is quite moving in its loneliness and sadness.

Other letters tended to praise the wholesomeness of the programme in contrast to trends in television in general. One letter revealed a woman's concern that a marriage in the soap should not end in divorce. She backed this up with a threat of discontinuing her viewing. The women thus felt that viewer loyalty should earn the right to have some say over what becomes of the show's characters. The woman spoke of how marriage requires effort for it to work. She felt that divorce was all too frequent in soaps. The woman seems to actually care about what happens, not so much to the characters, but how marriage itself is dealt with. She also suggested that her views reflect the opinion of a lot of viewers. However, as Tulloch points out, unlike, say, younger viewers of science fiction series, the elderly audience cannot mobilize a campaign to pressurize the producers of a programme. Furthermore, one might imagine that she would in fact have little idea as to what other viewers really think.

Courting the elderly viewer

For elderly people there is the problem that many soaps are under pressure to run stories involving young people. Tulloch said that elderly viewers would complain about the arrival of youth themes in a show that they had previously liked. In interviews with producers Tulloch found that enough themes were kept in to keep the elderly happy while more dramatic and contemporary plots were used to attract floating viewers. One producer of *A Country Practice* said that they generally contained younger themes in the show without alienating the elderly. A younger couple would be introduced for romance and would then get married and have children over a few years. It was felt that the elderly viewer would be aware of the cycles and see the arrival of the young people as reflecting part of the life/family process rather than as the intrusion of youth. In the end, though, a producer said, this couple will have to be written out so that a new romantic couple can be introduced. Apparently the elderly viewer did not mind this providing that it was not a divorce that led to them being of no more use to the show. This leaving can be seen in context of proper family processes where young people move on the world. What was a problem for the elderly viewer was when an older character was axed. Tulloch said that this was one major theme in interviews. He speculates that this may in some way reflect their own lives where they no longer feel of use.

Tulloch gives an excellent example of one interview where a woman, assuming that he had some influence over soap story lines, told him that she thought that one older character whom she had liked should be brought back. The problem was that this character has been killed off during a war. But this was no problem it seemed. Showing her fluency in genre conventions, the woman said that the character could turn up having lost her memory and been in hospital. She also maintained that it would be a good thing for her soap family who had not fared so well without her. She added that during the war people sometimes did turn up having lost their memories.

Television as an indication of cultural level

Tulloch said that the elderly viewers seemed to fall into two categories. Some watched television very selectively and had quite conservative views about its content, considering much of it as 'trash'. These viewers would normally talk about watching television for information or for 'quality' or 'cultural' programmes. Yet others, especially those unable to leave the home, were very dependent upon it to fill time. This suggests that cultural values are very important in determining viewing behaviour. Some of the elderly people were quite ashamed of the fact that they had become absorbed by certain programmes that they considered low-brow. One woman told of being brought a television set as a gift and then leaving it switched on but with a tea towel over the screen, until eventually, to her expressed regret, she did become hooked on certain programmes. She was keen to express the fact that she really needed all her time for such things as writing letters, activities for charitable causes, and other more culturally respectable pastimes.

While it is an important point that cultural values are important in influencing viewing behaviour, Tulloch's example in this case is limited because he relies only on interviews and not on ethnographic observation. How can we be certain that when the woman said that she needed more time for writing letters, it was not just her way of indicating that while she is drawn downwards in cultural activities by the television, she does still indulge in more sophisticated and literary activities? The tone that Tulloch takes indicates that he is aware of this fact. But this is something that he is unable to test out.

The need to state that one does not watch television mindlessly is illustrated by another interview with a mother and daughter. They said that while they watched television, they could not just sit in front of it all day. They pointed out that some people did do this which was a time-wasting activity. The mother and daughter said that they preferred to pass the time by travelling and looking around. They said that pointed out that other people really did not engage in this more detailed looking. The mother and daughter evoke an image of a generalized other who has a lazy and unenthusiastic gaze through which they are able to contrast themselves favourably. Again, Tulloch is unable to corroborate whether what these people told him was in fact true of their behaviour, although he does point out the way that viewing is clearly an indication of cultural level.

Another couple are shown to complain that some soaps do not show enough about the countries in which they are made, like Australia, for example. This emphasis on educational content clearly expresses a stance which contrasts pure entertainment with a more discerning and sophisticated eye. It allows the speaker to present themselves as a more demanding viewer.

Tulloch does speculate that such discourse is motivated by social class and that the criticism of soaps is made from a high cultural position which values factual learning and documentary-style presentation of information. But he is unable to show this. His data, I would argue, are therefore disassembled. That he does speculate about the nature of this discourse is evidence of an ethnographic gaze, but the data are not gathered with this in mind. They are generated in isolated contexts of interaction and need to be contextualized into the behaviour of these people more generally. Only then can we map out the discourses that these people use to talk about television. It is only through ethnography that we can solve the problem of knowing what this talk is really about.

Why we watch soaps

Tulloch's research also helps us to think about the way that soap operas draw people in so that they become regular viewers. Many of his respondents said that they had not intended to watch soaps, considering them to be trashy, but had ended up as avid viewers. Many of us will have experienced something similar.

Tulloch said that there are two ways that soaps get viewers hooked into what he calls 'willing complicity' (1989, p. 189). One of these is the way that soap viewers develop a knowledge about characters and their situations very quickly. Many of us criticize soaps for their repetitive and very basic plots. But regular viewers attend not so much to the plots as to the network of relationships between the characters and to the experiences of the individual characters. Someone not acquainted with the characters and their relationships will therefore only see what appears to them as a dull, predictable plot which is typical of soaps. Even those people who emphasized that they did not want to be involved in a soap, once they begin to gain access to the characters and the interpersonal relationships, will need to see what happens next. Interestingly, Tulloch revealed that it is not just people who have a high-culture perspective who view soaps in this way – as part of mass culture. Often people who were keen viewers of certain soaps would consider other soaps in this way.

Tulloch also looked at the way that television viewing can become part of the routine of the day, of the fabric of people's lives. Many of the people he interviewed talked about the way that they would organize their lives around viewing times. Viewing of soaps, like the news, can be one ritualistic point in the day where certain emotions are vented. As with other research which examined the way that people watch television, such as Lull (1990), Tulloch found that where elderly people watched in company, they would often talk about the programmes, particularly about contestants on quiz programmes, and offer comments about presenters that they liked and disliked.

One distinct way that the elderly engaged with programmes was in the context of the values of their generation. Tulloch says that while watching television with elderly people he would often hear references to the older people on the screen and the significance of this in terms of life in a broader sense. He suggests that since elderly people do not tend to have their own programmes due to their low advertising appeal, they have to find their pleasures in the characters that reflect their own interests in programmes that might be targeted specifically at younger audiences. Situation comedies are particularly good for this as they often use intergenerational conflicts as a source of humour.

The difference between gender and social class usage of television was another element revealed in the data. The people interviewed were very clear about the differences between male, action-oriented programmes and more touchy-feely female ones, although some men said that they had ceased to be interested in the news, for example, due to the violence, which formed part of a world they did not know. Again, as with the comments about soap operas being low-brow, I would suggest that it would be interesting to have examined this discourse about violence in society. We might find, for example, that since elderly people have less interaction with the outside world they will tend to take the mass media, with its emphasis on the dramatic, much more literally. Those of us who investigate the mass media are generally fairly active in the world. If an elderly person spends a lot of time in the home, does this mean that the news world will take on a different appearance for them?

When investigating class and gender differences Tulloch uses ethnographic triangulation nicely – meaning that he was able to get a broader perspective by looking both at what people say and what they do. He gave the example of a couple. The husband was from a much more middle-class background than the wife. While talking about what she liked in a soap opera the wife was interrupted by her husband who then dominated the conversation to be highly critical of soaps. While he was criticizing the soap *Coronation Street* she admitted that it may be a little low-brow. But when Tulloch later observed her watching the programme he found her laughing with her favourite characters. When asked about the soap she would moderate her likes into the cultural values of the husband. He felt that soaps like *Coronation Street* were antagonistic to people such as him with a clearly middle-class background and outlook. He also disliked programmes like *Dallas,* describing them as just parties and sex, like, he thought, the rest of contemporary society. These points are very interesting as it allows us a glimpse at the way that people's lives more broadly provide them a framework through which they interpret television. But I would still like to have known more about the discourses that the husband uses. He draws on conservative views of a permissive society. To what extent are these central to his life and how do they influence other viewing?

Tulloch gives the contrast of a working-class couple. Here both liked soaps such as *EastEnders* and *Dallas.* The husband had previously been involved in racketeering and the black market in London and liked the idea of people being involved in crime. They both liked the idea that *Dallas* was a lifestyle to which they might aspire.

Overall, Tulloch's research indicates how ethnography can give us insights into the way that people relate to soap operas and why they might be especially important for the elderly. The data are at their most revealing, however, when Tulloch combines interviews with observation. When this is done, he is able to give a clearer sense of the way that his respondents use particular discourses. Their cultural framework becomes more visible. To draw this out it would have been useful to have had more access to the way that particular respondents talked and behaved at different times.

For example, how did the middle-class man who saw *Dallas* as a symptom of an immoral contemporary society talk in different settings? This information would help us to have a sharper sense of this person living through culture and where television fitted in to this.

J. Tulloch (1990) *Television Drama: Agency, Audience and Myth*. London: Routledge

Tulloch (1990) offers an additional, important observation on this kind of data. He says that the way that people respond in settings must be understood as being due to the fact that television is always being reworked through discussions. The elderly couple have had discussions about characters, plots and different kinds of programmes. This will influence how each of them will think about and talk about them. What gets discussed will depend on the context and what is at stake for the speakers, both when they are alone and when they speak in the presence of the interviewer. People do not simply respond to television in isolation. The talk that the researcher encounters, then, must be understood as always being a unique 'textual situation' and that this will be influenced by the politics of that situation. In Tulloch's words, what we come across are 'reconstructions of television'. This is an excellent way to help us to think about how people always speak with a responsiveness to the people around them. They use cultural representations, such as soaps being low-brow, but they do this with a sense of what others who are present know and think. In this way we must never think of people's utterances as being separate from their vivid sensitivity to setting.

10 Adoring film stars

J. Stacey (1994) *Star Gazing: Hollywood Cinema and Female Spectatorship.* London: Routledge

This study lacks many features of what we might ideally think of as an ethnography – Stacey herself acknowledges that her ethnography is not ethnographic in the sense used in anthropology. Yet it is very much part of a phase research into audience uses of media that became known as the 'ethnographic turn' in 1980s cultural studies, by which Stacey is clearly heavily influenced. The book has a section where she looks at Morley's *Nationwide* (1980) and Hobson's *Crossroads* (1982) which both emphasized the active audience and the way that people bring a whole range of knowledge with them to the activity of viewing. Stacey also drew on the work of Radway (1984) and Ang (1985) which argued for the importance of taking care not to dismiss the pleasures of popular entertainments as simply reproducing dominant ideologies through mindless trivia. Ang, for example, looked at the different levels of watching *Dallas*. While the programme may show an absurdly glamorous world, this does not necessarily mean that women deny reality through watching. Ang suggests that rather it allows them to play with reality.

The approach characterized by these studies, which we looked at in more depth in Chapter 4, used the term ethnography to emphasize the attention given to the audience. This was something that had been largely neglected in media studies. Many of these studies did raise some fascinating points on how people interacted with different media, as did Stacey's, but they also show how we are left being somewhat uncertain about the nature of the data as they are all collected from one single setting. We are left with the comments of the respondents unlocated in the flow of everyday life. We rely on exactly that which Polanyi warned us not to expect – that people actually have access to the reasons why they do things. Stacey is to a degree mindful to this, although she seems to use this as a way of then rather avoiding the problem.

While this study would not be thought of as strictly ethnographic, it is important that we look at its methodology and findings in some depth. This is because this kind of study indicates the importance of getting as close to the audience as possible and it allows us to consider the way that the ethnographic gaze that we have been considering in this volume might have taken a different approach. Stacey's study is also very important because it looks at film audiences, which is something that has seldom been investigated. The huge body of work on film has been focused on the films themselves or on the industry.

What motivated Stacey's work in particular was the debate on the female spectator. Those writing on the subject had generally taken the position that women spectators had little to gain from feature films other than confirmation of themselves as passive adornments in a world where men busily and heroically go about making meaning. For example, Haskell (1973) looked at Hollywood women as passive sexual stereotypes, or as dangerous and inappropriate characters who were punished for making the wrong demands, being too intelligent or ambitious. The highly influential work of Mulvey (1975) had argued that feature films were made from the point of view of the male spectator. These films were basically about male protagonists and the viewing point of the film was organized around their experiences. Mulvey called this organizing principle the 'male gaze'. The male spectator could identify with the male protagonist, whereas females present in the story would be there as passive objects for the pleasure of both the protagonist and male spectator. The female characters were thus not realistic representations of women but were images tailor-made for the 'male gaze'. Women, Mulvey said, were defined basically in terms of how they looked – the female was simply spectacle while the male was meaning-maker. This all helped to confirm the male as active and the female as passive in a society where women are treated as objects by men.

Other writers like Doane (1987), in another very influential piece, argued that films often emphasize that being female is somehow deficient. She thought that even women in women's films were not like real women but were rather caricatures masquerading as women. Basically, in both of these studies it seemed that women's experience of film was the crushing reception of male definitions of femininity.

One of the problems with such work, which was typical of psychoanalytically driven analysis in film studies, was that there was no consultation with what the audience actually did when they watched films. Stacey, following from the work of Radway in *Reading the Romance* which used interviews, and Ang's work on *Dallas*, which used fan letters, was dissatisfied with the model of women as simply passive and wanted to investigate their experience of films empirically.

Research done in this ethnographic tradition had spoken of giving a voice to its subjects. Stacey's volume *Star Gazing* is therefore an attempt to find out what kind of pleasure women actually get out of films. The focus was on the way that women related to female stars. Stacey wanted to know what women found in these female characters designed for the male gaze. What do women make of these images and what pleasure do they get out of them?

For Stacey it was important not to treat the women as passive as had been done by previous textual analysis. She suggests that it may have previously been difficult within feminism to approach the actual female audience when film criticism had so angrily discussed Hollywood cinema and was so dismissive of the kind of pleasure that it brought. She also said that looking at the actual female spectators could also have been seen as raising uncomfortable issues regarding the relationship between the academic middle-class critics and the spectators themselves.

Stacey begins by saying that she would study women's relationship to female Hollywood stars of the 1940s and 1950s as this was one of her own interests. She also says that she wanted to locate her study in the British context where American culture was being assimilated in the 1950s, which she said allowed Britain a sense of identification with a white power as its own sense of ethnic imperial superiority declined. The period has become mythologized in British culture – along with World War II – as symbolizing British getting-on-with-it and community. It was also a time of change for women. Many working-class women remained in work despite the middle-class idea that they all moved back into domesticity.

Research methodology

Stacey started her research using files from the Mass Observation Archive at Sussex University. She looked at diaries that the project had asked people to keep during World War II. Cinema had been an important component of people's lives. There were also boxes of letters written to the British film magazine *Picturegoer*, where the largest proportion of them were about the stars, addressing issues of acting ability, general praise or criticism, and about 60 per cent were from women. She points out, however, that we cannot assume that printed letters will contain a representative sample of all letters sent. This is an important point. Can we take it that any magazine reflects the views of something called its 'readership'? One interesting thing about magazines or any media is the way that they construct their audience. Can we say that the features, editorials and readers' letters which appear in a magazine like *Cosmopolitan* reflects the lives and beliefs of its readership? Are these ingredients designed to create a particular kind of world or perceived community in which readers are invited to participate?

Stacey examined the letters that appeared in *Picturegoer* in order that she could look for changes over time. She said that common themes were national identity, sexuality, glamour, and acting abilities. She said that there were differences in the way that the British stars were talked about in terms of charm, personality and grace whereas American stars were seen as glamorous and artificial and as not really being actors. She says that Britishness also meant a level of sexual respectability, but that this also went along with social class distinctions where working class was associated with crudeness. She said that this polarity, encouraged by features in *Picturegoer*, was more pronounced in the 1940s when it was perceived that the two industries were in competition. After the 1950s the letters were still present but became heavily edited so that it was not possible to make comparisons.

Stacey then decided that she should send letters to four British women's magazines whose readerships were women of 50 and over. In the letters she asked keen film goers to write to her about which stars they had liked or which they had disliked and to give their reasons for this. The letters went to *Woman, Woman's Own, Woman's Weekly* and *Woman's Realm*. Two of these published the letter: *Woman's Realm* and *Woman's Weekly*. She initially received 350 letters.

This approach is not unlike that used by researchers at the Chicago School that we looked at in chapter three. These researchers would use archives, official documents and letters to help to create a sense of the context. However, what they would also do was carry out extensive periods of observation. This is something that Stacey did not do.

Interpreting data

What kind of status are we able to give to letters and to responses to questionnaires? Clearly we cannot think about this in the kind of model of ethnography offered by anthropologists such as Malinowski – not unless the letters were viewed as *one* source of data as part of the general flow of everyday life. Stacey did use something of what we might think of as the ethnographic gaze when thinking about the status of her data at the start of the book, although she then goes on to lose sight of this point somewhat and treat responses as 'real'. In the chapter on the idea of culture in the ethnographic gaze I argued that we need to move away from the idea of people producing real opinions or beliefs. Rather, we need to think about people using their cultural frameworks in settings, in order to make sense of the world in that moment and to find their place in that world.

Stacey's approach is consistent with this view when she comments that interpreting her data was difficult since what her respondents said would depend on what they themselves had come to know about the legitimate things that one can say about film – in other words, the available cultural discourses for talking about the subject. The film theorist Staiger (1992) has said that people's experiences of films should be understood in terms of the factors at any time which may have influenced people's readings of a film. Previously I gave the example of the way that films like *It's A Wonderful Life* and *Citizen Kane* were originally both critical and box office failures. Now they are both thought of as classics. When people talk about these and other films as classics, we need to understand how in society at a particular time films have been understood in certain ways. Film theorists might look at why we now think about such films differently.

To those who generally accept the validity of such qualitative data it might seem strange to say that people are constrained to talk about a particular topic by the kinds of ways that are available for doing so at any particular time. Surely, they might think, people simply talk about how they feel about films, and of course this will mean this reflects the attitudes of the time. But this is not quite what is at stake here. The anthropologist Evans-Pritchard (1937) made it clear that people may be able to give official reasons for why they do things, but we must really look a lot further into the way that people behave and talk to be sure if this has any bearing on their broader relationship to the phenomena about which they are talking. We can never get access to people's pure beliefs. Anthropology, as we looked at in Chapter 2, has taught us not to think about the way that people relate to culture in this way. We should rather think of a cultural tool kit which is used for practical understanding and interaction, allowing us to communicate and get along. By gathering the discourse of these respondents we are gaining access to the discourses that are available for people to think about film.

Stacey was also mindful of the problems involved in getting people to talk about the past. Memory does not just simply reflect the past neutrally. When anyone tells a researcher anything, it is a retrospective representation which involves cultural processes. It involves the way that people think about themselves through cultural discourses. And this cultural playing out of identity will influence recollection. Put simply, this will mean selective remembering and even construction of events and interpretations through current needs. This would certainly be the case when we are dealing with the classic Hollywood of the 1940s, which generally falls into the category of treasured memory. It is thought about in terms of a utopian golden past of movie glamour. Stacey points out that respondents would have perceived her request for letters about memories of Hollywood during this period in this very context. But she does not see this necessarily as a problem as it still allows us to look at the discourses that are available for these women. She says: 'Popular memories of the cinema ... replicate particular narrative and visual conventions of popular culture generally' (1994, p. 71). And, this, I feel is where Stacey shows the potential for greater understanding of her data than if she assumed that she had simply tapped in to people's true beliefs. Later in the book, however, Stacey deals with her data as if they do concretely reflect what women thought about a range of issues.

Stacey herself deals with the problem of people's letters and responses by saying that we should avoid either of two extremes. She says that we should not think about women's comments as offering a truth about the world or particularly films and how people make sense of them. To assume this, she argues, would miss the way that people talk as subjects in culture, history and setting. But we should also avoid thinking about what the women say as just another text, or fiction. In other words, we can assume that what people say in such settings does give some insight into the way that people can think about films. Looking at these accepted conventions of expression can itself be revealing.

Women and movies: escapism

Stacey felt that her data showed how important film is in the act of reminiscing and trips down memory lane. The women reported on their experiences of going to the movies as part of a charming thing that was part of a bygone era. Stacey found that the cinemas themselves formed an important part of these fond memories. The women would recall all the details: the lavish luxury, rich textures, fancy curtains, chandeliers and thick carpets. This all added to the 'other worldliness' of the cinema experience.

The women saw Hollywood films as being about this glamour in contrast to British films which were about acting, largely located in the drab Britain of the time. The war had brought hardship and emotional difficulties. For many women life was full of death, loss, shortages and dislocation. Hollywood showed a luxurious world of abundance when British women were having to 'make do and mend' while clothing was rationed.

Stacey says that this world of glamour brought expressions of femininity which were not available to women in Britain at this time. The cinemas, along with the films themselves, were an escape to a materially opulent world where there was outrageous style and luxury. She gives an example of one woman who said that coming down the stairs in a cinema was like a Hollywood female star descending into a ballroom.

The experience of the movies was also recalled in the context of the shared experience of watching the film. Stacey sees this emphasis on the collective experience for the women as being something particularly feminine, in contrast to masculine individuality. This sense of collective experience was heightened in popular memory because of the war. The women spoke fondly of the pulling together. In the cinema environment people could move collectively into a different world away from the war.

The Hollywood movies were also associated with an American culture of abundance of consumables. During the war American soldiers had appeared with products which were scarce or unaffordable in Britain. Often these products were simply preferred as they represented something other than traditional British values. They seemed associated with this escapist fun world. The women said that they just enjoyed looking at this far-away world, its landscapes, cities and houses.

Stacey says that the women in her study would have been young women or adolescents at the time and they often saw the female Hollywood stars as being in opposition to the older women they saw around them in Britain. The women around them were busy trying to hold things together and deal with the shortages. The Hollywood stars wore great clothes, had romances, attentive handsome leading men and danced in exotic locations. The stars offered a different kind of model for femininity. Their images were tied up with ideas of abundance.

Stacey suggests that currently American culture does not seem the same as it did during the 1940s. It was something very far away. Now it is something that has its place in everyday television, in burger chains on the high street. America can now feasibly be visited. This will have lessened the other worldliness of Hollywood and of the stars.

The stars

From the data we have summarized so far it is clear that Stacey felt that women were far from passive victims of Hollywood. In the book she goes on to use her data to challenge the psychoanalytical idea of identification such as expressed by Mulvey.

Mulvey argued that film only reflects patriarchal values and that women in films are generally passive sexual objects, leaving the female spectator with no choice other than to identify with this. Stacey found that the women in her study were often quite devoted to female stars, seeing them as having characteristics of strength and resilience that they would themselves have liked to have had. These stars were also appreciated for their beauty and many women became devoted fans for many years.

Part of this worship of stars was because they were perceived as being so far away from the ordinary world of mortals. Women would speak of not being able to take their eyes off their favourite stars. In some cases the women would say that they wanted to be more like a star, doing their hair in the same style perhaps. In other cases the star was seen as something to be worshipped from afar. Stacey says that some-times these bonds had a homoerotic quality to them. Sometimes the women would speak of liking a star because they resembled them in some way.

Sometimes women spoke of imagining themselves in the roles of the stars. They would speak of being there on the screen, of losing themselves in the film. This is inter-esting as much psychoanalytical theory talks about the spectator and the act of watch-ing as a voyeuristic activity. Stacey was concerned to point out that this losing oneself in romance fiction is something that the women felt embarrassed about. But this itself could be thought of as patriarchy where women's likes are dismissed as trivial.

Women would talk a lot about aspiring to be like the star – to have some of their screen qualities. This may have been because of confidence, for the clothes that they wore or just for their physical beauty. Star quality itself was associated with glamour, strength and confidence. The women would even mention getting high on a star, which Stacey sees as moments of intimacy between the star and the spectator. Interestingly, even where strong women film characters were killed off or punished for their strength and intelligence, the women did not remember this part but held on to the positive aspects.

Stacey was keen to point out that the women might also say that now they realize that these stars were just marketed images and manufactured commodities. But this would not prevent them from looking back fondly at the ability that they had to be drawn in to this glamorous world. This data allowed Stacey to challenge Mulvey's view of the 'male gaze' where women could either identify with the male protagonist or with the passive objectified female. Of course, since Stacey started out with the view of giving a voice to women, this is not surprising. Nevertheless it is difficult to refute the fact that the women in her study seem to have very empowering recollections of watching movies.

Consumption and Hollywood

Another thing that the data revealed was the way that the women related to the world of American products which were made desirable by the movies. These would include things like fashion accessories, household furnishings and general consumer-based lifestyles. Stacey wondered to what extent we might think of Hollywood as encouraging women to become passive consumers. The films clearly were showcases for this world. Stacey notes that cinemas were built near to shopping centres and matinee screenings would allow women to go straight out to shop.

Stacey suggests that along with identification and escapism, consumption was important in the way women expressed themselves. The women talked longingly about hairstyles, clothes and make-up. They seemed to relish sharing in the judgement of style, in what looked good, in what clothes went well together. This would allow them to feel an identification with the star. Women would talk about being inspired to buy things after seeing them in a film and could remember things in detail which they had seen over 50 years ago, which gave them a sense of pride. Many stars were remembered precisely for their fashion sense.

Stacey remarks that the comments of the women showed the importance of the stars and their fashions in the development of identity. This was at a time when there was no such thing as the teenage market. Therefore the female stars were sources of images of what femininity was all about as they offered various ideals. Particularly for these British women, the images of Hollywood stars seemed to offer much more scope for personal freedom, self-expression, and assertiveness than images of femininity available in Britain at the time. Many clothes were even named after stars who often wore trademark clothing. Stacey is convinced that the women were able to construct their individuality through consumption.

Stacey's study is an important one: it takes the somewhat unusual step of looking at cinema audiences themselves which allows her to take a different angle on some theoretical debates, like identification and consumption. The study uses qualitative data, in the style of some of the Chicago School studies. Stacey basically uses data from oral histories, from the long letters that she received, to give a sense of real people enjoying movies and stars. Clearly, the sample would be comprised of women who were motivated, for some reason or another, to write to her about their love of films. And we have the problem of relying solely on one source of data. Stacey had no way of corroborating what the women told her about themselves. And the point of ethnography in the anthropological model is that we consider the official reasons that people give for what they do, for example, that they liked cinema for escapism from a drab Britain, in the context of what people do and say more broadly. Only in this way can we get a sense of living culture. But as Stacey stresses, we can think about her data in terms of it showing the way that women can talk about film – the available conventions and discourses in a culture for talking about the subject. And, as Foucault (1966, 1969) has argued, these discourses go a long way in influencing how we think and therefore act. But when Stacey looks at the women talking about consumerism as liberation, is this really their true belief, or are they simply reproducing capitalist discourse from the time?

One characteristic of the study that stands out is the way that, through its concern to give the women a voice and to challenge the earlier constructions of the female spectator as passive, it says nothing about how capitalist consumerism changes people's lives. Nor does it have anything to say about whether the women are subordinate to dominant ideologies. In this way the study was typical of many of the other 'resistance studies' of the 1980s. Perhaps, on the other hand, it is difficult to swallow the truth that consumerism really does facilitate individual expression rather than provide a myth of it, which pathologically distorts our sense of ourselves and each other.

The important question for us to ask here is, how could we investigate this process to provide clearer answers? The answer here lies in looking at the way that people in living culture watch films, talk about them, how the film images relate to those in the broader culture. In short, we have, like Malinowski, to provide a whole map of a culture and way of life, or at least try to account for all the parts that might help us to understand the images we see in a film and the way that a woman might relate to them. For example, if we think about a film like *Coyote Ugly* (2001) or *Charlie's Angels* (2001), we will need to look at the representations of the women in the film. How do these fit in with other representations of women in the mass media and in society in general? We might find, for example, that consumerism at the time drew heavily on a mythological construction of a confident, lively fun-loving female, in the same way that it drew on clichéd images of hairy-chested masculinity in the 1970s, as embodied in the Marlboro ads. We would have to resist the temptation to assume that any of the representations were simply reflections of how women innately are. In other words we would have to make them anthropologically strange – think about them in the same way as we might view magic in the Trobriand Islands. The task would then be to find out the ways that women related to these images. We could find out how they talked about the film. We could observe how the mythology of independence and confidence as expressed in the film, etc., appeared in women's lives more broadly.

Making the present anthropologically strange for the purpose of research is not an easy task. It is more difficult to see the present in one's own culture as something that is arbitrary and constructed. The past – as the example of the medallion-wearing, hairy-chested, granite-jawed Marlboro man shows us – is much easier to view in a detached manner. But could we really in the future find out what the women who saw movies like *Coyote Ugly*, with their particular representations of women, think by asking them to write letters to us about what they saw and felt?

Using the Internet

11

D. Miller and D. Slater (2000) *The Internet: An Ethnographic Approach.* Oxford and New York: Berg.

The title of this volume speaks for itself. The book is an excellent study of Internet use in Trinidad. At the time the research was groundbreaking and much needed. There was no empirical evidence as to how the Internet was being used. All the literature on the subject was highly speculative and generally still spoke of the Internet in very romantic terms. Miller and Slater begin the book by commenting on the need to move away from the rhetoric of cyberspace and the virtual to find out how 'numerous new technologies [are] used by diverse people, in diverse real-world locations' (2000, p. 1).

Their plan was to look at how the Internet was thought about and used in a particular place. In their ethnography the place was Trinidad. The authors make the crucial point of saying that their ethnography will therefore tell us things about both the Internet and Trinidad, suggesting that it is not possible to understand one without the other. This is important. Audience studies have tended to look for effects or uses, or opinions on the media, in isolation from culture. Miller and Slater think that this is not possible. It would be like Malinowski looking at magic without considering anything else about the culture in the Trobriand Islands. This would ignore the place that magic, or television, has in a culture and how people think about and act towards it. In terms of the case of the Internet in Trinidad, the authors argue that they are not simply looking at its uses or effects of the new medium, but at how people in a specific place make sense of it.

The study was part of an 11-year project on Trinidadian culture and part of a much longer study of the Internet. The actual time spent in Trinidad studying the Internet was five weeks. The researchers interviewed Trinidadians in both London and New York. They spent time in cybercafés hanging out and interviewing people. Students were asked to fill out questionnaires which they followed up with in-depth interviews. The researchers would stay on-line for long periods – as long as informants. Therefore the ethnography on the Internet was informed by spending long periods of time in Trinidad to create the basis of an understanding of the society and culture. It also meant using the Internet in ways that it was used by Trinidadians and involved considering how the Internet had become involved in people's lives and what they thought of it.

Miller and Slater found that the Internet had been immediately accepted in Trinidad. This, they suggest, was because it fitted well with Trinidadian values such as 'national pride, cosmopolitanism, freedom, entrepreneurialism' (ibid., p. 2). Also it was naturally useful as the Trinidadian family is traditionally dispersed across the globe and has to communicate over distances. People showed no concerns about Internet content and their only real complaints were that things weren't changing as quickly as they should.

Little use of the Net was found that could be said to be virtual. Subjects treated chat, e-mail and e-commerce as real. Rather than looking at a new reality, as much of the earlier formulations on the Internet had excitedly announced, it seemed that we were dealing with new mediations for communication. The authors say that their findings indicate that e-mail communications or websites were thought of as basically concrete and mundane things which facilitated interaction rather than being anything virtual.

Miller and Slater say that the idea of the virtual is not new to the Internet. They mention Anderson's (1983) idea of the nation as an imagined community. Anderson put the newspaper at the centre of these imagined communities, referring to its power to give the reader the sense that there were many thousands, even millions, out there doing the same, even though they would never meet most of them. The implied public could be described as a virtual community.

The authors emphasize that it is important not to see the Internet in a way that is separate from the rest of people's lives. Early Internet mythology had presented a romanticized image of the cybersurfer as a virtual human being fragmented in cyber-space. But people go onto the Net as Trinidadians, as young people, and as business people. For example, a young man might live in a world where he likes MTV, certain television programmes and Nike. The websites that this person visits will reflect their off-line culture. The authors argue therefore that we should not reify the Net and study it as something which affects people. The Net is made up of people like those in their study. We should not look at the Internet as something that is separate from society. It is what we might think of, they suggest, as material culture.

Internet access

Miller and Slater found much more widespread use of the Internet than they had expected. While one in 20 households had access, around one-third had a regular user. Even in the lowest-income houses, people bought the best computers and modems. The Internet, they argue, had become part of being fashionable and stylish in Trinidad and its skills were being used as a way of bypassing traditional forms of qualifications. Since its arrival on the island in 1995 the Internet had been taken up rapidly by all sectors of society.

The researchers carried out a house-to-house survey to look at the extent of use in four residential areas, which they felt would be representative of the whole of Trinidad in terms of them covering a range of socio-economic areas. Some of these areas were where use would be expected to be low, rather than in the capital where use would be higher. They then focused on four households. Using their data as a whole they considered the relationship between use and factors such as gender, age and social class.

They found that the difference in Internet access was not as high as one might expect between richer and poor areas, although there was still a great difference and computers were still expensive even with subsidies. And even though the government was committed to the Internet in schools, some had taken longer than others and the prestige schools were able to raise funds from private sources.

Knowledge and skills in the Internet, even if learned informally, were seen as a way to access middle-class jobs. Many people, even the poor, would invest in Internet courses as education is seen as the best way to achieve social mobility. The researchers say that IT business had been much more open to demonstrable skills in place of formal qualifications. As technology changes quickly and courses may not necessarily keep up it would often be the enthusiastic home users who were the whizz kids. But getting jobs was not easy and would probably depend on contacts. Most independent webpage designers were the children of local businesspeople. And it was difficult to gain access to some of the latest and more expensive technology without having access to businesses using this.

No gender distinctions were found in home use. Young women were equally as likely to be seeking out a career in IT. The house-to-house surveys and the observations in the cybercafés strongly suggested that the Internet was used equally by males and females. But once in the work environment women tended to move into administrative work while the men did all the high-powered work. However, this was more often the case of the women who had returned to Trinidad. Greater equality in the workplace was experienced by those who went abroad.

The research uncovered some unexpected things. The main Internet service provider allowed people to sell on access from their own accounts. So while there were up to 25 000 accounts counted, sometimes a whole street would be hooked up from one of these. So actual access was difficult to measure. It was thought from speaking to people over the time of the study that it was safe to estimate that about 30 per cent of households had one user. The researchers were also struck by the way that pirated games and software were circulated rapidly among users.

Business and the Internet

Miller and Slater say that their data suggested that all visions of the future in terms of Trinidad's economic and social position seemed to revolve around the Internet. This was in terms of tourism, banking and the possibility of offering web design to North American companies. The Internet was associated with innovation, modernity and opportunity. The world of computers was generally seen as stylish and appropriate for Trinidad, which sees itself as the trendsetter in the Caribbean.

In every high street in Trinidad there were signs advertising courses in Internet use and IT. Everyone felt that the Internet would continue to grow. The government had abolished all tax on hardware and software and were offering interest-free loans for computers to all public sector employees, which had seen a massive take-up. The government was also committed to getting Internet access to all public buildings like schools and libraries.

Miller and Slater ask the question as to what all this meant to the average trades-person who put their goods on-line. They suggest that it meant that people do find themselves in a position where they are negotiating in networks which lie beyond their geographical location, which means that they will find themselves exposed to a broader range of cultural, political and economic factors. They state that: 'The bound-aries of market, nations, cultures and technologies become increasingly permeable, and require people to think of themselves as actors on ever more global stages' (ibid., pp. 18–19). They suggest that, practically speaking, for a retailer in a small town in Trinidad this meant that the idea of the local price is now being changed to include the idea of a single world-wide marketplace.

Dispersed families

The research found that the Internet was used to strengthen bonds between dis-persed Trinidadian families. This was particularly important in Trinidad which had long been characterized by the geographical dispersal of its people across the globe. Trinidadians have traditionally left Trinidad in search of work opportunities. Of 160 households surveyed, 101 had a member of their nuclear family living abroad. Trinidadians who lived in London, New York, Toronto and Miami said that they used the Internet to maintain a closer sense of involvement in their culture and with their families.

It was found that families had previously relied on the telephone to keep in touch, but this was seen as very expensive and would be used infrequently. The thing about e-mail is that chat can be mundane and everyday, and thus more like normal family life. Half the Trinidadians living in London said that they use the Internet primarily for this purpose. The telephone was still used but was reserved for special occasions such as birthdays.

Relationships

Men interviewed said that when they chatted to strangers on the Web this was always with women. They said that this was generally done in terms of flirtation. The men said that they would only chat to other men if they were searching for some specific information. The men talked about the challenge and the excitement, the chase and the thrill. Miller and Slater say that Trinidadians use a style of flirtatiousness that is not always in accord with the practices of other societies. They give the example of one woman who called herself Miss Sexy, which was misconstrued by many men as a particular kind of opportunity.

The Trinidadian women said that they were more interested in chatting with people from different countries – a sort of mediated tourism. They also tended to like to discuss personal issues such as family with people from very different cultures. Miller and Slater suggest that this confirms for the women the idea that somehow, despite the surface differences, we are basically all the same – a kind of global sentimentality. They said that lot of the women they spoke with had these on-line friends who were planning a visit.

One thing that earlier commentators on the Internet had talked about was the way that people have fragmented or dislocated identities on-line. By this they meant that we could pretend to be anyone or as many people as we wanted to be, and that no-one would ever know. Miller and Slater's research suggests that this is not necessarily the case. Both men and women spoke about the fact that trust is eventually built up despite anonymity through a continued on-line presence over time. It might also have to do with the amount of mundane life that someone shares with you. Some respondents had on-line friendships that had lasted several years and which were trusted as it was felt that long periods of time tend to try and test people. So while it was true that people may chat with someone not knowing anything about them, this will remain only as chat until a relationship has been developed. How much a relationship means to someone will simply depend on how much the relationship has developed. Miller and Slater use this evidence to reject the idea of virtual friends. These can be real friends. Respondents said that they were a little more cautious initially with on-line chatters but that since you cannot have non-verbal cues for deceit, you learn to track what they are writing.

The research found many examples of Trinidadians who had met their partners on-line. Miller and Slater suggest that this was probably because this was a country which is used to looking outwards as many Trinidadians end up living abroad. Marrying someone in this way also facilitates the possibility of a life abroad. They also note that for schoolchildren the Internet was a means of flirting with the opposite sex before dating or as a way to organize dating. This allowed them to be a little more forthright while they remained anonymous.

Trinidadian culture

We must understand the way that the Internet has taken off in terms of the country's history of slavery and indentured labour. The centrality of the idea of freedom and then of the idea of Trinidad as being self-determining are important features.

Government and businesses see the Internet as helping to integrate the country into the international community. It is seen as the essence of modernity and of the spirit of free access and movement, allowing the increase of people's potential. Miller and Slater say that there was no talk about regulation or problems with content even though many in the study believed that porn is still the main use of the Internet. And they say the international arena is one where the Trinidadians are used to competing.

As an ethnographic study of Internet usage this is extremely revealing. Its strength lies in the fact that the authors are able to locate the way that people speak about the Internet in the broader Trinidadian culture. As Miller and Slater point out, people interact with material culture in a way that is articulated through their own existing culture. If we wish to understand how people relate to the Internet, we cannot examine it in isolation. In previous studies looked at in this volume we have seen the importance of locating people's behaviour into the environment that they live and into the broader cultural framework that they use to make sense of the world. This was the case for the elderly people in Tulloch's (1989) study who related to and talked about soap opera in terms of existing discourses about high and low culture. The women in Stacey's (1994) study used available discourses to talk about movies and movie stars. The boys in Thrasher's (1927) study of gangs carry out acts of violence due to the way they have come to relate to the world. The Trobriand Islanders will cast magic spells on canoes, not because they are irrational but because this is part of the way that their culture understands the world. If we want to understand how any of these people relate to anything in the mass media, we would need to know more about the frameworks which they normally use as a reference for dealing with the world.

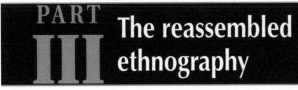

PART III

The reassembled ethnography

Data analysis

In this Part I look more closely at the kind of data analysis that would characterize the ethnographic gaze and the reassembled ethnography. This means collecting and presenting data, which reveals how people relate to the mass media, in a way that allows us to see this in the context of these people's everyday lives. These are real people who have real concerns to understand the world and to find a place for themselves in that world. They do this through a particular cultural framework which they use with a sensitivity to each other. Thus, the ethnographer must be able to show not only the knowledge that people have about the world but the way that they relate to each other. The mass media must be shown to be part of this process, how it draws on and feeds into this cultural framework, what frameworks people use to understand the media and how these unfold in social contexts.

In Chapter 12 I look at a media spectacle in Spain. Through ethnography we are able to understand why a particular set of events became so widely talked about that the whole of a province was gripped by hysteria and then itself turned on the very media through which they had originally been so keen to be informed.

In Chapter 13 I look at how ethnography can help us to understand newspaper circulations in Spain. These are extremely low and people are very loyal to one title which they never seem to read. This situation can only be understood by looking at the broader cultural framework and the way that this informs displays of identity.

In Chapter 14 I turn the ethnographic gaze to look at data from a project which would generally be thought of a focus group-based research, although in this case the talk is generated as the speakers participated in a role-play activity. I show how viewing these data with an ethnographic gaze allows us to gain much greater insight into what the participants are saying and how they relate to television. I show how it is important to reassemble the data back into the broader flow of the lives and cultures of the participants.

Chapter 15 details the procedures for carrying out an ethnographic study, drawing on the studies discussed in the book.

12 An anthropological approach to a news spectacle

In this chapter I present a study of newspaper reading that I carried out as an anthropologist in the 1990s (Machin 1996; Machin and Carrithers 1996). I have chosen this particular study as it clearly illustrates the ethnographic gaze and the idea of the reassembled ethnography. The approach taken to media audiences in this chapter addresses the call by researchers, such as Ang (1990) and Radway (1988), to find how to study audiences in a way that did not disconnect those audiences from their everyday lives. Ang suggested that we need to look at reception as 'an integral part of popular cultural practices that articulate both "subjective" and "objective" both "micro" and "macro" processes' (1990, p. 224). He stressed that we need to move away from the way that people become characterized as being static audience members who carry with them an unchanging set of readings of the media.

Radway (1988) argued that research needed to get away from thinking about reception in an isolated way, or of audiences as something that are external to the rest of people's lives. Rather than an audience member, she suggested, research had to think about people in terms of 'the active producing cultural worker who fashions narratives, stories, objects and practices from myriad bits and pieces of prior cultural production' (1988, p. 362). This is exactly what the anthropological approach that I take in this chapter does.

The data used in this chapter are from an 18-month ethnographic study of newspaper readers in Valencia, Spain. The study involved working with journalists in the fashion of Fishman's (1980). The data also comes from interviews with people about news and tape recording naturally occurring conversations both about the day's news events and other more general topics. While living in Valencia I also took work in a factory and in a bar. These settings gave me access to different groups of people whom I could get to know, and whom I could observe chatting.

One thing that stood out during my period of research was the way that people responded to a particular news spectacle. This was fascinating. The Spanish press is generally not sensationalist, but this particular set of events led to a temporary switch to a different kind of news presentation. Newspapers are generally filled with politics, and are considered impenetrable by many readers, which is one reason why they have some of the lowest national readerships in the whole of Europe. But for a short time they were filled with little other than stories about these events – events that I was told by the police were not necessarily that unusual. The data that I present in this chapter help to explain why this story became so important that it temporarily transformed newspapers in Spain.

The news spectacle I wish to focus on involved the disappearance and search for three teenage girls, and the discovery of their abused bodies in a shallow grave in the mountains. There was then the search for the two individuals believed to have raped and murdered them. The story was not that unique. But it became one of the biggest stories in the history of the Spanish press. The reasons for this are complex. First, let us start with the basic sequence of events that motivated the news spectacle. We can then move on to look at the way that people responded to the story.

When the girls had first gone missing, the story had created a modicum of interest in the press. Initially the story only appeared, the journalist told me, because there was little else happening. It would not be usual to report on the disappearance of young people. Later the story gained publicity partly due to the activities of one of the fathers of the girls who travelled to several different European countries to solicit the help of other police forces in the search. Photographs of the three pretty girls could be seen around the city of Valencia. People in general speculated as to the possibility of the girls being victims of a slave trade in Africa. This titillation helped it to reach into public consciousness as people wondered about shop changing rooms with hidden chutes. One journalist told me this was one reason that he ran the story. The story disappeared for a while to re-emerge at Christmas when the trauma of the ruptured family again generated news interest.

The story had largely disappeared from the news media until about a month later when the bodies were discovered. Each day the newspapers and other news media revealed more and more gruesome details of what had happened to the girls as forensic evidence was released. The newspapers filled as many pages as they could on the matter. Anyone vaguely connected with the case was interviewed. Graphics were used to help readers visualize the events. Circulations exploded, and for a while at least newspapers bore some resemblance to their sensationalist counterparts in other European countries such as *Bild Zeitung* and the *Sun*. Details were released that evidence had been found at the crime scene connecting two individuals to the murders, who it soon transpired, were on the run in Valencia.

The two presumed killers were from marginalized, non-literate backgrounds, lived in poor squalid areas, and had previous prison records. Stories appeared demonizing particularly one of them, who, it turned out, was out on release from prison which he had earned for good behaviour. The story became the subject of conversations all over the city. The sheer horror of the story and the intensive reporting created an atmosphere of tension and fear. Women said that they were scared to leave their homes. Journalist, pushed by their editors, searched for any possible angle on the story to maintain the high circulations. Many of the journalists themselves commented on the strange situation where the village which had been the home of the three girls had been completely taken over by an incredible number of journalists.

News articles were produced interviewing the families of the girls and especially people who had known the two suspects. One of the suspects was caught, although it was decided that he was more of a henchman. The real evildoer was a young man named Antonio Angles who was portrayed as having manipulated and controlled his weak-minded and easily led accomplice. Many stories were written describing just how evil Angles was. He was good-looking which seemed to emphasize his twistedness. His mother told how her fear of her son was such that she would sleep with her money inside her vagina. Unnamed sources in his village told of extortion, threats and lawlessness. One newspaper ran any vaguely connected story under the heading 'The search for public enemy number one' accompanied by a small photo of Angles. These would be other disappearances or the many debates that sprang up around related issues, for example, to do with prisoners being allowed leave for good behaviour. There were many student demonstrations regarding the right to be on the street without fear of harm.

It is from this point in the developing events that I want to look at how people were talking about the news stories. On the one hand, we have the texts themselves, but what did people make of them? And did people's responses themselves influence the style of reporting?

The following snippets of conversation have been chosen as they are highly representative of how people were talking about the story. They reveal something special about the way that people relate to culture and illustrate the importance of the ethnographic gaze and the task of reassembling the ethnographic moment back into the flow of everyday life.

The newspaper readers

The following slices of conversation were tape-recorded in cafés. I knew the speakers through work in a factory. The first comment is motivated by reading a news text about the suspect, Antonio Angles, who seemed to be showing almost supernatural powers to elude the police. There are six people present including the researcher. We were taking morning coffee.

> Ignacio: (11:15 a.m. Thursday) That guy is a bastard. They are just worse than animals these people. They are not satisfied with living by society's laws so we shouldn't treat them with the law. I say, give them the laws of the jungle that they want. Give them to the families of the girls. That would be a warning to others like them. They just want to bring society down to their level.

In traditional audience research, or even in the ethnographic turn, we might take what Ignacio says here to be his opinion on the subject. Ignacio *believes* that true justice should be done in cases of such criminals who are clearly not human. But later on the same day the speaker is involved in a different conversation. Here he is focusing his comments on a member of the group with whom he often disagreed in order to make himself feel and appear of higher status. This person was often used for this purpose by members of the group and was generally pretty inept at debate. Ignacio was always confident of his ability to outmanoeuvre this person. This individual had just commented on the details of what had happened to the girls.

> Ignacio: (9:15, Thursday) I think that the whole thing is shameful. For them [the newspapers] it is just a chance to make money as usual. It's just appealing to people's sense of [morbid curiosity]. What do people expect anyway? These underprivileged people are always involved in such things. Try putting it on the front page every time one of those people does something wrong. I want to know when the government will do something about it. It is things like this that allow them to hide the truth and hide the poverty.

This is clearly a very different position to take than is found in the first conversation. In the first case Ignacio speaks as part of a respectable social order which is threatened by evildoers whom he characterizes as animals. In the second the suspect is spoken of as a victim of social inequalities. This was another well-worn conversational manoeuvre in Spain. The Spanish flavour in this particular comment is contained in the idea that officialdom is not interested in ordinary people but serves its own interests. And Ignacio here aligns himself beside those who are intelligent enough to see through government lies. As he made both these comments Ignacio would look around at the others in the group taking the tone of what he was saying being publicly known knowledge.

Of course we might simply assume that Ignacio had changed his mind. However, the very next day Ignacio again returned to his former position.

> Ignacio: (11:15, Friday) They should just send in people to get rid of them. It's like in the area where I live. You can see all the rubbish [homeless people] on the streets. Everyone knows who sells the drugs. The police should just step in and get rid of them. Let's face it, they are just a burden. They should just say, sort yourselves out or goodbye.

Here we can see a return to the stance of lesser tolerance. Here Ignacio again speaks as a member of the honest, decent society. But in this case that society needs to be liberated from a burden rather than a threat. And here those who are the burden are not described as having the destruction of society as their conscious aim as they did in the first comment.

A short time after this comment, Ignacio responds generally to a comment by another member of the group.

> Ignacio: (11:35 a.m. Friday): You can't believe a word that the newspapers say anyway. Them and the politicians, what do they care?

The view expressed here is different from all the other samples. The other comments accepted the newspaper's stories, even though the second disagreed with its explanation. In this case newspapers cannot be believed. This is even though Ignacio himself often used them as a source of conversation. The theme of the comment is similar to the second sample where Ignacio aligns himself against corrupt official-dom. In fact, this idea that newspapers were full of lies was also a common theme in Spanish talk. Interviews with people about why they bought or read a particular title would often emphasize on the one hand that readership was seen as a respectable thing suggesting education and cultural sophistication. But in the same interview if asked to talk specifically about a news item, the same people would usually comment that all news was lies – being connected to the world of officialdom and power. This was a theme that would just not be heard in the way that, say, British people would talk about newspapers. In Britain there would be a certainty that there was a clear dis-tinction between the truth content of the tabloid and broadsheet newspapers.

Presented in this manner we might have a tendency to think of Ignacio as a weak or changeable individual. However, this flexibility in the way that people use cultural themes was characteristic of the talk that was recorded over 18 months in Spain. And this way of talking should not be thought of as revealing weakness or fickleness. People are concerned about understanding the world in which they live, and this understanding may be slowly changing. But people are also involved in a process of responsiveness to their conversational partners. They talk to achieve credibility, soli-darity, to compete and because it is enjoyable.

One objection to this idea might be that it seems that we are saying that there is no real Ignacio. Of course there is. But the point is that we experience ourselves through the alignments that talk allows. We cannot say exactly what any one person in fact believes although we might expect people with certain characteristics to speak using certain themes. These themes might be thought of as the bedrock of a culture. What is important in research is that we capture this movement. People improvise using their cultural tool kit, which provides them with a range of widely accepted explanations about how things work. The ethnographic turn in audience studies missed this process of improvisation. Consequently, as many of those writers themselves became aware, such studies tended to offer a monolithic view of a static culture. It is this very process of improvisation and mobility which is at the heart of change.

This view also has the power to allow us to see that what people say relates to the broader cultural setting and the more immediate setting of interaction. Ignacio uses some very Spanish themes regarding distrust of authority. He is also familiar with cer-tain views regarding the intolerance of evildoers. But when he uses these themes it is with a vivid sensitivity to the others around him. He can gain approval by holding a widely respected point of view and he can compete with his fellows.

Journalists

It would be reasonable to suggest that stories such as the disappearance and murder of the three girls, and the emergence of a murderer who can be presented as fairly colourful and charismatic are good, as they are high on drama and personality. They also allow a lot of morbid intrigue. But they are also important as they allow conversations through which people can align themselves in the manner we have just seen.

I now want to move on to the journalists themselves. The journalists can be thought of as generating their news texts through a similar process of sensitivity to the kind of improvisations being made by the likes of Ignacio, although, as journalists, their role is to emphasize the dramatic and the kinds of story and character that will move people to talk.

Felisa was a journalist responsible on her newspaper for all the stories being generated around the events surrounding the murder of the three girls. Felisa emphasized that when she wrote her stories she did so through spending time with people in bars, in the hairdressers, and other public places. One of her team, Guillem, said:

> Remember that we go to all the usual public places. We are bound to get caught up with the whole emotion of the situation. Then you take that with you when you write. Well, of course, we are under pressure by editors to write stuff, and of course you know that certain kinds of material helps to sell newspapers. People like their baddies to be real baddies. You have to provide a focus for the readers, something for them to get a handle on. But when the atmosphere has been as it has. As you know yourself, it has been really heavy: the woman in the shop tells you she is too scared to open up, your neighbour goes on about his kids having nightmares. Every day we find out more about just how horrific the murders were and everybody wants to run through it a few times. When it's like this, you write naturally. You can't isolate yourself from the way people feel no matter how much you want to be objective.

So, while this journalist is guided by professional requirements, news conventions and the ideology of his newspaper, he also composes his stories in a way that is sensitive to the improvisations being done by people like Ignacio. The journalist was aware of the way that people improvised using certain themes, or cultural representations. How the journalist responds to people is not exactly the same as Ignacio. Ignacio is only responsive to his immediate company. The journalists have to be responsive in a much broader manner. But they will then still produce news stories around these themes.

We find the mixture of this professional experience and the sensitivity to people's improvisation in the following comment by Felisa. She was commenting on a story that she had written headed THEY ATE BENEATH THE POSTER OF THE GIRLS.

> It is good to create a 'something must be done' feel. People feel that we live in a lawless society where the state is soft. When you hear people talking or passing comments, say in a bar, they are always wanting to know why something is not being done … And by showing lots of pictures of angry or grieving crowds during the coverage of [the events] we give the sense that we are the public face of that community that wants something to be done

... I will portray Angles in a way that emphasizes his difference from the community and the way that he represents everything that is a threat to the decency of that community. This generates people's interest. He is not just some nutcase, he is the enemy of all decent people. They have protagonists to identify with and they have good and evil ... The headline THEY ATE BENEATH THE POSTER OF THE GIRLS for me is an example of this kind of text. When I first heard the fact from the mouth of the bar owner I knew I had a story. Only the most evil of people could eat their dinner each day knowing what they had done under a poster which continually reminded them of it ... The bar owner recognized that and so will everyone else.

So Felisa comes across this story as part of a bar conversation. She is able to generalize from the example of the story she is told to think about good and evil. She knows from her experience how to form a narrative that will work for the readers. In this sense we can see that there is a responsiveness between the journalists and their readers. Like Ignacio she is able to produce an improvisation on the theme regarding the way that society is under threat by evildoers. Felisa herself expressed to me on several occasions that having visited and interviewed members of the fugitive's family she was 'shocked at how people in Spain live in terrible deprived conditions'. She said that such people live on the margins of society and its values. But she is aware of the way that the theme about the evildoers would allow the newspaper to be read and positioned.

In fact, by this point in the events people were already starting to tire of the story. The view expressed by Ignacio that the whole thing was grotesque sensationalism was starting to become more centrally heard.

Angles was never caught. In August of the same year, the news media reported that it was thought that he had drowned off the coast of Ireland. No body was ever found. Many people in Valencia could be heard saying that they didn't believe any of it. It was widely thought that there was some kind of cover-up. One view frequently expressed at the height of the story was that it was strange that the police had been unable to catch him at the time.

The fact that these particular events became a news spectacle is partly due to chance. It was also because the father of the girls was quite vocal at the time of the search. It was also Christmas time, one journalist told me, which made the story more newsworthy. But why it grew into the monster that it did can be explained by the way that the journalists translated everything that happened into a drama using the cultural framework that they were hearing in everyday settings.

I would now like to take a closer look at one of the texts written at the height of the story at about the time when we found Ignacio talking so strongly about the rubbish on the streets. In this text we can clearly see that the journalist has used some of the themes that people like Ignacio were using to organize some of the details that she has gathered. Intriguingly, like Ignacio, she does not need to think in terms of consistency between the themes that she does use.

Newspaper text

Here is one of the stories that was typical of the most intense period of reporting on the subject. In this text the suspect is described under the heading, I Slept With My Money in My Vagina. I will look in detail at the first few paragraphs.

To begin with, the headline is something that the journalist heard from the mother of the presumed killer and immediately recognized it as being something to which people could relate. In Spanish culture the mother is particularly revered. The headline, along with a photograph of Angles' mother looking beleaguered, would be particularly powerful. Even though other texts might demonize the whole of the family, this was particularly useful for this purpose, at a time when, the journalist told me, there was massive demand for the most extreme material and hatred. The text begins:

> With the face of a good boy and his appearance of never having broken even one plate Antonio Angles Martins has taken part in only one sport in the whole of his life: exercising terror and cruelty towards his fellows. Perverse to the hilt, selfish, primitive and incapable of submitting to any norm, the presumed killer of the three girls from Alcacer managed to even get out of doing his military service by feigning suicide. His mother had to hide her money in her vagina so that Antonio, who had already robbed his brothers, did not do the same to her. He would threaten to kill people on his 'good days'. He is illiterate, perverse and primitive and panic is the currency of exchange he used with those he knew. His closest and inseparable friend has always been a huge knife that he carried hidden in his sleeve.

In this text the journalist is presenting Angles as a complete evildoer, as is indicated from the headline which tells us that such was his twistedness that he had no respect for motherhood and therefore for the family. The text goes on to make any trait or action known about Angles to be an indication of his twistedness. His illiteracy and primitive nature were not seen as indications of his marginalized position in society, nor as possible contributory factors to this criminal lifestyle, but are indications of his worthlessness and moral corruption. Here any aspect of Angles' life can be used in this way, such as the fact that he had avoided military service. Most young men at the time found ways to avoid military service, especially those from the middle classes. It was universally seen as a complete waste of time. Yet here it is used as a further example of Angles' corrupted nature.

The sheer level of evilness is reflected in the fact that the family, particularly the mother, much revered in Spanish culture, had been abused. It is interesting that Angles is seen to be doing whatever he wants to do as he refuses to comply to any rule. The military service is evidence of this. This is interesting in terms of the way that Ignacio spoke about such evildoers as having the conscious aim of bringing society down. The journalists who wrote these stories did tell me that while they appreciated that such a person was from a particular background, which was always connected to crime, they themselves did get carried away by hatred while they were writing and as they spent time interviewing people involved and hearing the way that people around them were reacting. The journalist told me that while the fact that Angles carried a knife is referred to in the text, she knew that it was usual for people from such areas to carry knives or other arms. Angles' younger bothers had criminal records for possession of firearms. In this paragraph, however, it works better that they are victims. The journalist told me that she knew that people had an idea about particular kinds of people who are a threat to decency, and these people think that moral standards are falling because of this. In this story the journalist said that she was giving them just such a person.

The text continues:

> Antonio Angles, the third of nine children ... who because of their endless violent rages and cruelty have been stigmatized by people in their village, loved to dress well and care for his appearance. He had a weakness for designer clothes and was always able to match the colours of those he got hold of – often stolen at knife point or after waiting outside the village school in Catarroja on a motor scooter with the engine running, where he stole jackets, shirts and even shoes. This delinquent that no one ever dared to tun in had never had a girlfriend and those who knew him said that he was not homosexual.

This second paragraph is interesting as here the family of the suspect have ceased to be the victims of the evil but are now accomplices. The journalist told me that this would not be seen as a contradiction by the readers as it was just more evidence of the general evil of these people, and the readers at this point in the unfolding of the story wanted to read about evildoers. They wanted to feel angry and appalled. They would therefore be reading with this motivation above others.

Another feature of Angles which would also be characteristic of most young Spanish men is also used as an indication of Angles' twistedness is his like of expensive clothes. Yet in this case it is described as a weakness. His attractiveness as a whole was seen as somehow indicative of the perversion. One journalist told me that we could think of this as being like a typical baddie in a Hollywood film, where if an arch villain is particularly physically attractive, it is evidence of particularly extreme psychopathic characteristics. Normally we can expect the evildoers to be ugly. When they are attractive, we can be confident that there has been some particularly vicious twist of nature and can expect the worst kind of perversions from this person. Several journalists said that in some ways the reason that Angles had been seen as the arch-villain and the other suspect who had been captured and blamed everything on Angles, the henchman, was because Angles was attractive and his accomplice was ugly. The ugliness of the accomplice was somehow more natural for an evildoer. The attractiveness of Angles was more chilling, I was told. And the fact that something was out of place would make people react more powerfully. The journalist told me that when people imagine evildoers they imagine them as far away from ordinary people as possible. This is what she was doing in this story.

As well as being able to offer basically any trait as evidence of evil-doing, the journalist also told me that there was less requirement to be precise about sources. This is evident in the next paragraph:

> The source was familiar with the ups and downs of the delinquent who had no sense of law and order. They preferred to remain anonymous as the mere mention of the name of Angles filled them with terror.

The journalist told me that no one would question such a source as to do so would seem to be the same as questioning the nature of Angles' evil.

What we can say about this text is that it must be understood as being connected to the talk by people like Ignacio. The journalist had a keen sense of the stage at which such people were at in their response to the events, and was able to fuel them accordingly.

These ethnographic examples illustrate that one way to think about the relationship between journalists and their readers is as a conversation. They have a powerful sense of each other as interlocutors either through immediate presence or through imagination. This community should not just be thought of as a group which has shared ideas but in terms of its sense of mutual gaze and response. Rather than an *interpretive community*, which was the term used to describe categories of audience members in the ethnographic turn (Schroder 1994) we have a *community of improvisers*.

One thing that this method of looking at things does is allow us to think about the way that discourse for talking about things and topics of conversation might change. People do change their attitudes from moment to moment but these changes add up to much larger changes. The idea of the interpretative community seems to suggest that we can find groups of people with stable ideas. If Ignacio simply held the view that murderers were evil, then there would have been no room for the conversation and no possibility for the subsequent change of attitude.

The research which looked at interpretative communities, such as that done by Morley (1980) or even that done by Stacey (1994), went on the assumption that a number of utterances can be collected by the researcher. These utterances are collected and are then treated as though they were about the same topic and as if they came from the same speaker. The community of interpretation thus speaks with only one voice and in one setting. The flow and complexity of everyday life are broken down – it is disassembled into its parts, only some of which are then used as illustrations of the whole.

In contrast, the ethnography I have described here is sensitive to the way that people bring to bear a complex cultural framework to bear on the world as they move within it. This allows us to understand how they respond to the mass media and how the mass media responds to them.

13 Understanding readers' newspaper allegiance

Newspapers as an indication of character

In this chapter I want to show how an ethnography of newspaper readers in Spain allows us to explain certain distinctive features of newspaper circulation. In Spain, to the frustration of editors, newspaper sales are both very low and very static. The newspapers themselves are rather dull and formal in appearance but attempts to change them and make them more accessible have been met by resistance from readers. And an attempt to introduce a tabloid newspaper into this gap in the market was a disaster and resulted in heavy financial losses. So people do not read the newspapers that they buy because they are hard work, but do not wish to see anything different. The reasons for this, the ethnography suggests, are that in Spain there are certain cultural definitions of public and private space which do not apply in the north of Europe or America. These definitions influence the nature of what is perceived as appropriate for newspapers. This influences newspaper purchasing behaviour along with a complex interplay of the need to appear culturally sophisticated, and modern, and the legacy of political allegiance from the civil war and the dictatorship. All this sums up to newspapers being an indication of character. In northern Europe and America you might find that people like to be known to read a particular title which they feel says something about themselves. But in Spain this is slightly different.

The data in this chapter come mainly from interviews where individuals talked generally about their choices of newspapers. I also look at some instances of these people talking about news in their everyday lives. To begin with though I will create the ethnographic context by looking at the context of newspaper reading in Spain, by saying something about Spanish culture in general.

The press in Spain

There is no sensationalist press in Spain. There are no newspapers that resemble the big circulation dailies of Northern Europe such as the British *Sun* with about 3 million readers, and the German *Bild Zeitung* with about 5 million. The biggest Spanish title is *El País*, a quality broadsheet, with a circulation of about 440 000. One reason for this situation has been that the kind of people who form the bulk of the readership in other countries simply never acquired the habit in Spain. This is due to the fact that earlier in the twentieth century, while these other countries had a developed press, political upheaval, confiscations and censorship meant that there could be no consolidation in Spain. Later on after the civil war newspapers were expensive and hindered by limited communications networks and a dispersed population. And levels of illiteracy were still high in the 1920s. Before people acquired the habit of newspaper buying other media had taken over such as the radio and the cinema (Marin 1989). After 1939 40 years of dictatorship and control of the media did very little to bring the newspaper to the Spanish people. At the start of the twenty-first century Spain still had a highly politicized press aimed at more professional sectors of the population. A large proportion of newspaper circulation was accounted for by the many bars in the city which all have newspapers which will be browsed by the clients.

One reason that people are not attracted to newspapers in Spain is that they are very difficult to read. The majority of the pages are filled with local and national politics. The journalists who write these stories are aware that these stories will probably only be read by the politicians themselves. Some journalists I interviewed and observed even saw their jobs in these terms. The newspapers usually only carry about one page of human interest stories on crime and accidents. This is the most widely read part of the newspaper, along with the sport.

It might seem that one solution to the problem of low circulation would be to change the content and form of the newspapers – to include more colour, human interest stories, popular culture, gossip and large photographs. The German Axel Springer company, responsible for *Bild Zeitung*, saw this obvious gap in the market and launched a tabloid called *El Claro* in the early 1990s. It ran for two weeks and closed down. No one wanted to buy it. Also editors of existing newspapers have tried to change the format but have been met with resistance and criticism from readers. Editors of several newspapers told me that this was the paradox of the Spanish press. Even though studies show that people tend to read certain sections of the newspaper and ignore others, it is important that the proportions of these do not change. Editors also comment that it is very difficult to win readers over from other titles as people tend to buy or want to read newspapers on the basis of family tradition and politics.

Data from interviews and tape recordings of people talking about newspapers and news can give us an insight into why circulations cannot be increased and hints at what Axel Springer newspapers failed to see in their market research. This also shows that while the surveys done by the newspapers themselves can produce sophisticated demographic data, they are unable to provide information sensitive to the way that the newspaper is understood and used in everyday life. Here we will see how understanding this immobility in circulations requires an understanding of how newspapers fit into the lives of Spanish people. What we find is that newspapers in Spain are seen as being located in a particular kind of formal/public domain. Therefore they should be appropriate to that domain. And how people relate to them touches upon the way that character is acted out in terms of a particularly Mediterranean aesthetic. This is a culture where the public and the private, the formal and the informal are important planes for social action.

Why people buy the newspapers that they do

The way that people talked about newspapers in Spain had a flavour that one would not find in Northern Europe. This talk beautifully evoked many of the themes described in the classic ethnographic works on the Mediterranean, by Pitt-Rivers (1954), Du Boulay (1974) and Silverman (1975). These works describe a culture where social life is distinguished by the way that the individual displays themselves in a distinctive manner. For these writers an understanding of this was crucial to explaining how these societies work, for example, in terms of economics, social hierarchies and politics. Unlike in northern Europe and the West, where the individual is concealed/revealed in interaction, in the Mediterranean people display themselves as various characters in relation to a particular aesthetic (Sant Cassia 1991). Talk about newspapers, as we will see, shows people presenting themselves to express individuality. And this is indicated by displaying alignment with specific groups of others to show relative sophistication, dignity and honour – a sense of expressing being a category of person that is generally absent in northern Europe. This process is at the root of the problem with changing the nature of Spanish newspapers.

Methodology

The data used in this paper come from fieldwork in Valencia and Spain which was carried out throughout the 1990s, although much of the conversation sampled here is from interviews which took place in the early to mid-1990s. This in some ways informs the tone of some of the talk which was recorded just before the general elections which ended the long term of office of the PSOE Gonzalez government. The study began as an ethnographic style study of journalists and their readers, where I spent about 14 months following journalists and examining how they composed stories and how these developed in the context of how they were received in the public sphere. I also developed an interest in how people received and used news.

The newspapers read by the people interviewed were the regional newspapers – the right-wing *Las Provincias* and the left/centre *Levante* – and the nationals – the left/centre *El País*, the very conservative *ABC* and the then centre *El Mundo*. We begin by looking at how readers talked about why they chose newspapers. I had known these people for at least six months, lived with them and worked with them.

The conversation that I present here is all from tape-recorded interviews. I will introduce the individuals in turn, drawing out the important themes.

People talking about newspapers

Pepe

Pepe was 42 and was a security guard. He bought the right-wing *Las Provincias*. He said that he did not like *Levante* as it supported the left-wing government no matter what it did. In contrast, *Las Provincias*, he said, was critical of them. He told me that 'the socialists should not be in power. They have shown that they are corrupt and are now messing the country up'. He suggested that there was a need for fresh ideas as the socialists had used all theirs up. Pepe expressed this in the context of wanting to keep his job. His contract was renewable every three months. He had already been laid off from a number of other positions. The opposition party, the conservative PP, he suggested, would bring greater stability.

Pepe told me that he never read *ABC*, the national PP-supporting newspaper, as he preferred the newspapers with local news. In fact *ABC* did have local offices and included a local supplement. I had carried out interviews there. Pepe told me that his father had bought *ABC*.

So Pepe talked about his choice of newspaper in terms of his ideological stance and in terms of liking to be informed about local affairs. He assumed that the national newspaper could not fulfil the second of these criteria. And the reasons he gives are in accord with those known by editors: that people buy newspapers due to political allegiance and family tradition. Even though Pepe buys a different newspaper than his father, it is of a consistent ideology.

However, further discussions with Pepe allow us to see the reasons he gives slightly differently. I talked to Pepe about news articles he felt stood out over the past month. He recalled mainly human interest stories, such as a highly publicized murder and the story of a teacher who had eloped with a pupil. He mentioned the war in Yugoslavia but laughed and said he had no idea what was going on or of the different groups who were involved in the conflict. He couldn't recall anything from the politics pages, not even from the previous few days. He told me: 'Well, I never read much of the politics anyway. It is pretty boring. You know what politicians are like.'

I asked him if he thought that *Las Provincias* was relatively more accurate or truthful than the socialist *Levante*. He said:

> Well, more than *Levante*, yes. They only want to support the government. I think the international news is pretty accurate, well, it's just news, isn't it? But I think a lot of the local stuff, the things people say is often dubious … most of the politicians are just self-interested. They're not bothered about ordinary people like us.

I asked Pepe about the political issues which *Las Provincias* supported and how these differed from those of the socialist party. He said that generally it was 'just time for a change'. He went on to say that anyway all politicians were the same. Later in the interview though he returned to his political reasons for buying *Las Provincias* by saying that *Levante* did not deal with the political issues directly enough.

I had been working at the factory where Pepe worked for about four months. I often ate breakfast with him and he might comment on the day's news stories. I never heard him speak specifically about a political policy overtly. His ideology was based on a sense that society was not going well, particularly in the sense that he lacked job security. This was often expressed through a discourse which referred to a mythical period of social harmony and security during the years of the dictatorship. He was particularly infuriated by the running local problem of drug addicts occupying properties in the historical centre of the city.

So Pepe talked about his newspaper buying in terms of political allegiance. He knew or read very little about actual policy but preferred the ideological stance associated with the PP. He, in fact, and like many of those who supported the PP at the time, knew nothing, in my experience, about any of their policies or their implications, but thought it was time for a change. He also criticized the PSOE for corruption. In a different conversation Pepe had been quite pleased to tell me about the way he accepted money for overlooking particular occurrences in his job as a security guard – a job which he acquired through a relative. I do not mention this to suggest that he was somehow hypocritical but rather to point out something of the nature of reasons for newspaper buying that I found in Spain.

We can see that there are a number of themes in Pepe's conversation that form his talk about why he buys a newspaper. In one of these he presented himself as an informed person who was literate – being a 'reader' is something which in itself has prestige in Spanish culture. But in my experience Pepe rarely engaged with the politics pages. When I observed him reading it was invariably the sports pages – the largest-selling Spanish titles are sports paper such as *Marca*. Yet his political allegiance was important to him. Pepe is generally conservative, and comes from a conservative family who had been in favour of Franco. His decision to purchase *Las Provincias* may thus be ideologically motivated if only in a sense that he sees the newspaper as a symbol of allegiance, while not really having much idea about how its contents actually differ from *Levante*. When I asked him specific details about politics and political angles of reporting, he would not, of course, have been able to say that he had no idea. We simply have to have reasons for doing the things that we do. We would not feel comfortable with people saying that they simply did not know why they did something which obviously involved some kind of decision. Nor are we able to say, for example, that we have no idea of the specifics but we buy a newspaper as it is a symbol of what we believe in. In Western cultures this would not be acceptable (D'Andrade 1987). Therefore, when asked about the differences between the two newspapers Pepe used the representation of all politicians being the same, in which case any differences are purely superficial.

The conversational manoeuvres used by Pepe are highly Mediterranean in their flavour. In the first instance Pepe is concerned about display. He is not highly educated yet is keen to express that he is informed. This way of demonstrating an educated and informed manner reminded me very much of the classic studies done in the Mediterranean by Silverman (1975), Belmonte (1979) and Lison-Tolosana (1966). Among other things, these authors discussed the importance of clothing and other consumer purchases in the Mediterranean, despite underlying poverty, to avoid the shame of the appearance of not being able to do so. Lison-Tolosana, writing on his own Spanish culture, said that it was 'important for the less prosperous strata to show a more-than-ordinary effort' (1966, p. 101). I found that particularly in the case of working-class newspaper buyers, there was a sense of demonstrating a superiority of cultural level.

Observers of Mediterranean culture have emphasized that the roots of this need to publicly demonstrate cultural level lie in the way that self-evaluation is very much in the public domain. Pitt-Rivers, summing up works on the region, observed: 'Students of the minutiae of personal relations have observed that they are much concerned with the ways in which people extort from others the validation of the image which they cherish of themselves' (1965, pp. 21–2). Hence to understand Pepe's discourse we need to be mindful of his cultural tendency to think in terms of character authorship. And a university researcher might call for a particular part of his cultural aesthetic to be emphasized, a particular conversational manoeuvre. The fact that Pepe uses this representation of himself as a manoeuvre is drawn out by the fact that in a different moment he says that all politicians are self-interested and that newspapers are full of lies. This kind of statement was another of Pepe's favourites. Again, he presents himself as a knower, but here he aligns himself with a different group.

The dislike of authority and officialdom is very much a collective representation in Spain and may be a legacy of the country's relatively recent history as an essentially peasant society (Pitt-Rivers 1954; Kenny 1968). People can often be heard saying that officialdom is very much against the interests of the ordinary person and that society is run by individuals whose objective will not be the performance of their allocated tasks. In a way this is because, among other things, everyone in the Mediterranean knows that 'nepotism is an obligation not a moral fault' (Campbell 1964, p. 257). In, say, Britain it might be possible to hear someone saying that politicians lie, but it is not with this same conviction of complete lack of faith in officialdom. This is reflected in the way that British newspaper readers would be unlikely to say that newspapers are full of lies. Importantly Pepe's use of this representation, while allowing him to avoid having to say that he does not really know that much about politics, also allows him to make another alignment. Here it is alongside the ordinary person and common sense. Here the newspaper, in the first instance, the symbol of being informed and educated, becomes part of the smokescreen of officialdom.

Both of these representations of newspapers allow Pepe to act out the roles of different characters. This is done as he aligns himself alongside categories of others. Pitt-Rivers (1965) commented on how Mediterranean people, as a means of presenting themselves, are keen to distance themselves from certain groups, to align themselves with a particular kind of person. He wrote: 'Social groups posses a collective honour in which their members participate' (ibid., p. 35). In the first instance Pepe aligns himself alongside a kind of person who is educated, sophisticated and who lives above the petty shames of gossip and illiteracy – the worst of peasant life. In the second case he aligns himself alongside ordinary people who have common sense. These people have a street-wise honour and decency.

From this first example we can already see that the newspaper can be used in talk and thought about in terms of the way that it allows a person to align themselves. In the words of the Mediterranean anthropologists, it can be an indication of character. But the newspaper itself also can be seen as being located. The newspaper exists in the public domain. But this public domain is a formal, rather than informal space. I will develop this point shortly. First, I want to continue by looking at more newspaper readers.

Violeta

Violeta was 56, and was a housewife. She was an *ABC* buyer. She told me that the socialists had made a crime-ridden society where young people were unable to find jobs: 'during Franco's times they would have dragged those villains off the streets and sorted them out'.

Violeta expressed pride at her daily purchase of *ABC*. She told me that she could not tolerate the news on the TV. She said:

> You can believe newspapers more. They are more responsible. On the TV they just want to shock you with all those pictures. They are shameful. I know a lot of people really like that. It is just so indecent.

Violeta's account of a majority who like tabloid, cheap, low-brow television news allows her to present herself in a contrasting light. These people, she said 'just sit like cabbages in front of the TV. Me I read everything. If I see a piece of paper on the pavement with something written on it I just have to read it. People don't read enough these days.' So Violeta contrasts herself with a rather ignorant community of non-readers. And, unlike these people, she is concerned with the more sophisticated kind of news offered by the newspaper rather than the television. In general conversation Violeta was fond of talking about a general moral decline in society. And this shameless and ignorant category of person was responsible for, or at least part of, the problem.

Of course we might simply accept that Violeta *is* concerned about a dumbing down of culture and an associated moral decline. And indeed she may be so concerned.

However, as with Pepe, it seemed that Violeta was also talking about newspapers with a sense of presenting herself as an educated individual. In interviews with her sons I asked them who read most in the household. One told me, 'Well, no-one does really. We buy the paper which we never really look at and Mum reads her glossy magazines and the occasional biography.' I had been in the house many times and generally found the family sitting round the television. And on excursions to the beach I had seen Violeta reading glossy gossip magazines, such as *Hola*. I had occasionally picked up the newspaper in their house and it was usually pristine and hardly touched.

As with Pepe, Violeta's behaviour might be thought about through a performance which emphasized education and sophistication. Violeta might have been particularly inclined to talk this way knowing that I was a university researcher. To show her higher cultural level she also uses another cultural representation which has a particularly Mediterranean feel. This is a representation, again one commented upon in many of the classic works on Mediterranean culture (Sant Cassia 1991; Peristany and Pitt-Rivers 1992), where the individual should not openly show a concern for the personal lives of others. While they might actually do this, it is important that a person is seen publicly to be above such a thing. This means that a person should not be seen to be enjoying the sensational. The dry, formal world of news is the appropriate way for a person to take an interest in events happening out there in the world.

For Violeta newspaper readers are much more sophisticated since newspapers are predominantly about official culture in contrast to the television news, which is considered to be much more base and personal. The television viewer here represents the category of person who is not above petty gossip and the sensational. Violeta can therefore invite me to think about her as much more intellectual, thoughtful and sophisticated – to think about her in terms of a particular aesthetic.

We might ask that if it is the case that no-one in the household reads the newspaper, why does then the family still buy *ABC*? Violeta told me that her husband, when he was alive, had always bought *ABC*, but that now she wanted to buy the paper. So I feel that the answer is simply one of tradition. *ABC* did, and still does, fit with the politics of the region where Violeta had lived during the dictatorship where Franco was supported. Violeta still bought the newspaper, as many families do, as a tradition, although in some ways the newspaper did reflect some of her political views. It supports strong law and order and warns against the dangers of a permissive decadent society. This is a discourse that Violeta frequently produces. However, she could also often be heard complaining of the restrictions of the dictatorship period particularly for women, revealing some bitterness:

> When I was with my husband you had no freedom. Women didn't have the freedom like they have today. In those days you had to agree with everything the man said. Remember that women had no legal rights and the husbands had to sign for everything. We didn't have the freedom that you have now.

On the one hand we see that Violeta may be buying the newspaper as part of a household tradition, which seems to be an important factor in newspaper buying in Spain. We can also see that while she recalls the times of Franco as being characterized by law and order, she is also aware that these were also times of restricted freedom. The discourse that she produces, while she might at the time be committed to each, depends on what she wants to achieve through them. Both can bring a certain amount of pleasure. Newspaper readership surveys in Spain are quick to level politics against choice of newspaper. If I asked Violeta what her politics were I know what the answer would be. Yet much of her discourse contains a bitterness about lost freedom, control and oppression. She was fond of pointing out how she would like to have been born 40 years later, 'when people could have more dignity and freedom'.

We are beginning to see how Spanish newspapers are located in people's lives in a way that is indicative of character. I have still not said exactly why this means that newspapers cannot change and why there is no room in the market for a tabloid. The clues are already there in that people should not be seen to be taking an interest in the lives of others and that the newspaper is an indication of cultural sophistication. But there is a last piece of the puzzle which the next example helps us to draw out.

Isa

Isa was a lab technician in a ceramics factory. She was a university graduate and lived with her husband and two children. She bought *Levante* every day. She said that she bought this particular newspaper as she did not like right-wing politics. She said in this context that: 'Spain has come a long way since Franco but still has a lot of ground to cover.' She thought that the PSOE were still the best party to govern, 'I still remember the moral oppression in which I grew up: the Catholic all-girls schools, the censorship.' Isa told me that they had always bought *Levante* in her family. Her parents had always done so. 'It is a sort of tradition,' she said proudly.

So the reasons Isa gave for buying *Levante* were ideology and family tradition. She presented this to me as evidence of a family tradition in socialist ideology. She was unaware that the newspaper *Levante* had been the official Franco paper during the Dictatorship. We might ask the question as to whether Isa would have changed newspaper had her family brought *Las Provincias*. The likelihood is that she would not. And as we shall see, she was not completely clear as to the nature of the contents of *Levante* in terms of what distinguished them from those of *Las Provincias*.

I asked her why it was important to buy a newspaper every day. She said:

> I think it is important for the children. They should know about what is going on in the world … it's too easy these days for the kids to just get stuck in front of the TV. The papers are good because you have to interact with them. The TV news can just pass through you.

She said that it was important for us to know what is going on around us, especially in the case of children:

> Many of the problems in contemporary society are caused by parents not bringing up their children to know about the world or what is right and wrong. If you know about the world you have common sense. Parents just don't give it to their kids these days. They just stick them in front of the TV or give them those stupid video games. You have to tell them what it is all about, give them values.

Like Violeta, although not quite as vehemently, she talked about reading as being a valuable and moral activity in the face of otherwise falling standards. Again, as with our previous buyers, Isa contrasts herself with those who are ignorant and whom she associates with popular culture. This is also a more traditional Spanish theme as reading is still considered as a somewhat elite or intellectually sophisticated activity.

But she said that she herself was usually too tired to look at the paper. When I asked her what she did read she said:

> I generally look at the international news, well, at least the headlines and also (laughing and mock embarrassment) I usually read the *sucesos*. They are easy to read. You don't always want to know about the activities of politician X or Y. Although sometimes I don't like the *sucesos*. Sometimes they go too far. Some people like that though.

I asked Isa in what ways *Levante* was better than *Las Provincias*. She said that *Las Provincias* got on her nerves as:

> All they do is criticize the PSOE. Surely they have to admit that all they do is not bad. Most of what they say is made up and exaggerated anyway. Mind you, that is the game of politics, isn't it? One side makes things up about those, then they make up things as well. In the end you don't know who to believe. Most of the time you just know it's all a load of rubbish. That's why I just don't bother reading sometimes.

As with our previous speakers, we find that Isa uses the Spanish themes of knowledge and literature against politics as lies and corruption. She was able to talk about her decision to buy a newspaper in terms of education for the children and having knowledge freely available around the house. Leaving aside the issue of whether her young children would ever go near the newspaper, we can again see the importance of the newspaper as an expression of social status. Lison-Tolosana (1966) wrote about display in terms of clothing and consumer goods, where Spanish peasants dressed up in order to take on the character of the affluent and sophisticated. Similarly Isa uses the newspaper as an indication of her sophistication and ranking. She sets herself against a category of common and ignorant people who are part of the problem of falling moral values. This was a theme commonly used by newspaper buyers. Yet later in the interview she aligns herself alongside a common-sense knowledge where ordinary people know that officialdom serves its own interests.

It would be tempting at this point to ask which of the two representations of news that Isa uses – that of newspapers as information and symbol of cultural sophistication, or that of newspapers as containing the lies of officialdom – is what she most believes about newspapers? But I would suggest, in fact, that this is not the question that should be asked. Watson (1991) and other ethnomethodologists have taught us to regard such representations as tools which can be used when appropriate – they are shared common-sense representations. Isa used them in an 'everyone knows' manner. And these representations do not have to form a coherent whole.

Which one of the representations guides her behaviour, we might ask? It would seem that if she really *believed* that newspapers were all lies, then she would surely cease to buy them. Since she continues to buy newspapers we might conclude that she actually *believes* that newspapers are informing. I would go along with the likes of Watson and suggest that both are simply cultural representations which she is able to draw upon which help her to organize her experiences. These are the discourses about newspapers that saturate Isa's society. In fact it may be the case that she buys the newspaper partly through tradition in that it is the paper which her father always bought. And at times when she contemplates the newspaper's presence or anyone asks her about it, then she can talk about its importance in terms of providing a source of knowledge provided by a socially responsible and educated parent for her children. However, she is also able to use the news as officialdom and lies when called upon. And she is still able to reflect upon her behaviour where she rarely in fact takes much notice of the newspaper even to find out what is in the politics pages. All these form the parts of the way that the newspaper fits into Isa's life.

Another thing that is striking about the data that I have presented here is that these people are not practised in speaking about such things in the manner that I was demanding. People could produce what they took to be the commonly held explanations but visibly struggled when I wanted to explore these. This is one clear example of Polanyi's (1958) point, that we looked at in Chapter 2, that people generally do not have access to the reasons for the things that they do. What we generally find is that they will produce the official reasons, or the common-sense reasons, for doing such a thing in that particular culture. People are generally accustomed to using these reasons in a way that allows them to respond to others, to align themselves in the world, not to deal with the awkward questions of a researcher.

From the examples we have considered, it is becoming clear that one important way that people think about newspapers in Spain is in terms of what they reveal about the buyers. Most of the people I spoke to who bought, or who expressed a preference for, a particular newspaper did so out of a sense of family history and ideology, which was more connected to tradition than to the finer details of the way that events were depicted in the newspapers. Of course there were people who did show a greater awareness of the nature of the content of the newspapers, but these were very few.

Most journalists which whom I spoke were well aware that most of what they wrote would be read by very few people.

How people are connected to newspapers, because of tradition and ideology, helps to explain why people tend not to shift newspaper allegiance. And the way that people are so concerned to talk about themselves in relation to others who are uneducated, or show too much interest in sensationalism, offers a hint to why, although people clearly like to read such material, there is resistance to newspapers moving in this particular direction. Newspapers belong to the formal public domain. It is inappropriate to be seen to be taking an interest in gossip and the sensational in this domain. In this context, given the importance of display, who would want to be associated with a newspaper which was clearly being inappropriate?

Talking about news

I now want to briefly locate the way that people talked about news in an everyday life situation. This helps us to see clearly both the interest in the sensational and the importance of publicly condemning this. It also helps us to understand why, in contrast to newspapers, which should remain formal, Spanish people are much more comfortable with sensationalism in glossy magazines. Here are two comments made by a woman talking about the day's news. First, here is what she had previously told me about newspapers.

Eva was 51 and worked in a small grocery shop. She said that she would not buy newspapers, although I had seen her reading them in the local bar. She told me that she would not buy them as she didn't like all the sensationalism. She said that it made her nervous: 'Why should a person want to know all the business of others?' This was a time when newspapers had, for a short while, reported on the details of the murder of three girls – which was the subject of the previous chapter. She told me of a story she had recently read saying that it was disgusting that people could take an interest in such things. She spoke at length about her dislike for people who should take more interest in things happening in their own lives. Referring to the murder of the three girls, she said that it was terrible that the politicians did nothing about it apart from give themselves more money. Again we have the theme that officialdom is corrupt and self-serving. There is also the important comment, that is now familiar through our previous examples, that *other* people are shameful for their interest in the lives of others.

Eva talking in her shop

In these samples of conversation Eva is talking with another woman, probably about 50 years of age, who was purchasing things from the shop. Eva clearly knew the woman.

Eva: (10:30 a.m.) I want to know how he did that. How did he manage to do all those things to those bodies? The newspaper doesn't tell you that. I tell you they are hiding something.

Eva: (10:35 a.m.) It's a disgrace that they put all this stuff in the newspapers. People have such *morbo* [morbid curiosity]. Why do they waste their time with it? They would be better putting their energies into something more productive.

Here we have a clear example of alignment with kinds of others. In the first place Eva, like many other people at the time, was expressing the usual distrust of officialdom. We could take this to be her fixed opinion on the matter. And we might think that she was simply concerned to know more about the case and was critical of the press. But later Eva rejects any association of having such an interest. In both cases these are conversational manoeuvres through which Eva is quickly able to connect with the woman in the shop. In the first case the women nodded at their shared wisdom at the expression of the widely held belief that officialdom was corrupt. But then soon, after a period of musing about the events, the conversation turned to a criticism of the kind of people who take prurient interest in such matters. This is expressed by the word *morbo*. In each case the two women nodded at each other as they sided against the shameless in society.

This is where we can see that sensationalist reporting, while it is clearly enjoyed, cannot be openly liked, at least not in the long term. Even though circulations soared with the murders of the three girls we looked at in the last chapter, the newspapers quickly returned to their usual impenetrability under a barrage of criticism and sanction from the very people who had been buying them.

It is not simply the case, however, that people do not want to read sensationalist stories and gossip. They can do this if it is in the right place. In Spain there is a massive market for glossy magazines such *Hola*. Many of these magazines take a quasi-news type of format. They summarize the week's news events along with gossip and colour photographs. But they in no way present themselves as newspapers. They are magazines and are feature based. In interviews people would tell me, usually self-mockingly, that were regular readers of these magazines.

Clearly magazines are located in a different kind of public space than newspapers. Therefore different rules of concealment and display apply. It is more acceptable to take an interest in the affairs of others providing that this is done in the appropriate domain. The magazine deals with a more informal world where display has a different status. Due to its history the newspaper has traditionally dealt with the highly serious and formal world of politics and public affairs. Newspapers are thought about as formal avenues for the presentation of information. Generally this means that a newspaper which includes too many photographs or gossip is seen as inappropriate. Likewise, the readers themselves should not be seen to be taking pleasure from this prying into the affairs of others, particularly in this formal public domain.

Practically for the newspaper editors who wish to win over readers from other titles or to attract new readers, this raises difficulties. Newspaper buying, while being associated with family tradition, is also associated with a statement about one's level of culture as against others who are not informed, who prefer popular culture, and who are inappropriately interested in the private affairs of others. Buyers will therefore be concerned when their newspaper starts to change.

Conclusion

The data used in this chapter from interviews and a shop conversation allow us to understand something about Spanish newspaper buying. The chapter illustrates the importance of treating even the interview data with an ethnographic gaze. What people say has been treated as the utterances of people who live in cultures who have an available cultural tool kit or range of cultural discourses. Therefore we treat people as making meaning and locating themselves as regards the social world. We could have treated what people like Pepe said initially as his beliefs about newspapers. Yet what we find on closer inspection is that he has a range of discourses through which he can think about newspapers. These allow him to account for his behaviour in a way that allows him to appear a reasonable actor. But we can see, as Polanyi (1958) pointed out, that he does not have access to the actual reasons that he does things. He does not talk about Spanish press history when talking about newspapers as this is not part of the discourse that is available to him. Nor does he choose to talk about the Mediterranean themes of display and alignment with types of generalized others. But the discourses that he does use mean that newspaper editors are stuck with their low circulations.

This chapter has placed the newspaper reader into culture in the same way as did Malinowski (1922) with Trobriand magic, Thrasher (1927) with the gang members, and Herdt (1987) with homosexual practices in the Sambia. In each case the researcher was looking for the framework which allows the people under study to make sense of their worlds. This framework allows those people to make sense of the world in a way that is intelligible to them as a collectivity. It provides common-sense shared meanings. Even with something as familiar to us all as newspapers, we must not assume that there is anything natural about how people will relate to them. In Spain the official model of journalism is, as in the West, one of the Fourth Estate. But this does not mean therefore that people should live out their lives according to these official representations. The only way to find this out is to look at what people are saying and doing. As Malinowski said, we must find the native's point of view.

The ethnographic gaze in non-ethnographic research

Role play

Throughout this book I have been emphasizing how the ethnographic gaze means thinking about human behaviour as people using their cultural tool kit to make meaning out of situations in a way that allows them also to make meaning of themselves. As we navigate our way through the social world, in the words of Bruner and Weisser (1991), we also navigate a sense of self. It is through their cultural framework and how they use it that people experience themselves. The ethnographic gaze involves seeing everyday situations as complex accomplishments as people apply this complex framework to understand situations to communicate, to act, to plan and carry out being a meaningful social actor.

I have also emphasized that we must be mindful of the fact that data are collected in a particular place at a particular time. People use their cultural tool kits with a responsiveness to others, and different situations often come with their own set of localized rules governing the way we should behave. Therefore when we collect data from these settings we disassemble them from the flow of sociality. What we need to do when we analyse them is to complete a subsequent act of reassembly. This is what I did when we looked at newspaper readers. It would have been tempting to have looked at what people said about newspapers or events in any one moment as being their belief or opinion. If a person says something like 'drug addicts are rubbish', we might be tempted to think about this as a person's opinion. But when we looked at different settings, or looked more broadly at what people said, we found that the idea of opinion or belief would not have been a satisfactory way to characterize how they talked. This observation could only be made because of the subsequent act of reassembly. Only thus can we show how people use the mass media and the images they produce in the flowing complexity of their everyday lives.

In this chapter I will look at some examples of data which are taken from research that we would not think of as ethnographic. These data were generated through the use of focus groups. The assumption generally behind the use of focus groups is that we can get people to discuss a topic and reveal exactly what they think about it and what motivates them. In this particular case the focus groups were used to find out what children thought of television. I want to show that if we apply our ethnographic gaze and are mindful of the disassembled nature of the data, these can be much more informative.

One criticism of focus groups is that the talk generated is done so in an artificial environment. Can we assume that the same people would talk in the same way in a more natural setting, the argument goes? It is more fruitful, however, to think about this in a slightly different way. All humans ever do is interact in settings. There is no interaction that is free of what psychologists like Wertsch (1991) have called speech genres, which are appropriate for settings. He gives the example of how children have to learn a formalized way of speaking that is deemed legitimate for the schoolroom. There is no interaction in which we participate that is free of the requirements of that setting. Without these rules we would never quite know what to expect, although that is not to say that sometimes, such as in schools, the legitimate genre might not be skewed towards the cultural definitions of powerful groups. This is the quality of social interaction. The very idea of the natural setting in this sense is quite peculiar. Where might we find a setting that shows how people really are, or what they really think external to the way that they behave in that setting?

In the last chapter we saw how newspaper readers talked about a certain set of events in different ways at different times. We concluded that it might not be useful to think about what people *really* believe or think. If we take this approach to the data generated in focus groups and look much more closely at people involved in meaning making, finely tuned to others and what is happening around them, concerned to indicate the kind of person that they are, we have a much more useful approach.

Children's talk about television from a BBC project

Towards the end of the 1990s I was involved in the data analysis of a large project commissioned by the BBC to look at children and television (Davies and Machin 2000a, 2000b). The project took place in 19 schools around England and Wales involving 1,300 children aged between 5 and 13. The schools, as well as covering a huge geographical range, also covered a range of types of school (inner city, outer city, rural) which were attended by pupils from very different sociocultural environments.

The project generated quantitative data about such things as numbers of programmes watched, how many homes had satellite television, etc. It also generated some fascinating qualitative data. The project coordinators wanted to get children to discuss television programmes and assess what their qualities were. The idea was to discover how the children themselves assess television.

At the time a number of researchers had taken up the task of challenging the basis of the current policy-making as regards children and television (Bazalgette and Buckingham 1995; Davies 1989). Much public debate on children and television had taken the form of moral panics where innocent and vulnerable children were passively corrupted by inappropriate programming. In the 1990s volumes like James and Prout's *Reconstructing Childhood* (1990) developed the view that the West had a highly romanticized view of children as innocent. They drew on the views of Aries (1962) who argued that in Western cultures, and in those influenced by them, we view children in two ways. One of these, he says, has its origins in the Romantic movement epitomized by Wordsworth and Blake. Here children emerged somehow closer to the Garden of Eden, untainted and pure. These writers were part of a movement that was keen to move away from the scientific rationalism of the Enlightenment and a return to the human spirit. The other view, characteristic of the Victorians, was that children were potentially savage and uncivilized. They therefore needed a strict regime to prevent the barbaric seeds in them from developing. This could be learned through appropriate self-restraint and discipline. These views, it was argued (Bazalgette and Buckingham 1995), coloured the way that children and television were thought about. This is why public debate often harked back to an age of innocence when children were appropriately protected. Such writers argued that policy should be made on the basis of research into what actual children do with television. Buckingham (1996) looked at the way that children understood horror films in the wake of the murder of a young child by two boys in Britain in 1993 which, at the time, was blamed largely by the press and politicians on the influence of video nasties. Buckingham found that the children in his study were highly literate in the visual media. They were wise to television and film conventions. They did find horror films scary but also took pleasure in talking about the ways that they were put together in terms of special effects and genre conventions. These children appeared to be shrewd and active viewers, unlike the passive innocent sponges depicted in the press. The research data I look at in this chapter can be understood as being part of this concern to generate policy based on empirical findings rather than the mythology of childhood.

The main difficulty that faced the researchers in this project was to get the children to talk openly. How do you get children to express themselves in the face of a researcher asking them about what they think about something like television? One solution to this was to use role-play situations. A number of ideas were thought up. One was where the children were to act at channel controllers, choosing a schedule of their best programmes, and then having to trim that schedule, discussing the programmes that were to be thrown out. Another involved the children taking on the roles of teachers, parents, and regulators and giving their views of issues of rescheduling of adults' programmes.

The role-play activities generated some fascinating data. The children surprised the teachers as to their confidence and ability to take on the roles allocated to them. The data I want to look at here came from a role play that took the following form: the children were divided into groups in the classroom. They were told that they were television programme controllers. At first the class collectively came up with a list of their favourite programmes. They then divided up in to smaller groups and were told to create a schedule from these programmes. They were told that due to financial reasons they had to drop one programme giving their reasons for this. Once they had done this the process was repeated with further budget tightening and further decisions about which programme to drop. All the discussions were recorded and transcribed. The children were then taken outside of the classroom to take part in small group discussions about the programmes that they personally liked to watch. The children responded with enthusiasm to their roles as television programme controllers.

The list that the children came up with was comprised of mainly children's programmes with some adult scheduled programmes such as *The X-Files* and an adult soap, *EastEnders*. When the children were asked to discard programmes, the reasons that they gave were very interesting.

Interviewer: In respect of the programme *999*, the argument for keeping it in is?

Mathew: If you think of all the people in the world who have problems and it shows what kinds of problems there are.

Interviewer: And *Animal Hospital*?

Stacey: *Animal Hospital* we can get rid of.

Dawn: *Animal Hospital* can stay.

Mathew: Yes, because that is sort of helping people learn about animals.

Girl: *The Bill* [adult police drama] should go then.

Boy: *The Bill*, Bye, Bye Bill.

Interviewer: Why do you want *The Bill* out?

Mathew: Because it's teaching people to sort of like – do things like commit murder. Someone might watch that and think, oh, that looks like a load of fun and go out and do it. Yeah.

These comments are typical of the way that children discussed television programmes. All of them were valued or rejected on the grounds of whether or not children could learn something worthwhile from them and whether therefore they were contributing to the good of society. Of the programmes discussed above it may not be surprising that programmes such as *999* and *Animal Hospital* were discussed in terms of them being good for children. Both could be said to about learning and about caring. But why should the children be so concerned about television being valued in this way? At no time in any of these discussions did any of the children simply say that they would keep a particular programme because it was fun or entertaining.

The way that the police drama *The Bill* was evaluated was also very typical. It is not immediately clear why the children should see such a programme as having no educational value. The series does not treat criminal activities positively. And it often locates crime in social contexts of depravity and struggle. We might speculate that the children felt uneasy about the programme as its stories are not always resolved. The main villains are not always brought to justice. And some of the police characters are not particularly nice people. That the programme suggests that the blame for crime may often be difficult to place may seem ambiguous to children who are accustomed to more definite moral messages in the mass media where good and evil are clearly identifiable.

In contrast to *The Bill* the children's comedy drama *Clarissa* was spoken of favourably:

> Girl: It explains about growing up and everything. Yeah. How to deal with your brothers.

This comment was widely supported by the children. But such a position could seem a little strange as the programme was hardly realistic and would be better thought of as very light entertainment. But we might simply accept that this is what the children believe. For them programmes like *Clarissa* might be valued for their educational qualities. Why, in fact, should we not accept this? The way that this idea of social value and learning is applied to the following two programmes is revealing.

Here the children are talking about the anodyne prime-time chart music programme *Top of the Pops*. The children had decided that the programme should be ejected from the schedule. They give their reasons why.

> Bethan: A lot of the songs have got swear words in it.
>
> Lewis: And there's drinking on stage and alcohol and stuff.
>
> Bethan: Most of them, some of them pop singers take drugs and that might influence young children.
>
> Rhodri: The thing is, on *Top of the Pops* they just show you the music, they don't really tell you the background of the band so you're not learning – not like *Live and Kicking* when the guests come on. On *Live and Kicking* they ask them all about them.

This is interesting. Surely the children do not switch on to watch such a programme with the main intention of learning? It seems apparent that this is how the children feel that television should be assessed. The next example shows the application of this model becoming ludicrous.

Here the children are musing on whether to reject *Man o Man*. This is a cheap cable-television quality programme. A number of men have to carry out silly tasks in front of studio audience of 'fun-loving' young women who have to assess their performances. The programme is cheap laughs, titillating and undemanding. But this does not in itself seem to be an issue for the children.

> Mathew: I don't see any point in the programme, it isn't like it's a game show as well, it's just that I don't think it is like a programme.
>
> Interviewer: Who's going to speak for the programme, who thinks it should be in?

Jennifer: I will. I think it should be in, because it helps women make their decisions for what man they want to go out with.

Initially Mathew is concerned as the programme is not easily categorizable. But then Jennifer expresses a view, that was quickly supported by others, that the programme could have a purpose. In the context of the nature of the programme this is an amazing point to make. The only real purpose of the show is mild titillation.

We might begin to think that one explanation for the way that the children are talking is that they are saying what they think they expect the adults want to hear. But I think that it is slightly more complex than that. The data, if we look more closely, suggest something different.

There are several reasons why the children speak in the way that they do. To begin with, this way of talking about television is very much rooted in British society. It lies at the heart of the idea of public service broadcasting. The granting of licences even for commercial channels such as Channel 4 have been under conditions of providing services which match certain of the ideas of public service broadcasting which were articulated by the founder of the BBC, Lord John Reith. Back in the 1920s he made clear his vision of broadcasting in Britain. The aim of the BBC, he believed, should be to educate the British people and contribute towards a better society. He held the view that the people might not themselves know what was good for them and it was up to the BBC to decide that on their behalf. It is fascinating that this view can still be found in children talking nearly 80 years later. What is interesting is that the children seem to use Reith's model for its own sake, as is illustrated by the fact that they apply it bizarrely to all programmes.

Another thing which influences the way that the children talk is that they are speaking in a formal classroom setting which sanctions particular kinds of talk. The psychologist Wertsch (1991) studied how in the classroom certain forms of talking about the world are considered appropriate. He looked at how from right at the beginning of their school career children learn that in the classroom there are legitimate forms of knowledge and legitimate ways of expressing oneself. In this sense the Reithian model fits with the school definitions of impersonal and formal analysis that are considered particularly suitable. British children are also familiar with the conservative discourse of helping, social conscience and being sensible that saturates their school life. In this sense the socially responsible discourse is what children associated as being favoured in the classroom.

We might still feel the temptation to argue that this is what the children actually think – that while they may not use the Reithian model particularly well, that this is really what they think that broadcasting should be all about. The study was not ethnographic so it was not possible to look at how the children behaved more generally. The data we had were disassembled from everyday life. However, the children were also asked to discuss their own personal preferences in small groups outside of the classroom. Here something very different happened. The children, for example, said that their favourite programmes were *The X-Files* and the prime-time British soap *EastEnders*. The following are typical of the way that children talked about programmes when asked to say what they most liked about them.

> Child: I like watching *The X-Files*, it makes me jump all the time and makes me feel ill and sick.

In this less formal setting the children used much less lofty standards for talking about programmes. However, the assessments in this new setting were typically made up of exaggerated comments. The child above says that *The X-Files* makes them feel ill and sick.

When asked what kinds of programmes they prefer the children answered typically:

> Daniel: Lots of violence.

> Stephen: Action-packed and bloodthirsty.

> Researcher: Who is your favourite character in *EastEnders*?

> Girl: Joe, because he is a bit nutty.

> Zoe: Grant and Phil because they are a bit rough, they can be nice but they are alcoholics and things like that.

Here the children's talk was very different. Is this their real opinion? Many children talked about liking *EastEnders* because of the violence. In fact, the programme is hardly ever remotely violent. The children were clearly keen to shock the interviewer. It is also interesting that in this case the girl says that she likes the character Joe because he is nutty. In fact Joe was a very pretty young man inserted into the programme for the very reason of attracting such young female viewers. His character had started to suffer from mental problems which might have been brought on by his traumatic family experiences. But it is unlikely that the girl likes him just because he was nutty. But this response went along with the fun and controversial way that the children were then talking.

In fact, the children often came out with answers that would seem strange by adult standards. One girl said that she liked the soap opera *Emmerdale Farm* because it has animals in it. It may take place in a farming village but there are never any animals in it. *Emmerdale* centres on the usual soap ingredients of affairs and family squabbles. But to the girl this seems like a reasonable answer, or at least it was an answer. And as in the case of liking Joe because he was nutty, it shows her to be a little bit playful and not sensible.

One way to think about what is happening is that in the classroom discussion the children were in a formal setting. So immediately a formal and responsible discourse might be seen as an appropriate way to talk about television. Also this discourse allowed the children to demonstrate maturity. The classroom discussions were full of references about protecting younger children. For example:

> Boy: *The X-Files* is too scary and a bit hard to understand, like doctors and autopsies, a five-year-old kid is not going to understand something like that.

But again the data revealed that this was clearly part of the way that the children wanted to present themselves. As previously discussed in the Introduction, the comments made by Nikita in one of the small group discussions is evidence of this. Initially when talking of cartoons she says:

> Nikita: My brother, he sort of watches cartoons like Tom and Jerry and stuff like that. I used to like it when I was young but I don't like it now. I've grown out of it because they sort of keep repeating them and you always know who's going to win.

But shortly afterwards the conversation has moved on to scheduling and how this can sometimes be inconvenient. The children were talking about this in a way that showed how they were often assertive in watching what they wanted when they wanted.

> Nikita: The best thing is in the mornings when they put on cartoons and they put them on at six in the morning and my mum says, 'Right, you're not watching until you're totally ready for school.'

In the first instance she talks about cartoons to show her maturity. Here they are just for little children. She has grown out of them. In the second instance we can also see that Nikita uses the topic to give a sense of who she is through her awareness of the way that children have to battle with adults. In this case she was proud to talk about something that she did which annoyed her mother. What is Nikita's real opinion or belief? Does she like cartoons or not? As we saw in the last chapter it is not productive to approach our data with this kind of question. What is important is that we acknowledge that Nikita, like other speakers, experiences herself through the alignments that she makes through her interactions. In both of these cases Nikita is able to present a particular kind of agency.

There are further reasons why we might find the children talking in the way that they did in the two cases. These can be drawn out if we think about broader discourses about children and childhood in Western societies. The discourse of caring for society and other children is also made appropriate for children due to the fact that much public discourse about children in Britain positions children as 'the future' and having a clear vision, being untainted by the cynical adult world. Sociologists of childhood like James and Prout (1990) looked at the way that in British society public discourse about children is suffused with this ideology. The desire to challenge such representations was partly what motivated the project which generated this data. In this view children are untarnished and pure. This is reflected in much children's fiction, where it is adults who rediscover moral awareness from children or where it is only the children who have the true clarity of vision to perceive the danger as the adults have become sidetracked by the triteness of the world that they have created (Bettelheim 1976; Zipes 1997). These stories remind us of the way that adults lose contact with essential human values. In the classroom context this is why the discourse of caring seems suitable for the children. In the schoolroom they are familiar with reading geography books which present children across the world as basically the same, untainted, with a simple vision of world harmony. Children's magazine programmes on the television are filled with material on the environment, although this is completely depoliticized. They encourage them to collect rubbish to generate money to help children in the Third World. But these problems are removed from the issues of national debts and post-colonial chaos. Coward (1996) talks about the way that issues that are often seen as appropriate for children are generally wrapped up in a 'language of public responsibility and caring' (ibid., p. 356).

The BCC has itself made this romantic image of childhood the centre of its campaigns to maintain the right to state funding. In Britain in 1998 the corporation produced a short promotional film called *Future Generations*. The aim of the short film was to show that the BBC was still needed to offer a nurturing broadcast environment for children. The film contained images of a small schoolboy dressed in an oversized school uniform which evoked the 1950s. The boy is round-faced and could himself have come out of classical children's fiction. He is cheeky, bright and loveable. With the aid of computer and other effects he takes the viewer on a brief life-size tour of BBC children's television from the 1960s and 1970s. All these programmes, usually shown as part of the BBC's *Watch with Mother* package, offer soft puppet-populated landscapes. The worlds inhabited by the characters were apolitical and without conflict, often emphasizing conservative and idealized images of community.

The point is that children are aware of all these discourses which suffuse the culture in which they live, which people use to talk about both television and children. This discourse appears to the children as common sense and as naturally reflecting the way that the world is. It influences how they themselves will think about what childhood is all about. The children feel that they can position themselves as being mature in the formal setting by showing the kinds of exaggerated and depoliticized social sensitivity that the wider society makes available to them.

The children also use very standard discourses in order to express agency by rejecting all the romantic imagery. They typically say that they like bloodthirsty things. This imagery itself draws on standard set of discourses about children as cheeky rogues who reject the adult definitions of childhood. A whole industry of toys, comics and cartoons draws on just such a repertoire.

Conclusion

One way that we could have treated the data in this study was as the beliefs of children as regards television. Yet if we take the approach of thinking about the children as using their cultural tool kit in settings with a responsiveness to those settings, something different emerges. And if we also think about that talk in the context of the broader culture, then we are much closer to understanding how children relate to television. This would only be the beginning of an ethnographic study but already we have located television in the discussion that is society.

What we have achieved in this approach to the data from the role-play situations is that instances of social interaction, that were disassembled from the flow of everyday life as data recorded in settings, have been reassembled back into the flow. In this way we were able to get a slightly better understanding of what was happening. The flow is not complete as we only have limited data. Our understanding could be enhanced by observing the children in different settings to see, for example, if it does seem the case that they take on certain behaviour that they see on television. But the way that I have analysed data in this chapter indicates that the ethnographic gaze is as much a means of viewing behaviour as a set of procedures.

15 Carrying out an ethnographic study

In this book so far I have focused explicitly on the way that ethnography should be thought of as being able to reveal things about human behaviour due to the model of behaviour that it follows. I have left it pretty much to the reader to follow the ethnographic examples in order to develop a sense of how such research should be carried out in practice. This is because the best way to understand ethnography is not by studying a set of methodological procedures. It is also because each case will be unique. The anthropologists and sociologists who first used ethnography took the step of accepting that we may not know the kinds of questions that we should even be asking of a particular social context. We may be completely ignorant of the main features which make that world tick. Ethnography should be thought of, therefore, as being a methodology which is characterized by improvisation.

Procedure

Of course all the ethnographies of the mass media and audiences that have been looked at in this volume have certain characteristics in terms of practical procedure. I would like to briefly look at these.

Deciding on an area for investigation

The best way to get a sense of the kinds of projects that are suitable for an ethnographic study is to look at the studies in this volume. They range from looking at use of the Internet, how journalists produce news, young people's relationship to consumerism, why women like cinema, why a certain story became a media spectacle, among others. All these have in common the idea that we can uncover things about the way the mass media fit into people's lives by looking at their lives more broadly. They also take an approach of focusing their point of study. Let us take as an example the way that people use newspapers as a source of information. One thing that would not be possible for a single ethnographer to do would be to look at how people in America as a whole used newspapers as a source of information. The project should have as its basis a manageable group of people. This might be a group of workers at a factory. It could be a group of female friends and their families. The aim is not to make statements which allow us to generalize about all people, but to reveal something about the way that particular people behave in the world. This will give us insight into some of the characteristics of the way that people, in this case, use news as a resource for information.

This does not mean that we can only use data that derive from the exact chosen sample. The ethnographic studies by Fishman and by Miller and Slater, that we looked at in Part II, used anything that they came across that seemed relevant. These studies used in-depth interviews which they interrelated with observations and comments made by people while they were in their sites of study. In ethnographic research anything can be data.

Asking a research question

When you are choosing your area for investigation, you may come up with a theory about what is going on and then go out and test it. This would be called a deductive approach. For this you will start with a hypothesis. This is often referred to as the hypothetico-deductive approach. For example, if I wanted to look at how young women responded to advertising imagery of independent young women I might hypothesize that such images become an important resource for the way that young women like to think about themselves.

If you do not have a hypothesis you will take an inductive approach which means that you will basically go out and explore. This would be used if, say, you wanted to see how people used cybercafés. You might not have any particular theory about this. Therefore you will simply observe with a view to learning about patterns of use. This would also be the case if you just wanted to think about how young women used images in advertising if you did not already have some theory which you wanted to test. This latter approach is the one that is usually used in ethnographic and in most qualitative research, although the researcher will generally have some kind of unformulated theory as to what they might find.

Finding respondents

The issue of finding respondents brings two problems. One of these is actually physically gaining access to places where these might be. The second is getting them to communicate with you. These may not be such a problem if you are going to look at what your friends think about news programmes. But they will be more of a problem if you decide you want to do an ethnographic study of the producers or writers of soap operas. In this case you will need to write to these people or find some kind of job which takes you close to them. The latter is the approach taken by many ethnographers as this allows them to be around people in different contexts.

The issue of finding respondents might also be more difficult if the researcher does not personally know the kind of people they wish to study. One group of undergraduates in one of my research classes carried out research on theatre attendance. In order to meet theatre goers they carried out very simple questionnaires in the entrance halls of theatres where they attempted to make contact with people for further interaction. Another researcher I supervised wanted to look at television as an influence on expectations for pregnancy and childbirth. This researcher wrote to a range of community groups such as the local National Childbirth Trust where she generated a number of contacts which later increased once she became involved, mainly as women introduced her to their friends. As with my own research into journalism, it is important to gain the trust of those people you study in order to gain access to a wider repertoire of behaviours.

Researchers have long talked about the Hawthorne effect which describes the way that the researcher can affect what people do through their very presence. In fact, the way that people respond to a researcher can itself be a valuable source of data as this often results in people offering the reasons that they assume are widely held and common sense – reasons that we might not find openly expressed in other interactions, as I showed in the previous three chapters. Also I have argued throughout this book that there is no such thing as a neutral, natural setting of interaction. There are only settings. But nevertheless, if the researcher is to gain access to a range of behaviours, they must be accepted as being a natural part of those settings. This will basically mean that you get the people you are studying to trust you. You really need to make it clear that you will not abuse the privilege of sharing their experiences and that you are interested in them as people. If they feel that you bring a sense of academic superiority with you, you will have very little chance of gaining access to a range of settings. All will be governed chiefly by your own presence.

Recording data

Once the topic has been decided it is just a matter of taking as many notes as possible about what people say about anything. Use tape-recordings if you can. Look at how the people you have decided to focus on deal with the world. Attempt to find out their cultural tool kit. What do they think that other people believe about the world? They can be interviewed specifically on the topic. But we have to be mindful that what we have recorded is only one source of data which should be thought of as belonging to a particular place and moment. We need to look at how they behave and at what they say at different times. As I did in the chapters on newspapers, we could look at how these people talked about a certain news story. How does the way that they talk about this relate to widely accepted social discourse? All along it is important to remember that all the talk is not natural but is composed through improvisation using an arbitrary cultural framework. It is done with a sense of the place of the self in relation to the world and with a deep engagement with what other people believe about the world.

In the case of the Spanish newspaper readers, and in Miller and Slater's (2000) study, there is also a sense of connecting the use of newspapers, or the Internet, to wider cultural values. The way that Trinidadian culture emphasizes entrepreneurialism, modernity and international community means that how people think about the Internet must be understood in this context. Likewise, it would be impossible to understand the way that people in Spain talk about newspapers unless we know things about Spanish culture. Tulloch's (1989) study of soap opera viewers showed that we would need to understand the nature of certain cultural representations regarding high and low culture and creativity if we were to understand how people talk about soap opera.

This process of connecting what people do and say to wider cultural representations is more difficult in our own culture, where things seem much more natural. The researcher really needs to be able to take one step back and reassess the way that they think about everything that they come across. This is the most difficult thing in ethnography and this is why I have spent a large part of this book dealing with this.

What the ethnographer should avoid is immediately chasing one idea that they have about what is happening and what is at the heart of what someone is doing. We need to record data, take notes and then reflect on these at a later time. It may take some time to see patterns but the researcher will find that they will begin to develop a feel for the subject and the people that they are investigating.

Another source of data for our ethnography might be the mass media themselves. This might be through spending time with the producers. Again we would be looking to understand why they produced the programmes or news stories that they did. We might find a range of practical reasons, but we would also find cultural frameworks. These will influence what they think that people believe and want.

The researcher will also have to decide whether or not they wish the people that they are researching to know that they are being researched. In my own experience this will have to be decided with a sensitivity to each context. While in Spain doing ethnographic research, I worked for a while in a bar where I would overhear many fascinating conversations. I would use my waiter's pad to take notes. Some might raise the question as to whether it was ethical to use such data without letting people know what was going on. On the other hand if I approached a group of people sitting at a table and asked if they minded if I took notes on their conversations, even if they consented, it is likely that the conversation would continue with a slightly different shape.

The conversations I presented in Chapter 12 are all from naturally occurring conversations. I had, prior to making tape-recordings of these conversations, interviewed all my colleagues. I had asked them if they minded if I recorded the conversations that we had in the bar. They seemed pleased that I was taking an interest in them and their points of view. I told them that when I started to record conversations I would not tell them as this might make them self-conscious. Sometime after I had started to record conversations my colleagues asked me if I had in fact done so, and wondered if they could hear one. I played one recording to the group which they liked. They laughed and the conversation leaders especially took pleasure in the way that the recordings represented them. But I was lucky that this group of men were so easy-going. Many ethnographers end up relying on note-taking.

Feasibility

One thing about ethnography that seems off-putting is that many of the classic studies seem to take a long time. Some of the anthropologists spent years in the field as did the researchers in the Chicago School. But there is no reason why an ethnographic study should take any longer than the time needed to design a questionnaire, providing the ethnography is carried out in the researcher's native culture and language.

An ethnographic study would take longer than focus group-based research which basically only requires the time to organize the focus group and the time taken or allocated to hold the discussion. This is one of the main attractions of the focus group. But in ten weeks there is no reason that an ethnographic study could not be carried out. Although, just as it is difficult to be specific regarding methodological procedures for ethnography, it is difficult to be specific as to timescale, as this depends very much on what is being investigated. Let us say I wanted to look at how a group of female undergraduates related to the imagery of young women in advertisements. I could collect a selection of adverts from magazines and television. I could get the women to take a look at these and record how they talk about them. I could interview the girls individually. I would need to spend as much time with them as possible in order to find out how and what they talked about at different times. This would allow me to build up a sense of their world-view and what they think other people in society believe. Such a piece of research could be highly revealing regarding the way that representations of young women in advertisements – as glamorous, as independent and confident, with all the constructs that are used to signify this, become adopted by these young women. Providing the research was done intensively it could be done over a relatively short period of time. Most importantly the quality of the ethnographic work would depend upon the degree to which the researcher had come to see the world through an ethnographic gaze.

Conclusion

I once heard a colleague in an anthropology department say that no-one knows what ethnography is. While this is certainly true as regards what methodological procedures correctly constitute ethnography, there is something that does lie at the heart of the approach. Ethnography does not provide a transparent window on the world. But no methodology offers this, although some strive to create the impression of it.

What ethnography does do is create an intimate social knowledge. It gives us access to the standards, ideas and traditions through which people carry out their lives and their relationships. Ethnography allows us to examine how intelligent human beings use these creatively to live in and make culture. It allows us to get to the heart of the way that as people do this they are routinely interdependent upon each other and deeply engaged with what everyone else thinks in the mutual enterprise of social life. It seems natural to me that if we are to understand the mass media, then it will have to be so in this very context. In many contemporary societies the mass media have become very much a part of the very processes to which ethnography is so tuned.

Maurice Godelier wrote that: 'human beings, in contrast to other animals, do not just live in society, they produce society in order to live' (1986, p. 1). The mass media are now very much a part of how we produce our societies. They are part of the way that we share what becomes defined as the 'commonly known'. As humans we behave with a vivid sense of what everyone else knows. This 'everyone else' is now also present for us through the imagined communities who we assume share our viewing, reading, listening or spectatorship. Therefore it is reasonable to suggest that to understand how the mass media and their output fit into people's lives we must think about it in terms of the way that people make their lives and their societies.

In the Introduction to this book I offered Kenneth Burke's image of interlocutors in a parlour to evoke an image of society as being like a conversation. Participants arrived in the parlour, listened in order to get the gist, put in their oar's worth and then left. This conversation was about what life and the world is all about. It was about how we can be human beings. Throughout the world there have been, and still are, an incredible abundance of ways of doing this – a vast range of conversations. The collective anthropological research, to some extent, could be seen as an archive, or celebration of this diversity. In our own cultures the mass media must be thought of as being very much a part of our own particular conversation and of the way that we make our societies. Only a methodology which allows us to think about this conversation in its entirety, which allows us to follow wherever we need to go in order to obtain data, which allows us to look at social life as it happens, can provide us with the intimate kind of knowledge required to understand that great conversation.

Bibliography

Adorno, T.W. (1941) 'On popular music', *Studies in Philosophy and Social Science* IX (1).

Adorno, T.W. (1991) *The Culture Industry: Selected Essays on Mass Culture*, London: Routledge.

Althusser, L. (1984) *Essays on Ideology*, London: New Left Books/Verso.

Anderson, B. (1983) *Imagined Communities*, London: Verso.

Anderson, N. (1961) *The Hobo*, Chicago: University of Chicago.

Ang, I. (1985) *Watching Dallas: Soap Opera and the Melodramatic Imagination*, London: Methuen.

Ang, I. (1990) 'Culture and communication: towards an ethnographic critique of media consumption in the transnational media system', *European Journal of Communication*, 5, 239–60.

Aries, P. (1962) *Centuries of Childhood*, London: Pimlico Press.

Asad, T. (1986) 'The concept of cultural translation in British social anthropology', in Clifford, J. and Marcus, G.E. (eds) *Writing Culture: The Poetics and Politics of Ethnography*. Berkeley, CA: University of California Press.

Barrat, D. (1986) *Media Sociology*. London: Tavistock.

Bazalgette, C. and Buckingham, D. (1995) *In Front of the Children: Screen Entertainment and Young Audiences*. London: BFI.

Becker, H.S. (1963) *Outsiders: Studies in the Sociology of Deviance*. London: Collier-Macmillan Ltd.

Becker, H.S. (1986) *Writing for Social Scientists*, Chicago: University of Chicago Press.

Belmonte, T. (1979) *The Broken Fountain*, New York: Columbia University Press.

Belton, T. (2000) 'The "Face at the Window" study: a fresh approach to media influence and to investigating the influence of television and videos on children's imagination', in *Media Culture and Society*, 22: 629–43.

Benedict, R. (1934) *Patterns of Culture*, Boston: Houghton Mifflin Co.

Bettelheim, B. (1976) *The Uses of Enchantment: The Meaning and Importance of Fairy Tales*. New York: Random House.

Blumer, H. (1933) *Movies and Conduct*, New York: Macmillan.

Blumer, H. (1969) *Symbolic Interactionism: Perspective and Method*, Berkeley, CA: University of California Press.

Blumer, H. and Hauser, P. (1933) *Movies, Delinquency and Crime*, New York: Macmillan.

Boas, F. (1921) 'Ethnology of the Kwakiutl based on data collected by George Hunt', *35th Annual Report of the Bureau of American Ethnology*, Pt. 2, 795–1481.

Bordwell, D., Staiger, J. and Thompson, K. (1985) *The Classical Hollywood Cinema: Film Style and Mode of Production to 1960*, New York: Columbia University Press.

Bourdieu, P. (1977) *An Outline of a Theory of Practice*, Cambridge: Cambridge University Press.

Bourdieu, P. (1984) *Distinction: A Social Critique of the Judgement of Taste*, London: Routledge and Kegan Paul.

Bruner, J. (1990) *Acts of Meaning*, Cambridge, MA: Harvard University Press.

Bruner, J. and Weisser, S. (1991) 'The invention of self: autobiography and its forms', in Olson, D.R. and Torrance, N. (eds) *Literacy and Orality*, Cambridge: Cambridge University Press.

Brunsden, C. (1991) 'Text and audience', in Seiter, E., Borchers, H., Kreutzner, G. and Warth, E. (eds) *Remote Control*, London: Routledge.

Buckingham, D. (1996) *Moving Images*, Manchester: Manchester University Press.

Bulmer, M. (1984) *The Chicago School of Sociology: Institutionalisation, Diversity, and the Rise of Sociological Research*, Chicago and London: University of Chicago Press.

Burke, K. (1944/1971) *A Grammar of Motives*, New York: Prentice-Hall.

Campbell, J.K. (1964) *Honour, Family and Patronage: A Study of Institutions and Moral Values in a Greek Mountain Community*, Oxford: Clarendon Press.

Carrithers, M. (1992) *Why Humans Have Cultures: Explaining Anthropology and Social Diversity*, Oxford: Oxford University Press.

Chicago Commission on Race Relations (1968, original 1922) *The Negro in Chicago*, Chicago: University of Chicago Press.

Clement, D.H. (1982) 'Samoan folk knowledge of mental disorders', in Marsella, A.J. and White, G. (eds) *Cultural Conceptions of Mental Health and Therapy*, Dordrecht, Holland: D. Reidel Publishing Company.

Clifford, J. and Marcus, G. (eds) (1986) *Writing Culture: The Poetics and Politics of Ethnography*. Berkeley, CA: University of California Press.

Collet, P. and Lamb, R. (1986) *Watching People Watching Television*, Report Presented to the IBA, London.

Comte, A. (1854) *The Positive Philosophy* (translated and condensed by Harriet Martineau), vol. 2, New York: D. Appleton and Co.

Coward, J. (1996) 'Reading children's books', in Coward, J. (ed.) *Only Connect: Readings on Children's Literature*, Oxford: Oxford University Press.

Curran, J. (1990) 'The New Revisionism in mass communication research – a reappraisal', *European Journal of Communication*, 5 (2–3).

Curran, J., Gurevitch, M. and Woolacott, J. (1982) 'The study of the media: theoretical approaches', in Gurevitch, M. *et al. Society and the Media*, London: Routledge.

Dahlgren, P. (1992) 'Viewers' plural sense-making of TV news', in Scannell, P. *et al.* *Culture and Power: A Media, Culture and Society Reader*, London: Sage.

D'Andrade, R. (1987) 'A folk model of the mind', in Holland, D. and Quinn, N. (eds) *Cultural Models in Language and Thought*, Cambridge and New York: Cambridge University Press.

Davies, M.M. (1989) *Television is Good for Your Kids*, London: Hilary Shipman.

Davies, M. M. and Machin, D. (2000a) 'Children's Demon TV – reality, freedom, panic: children's discussions of the Demon Headmaster', *Continuum: Journal of Media and Cultural Studies*, 14 (1).

Davies, M. M. and Machin, D. (2000b) ' "It helps people make their decisions": dating games, public service broadcasting and the negotiation of identity in middle-childhood', *Childhood*, 7 (2).

Doane, M.A. (1982/1990) 'Film and the masquerade: theorising the female spectator', in Erens, P. (ed.) *Issues in Feminist Film Criticism*, Bloomington, IND: Indiana University Press.

Doane, M.A. (1987) *The Desire to Desire: The Woman's Film in the 1940s*, Bloomington, IND: Indiana University Press.

Du Boulay, J. (1974) *Portrait of a Greek Mountain Village*. Oxford: Clarendon Press.

Durkheim, E. (1952) *Suicide*, London: Routledge and Kegan Paul.

Evans-Pritchard, E.E. (1934) 'Levy-Bruhl's theory of primitive mentality', *Bulletin of the Faculty of Arts*, University of Egypt.

Evans-Pritchard, E.E. (1937) *Witchcraft, Oracles and Magic among the Azande*, Oxford: Clarendon Press.

Fishman, M. (1980) *Manufacturing the News*, Austin and London: University of Texas Press.

Fiske, J. (1984) 'Television quiz shows and the purchase of cultural capital', *Australian Journal of Screen Theory*, 13–14.

Foucault, M. (1966) *The Order of Things*, trans. R. Howard, London: Tavistock.

Foucault, M. (1969) *The Archaeology of Knowledge*, trans. A. Sheridan, London: Tavistock.

Frazer, E. (1992) 'Teenage girls reading *Jackie*', in Scannell, P. (ed.) *Culture and Power: A Media, Culture and Society Reader*, London: Sage.

Frazer, J. (1922) *The Golden Bough: A Study in Magic and Religion*, New York: The Macmillan Co.

Garfinkel, H. (1967) *Studies in Ethnomethodology*, Englewood Cliffs, NJ: Prentice-Hall.

Geertz, C. (1973) *The Interpretation of Culture*, New York: Basic Books.

Geraghty, C. (1988) 'Audiences and "ethnography": questions of practice', in Geraghty, C. and Lusted, D. (eds) *The Television Studies Book*, London: Arnold.

Glasgow University Media Group (1976) *Bad News*, London: Routledge.

Godelier, M. (1986) *The Mental and the Material*, London: Verso.

Goffman, I. (1961) *Asylums*, Garden City, New York: Doubleday.

Goffman, I. (1969) *The Presentation of Self in Everyday Life*, Harmondsworth: Penguin.

Goffman, I. (1974) *Frame Analysis*, New York: Harpers.

Golding, P. and Middleton, S. (1982) *Images of Welfare*, Oxford: Mark Robertson.

Gomez Mompart, J.L. (1989) 'Existio en España prensa de masas? La Prensa en torno a 1900', in Timoteo, J. *et al.* (eds) *Historia de los medios de communicación en España*, Barcelona: Ariel.

Gramsci, A. (1971) *Selections from the Prison Notebooks*, edited and translated by Quintin Hoare and Geoffrey Novell Smith, London: Lawrence and Wishart.

Hacking, I. (1983) *Representation and Intervening: Introductory Topics in the Philosophy of Natural Science*, Cambridge: Cambridge University Press.

Hall, S. (1980) 'Encoding and decoding in the television discourse' (originally published in 1973) in Hall, S. *et al.* (eds) *Culture, Media, Language: Working Papers in Cultural Studies, 1972-79*, London: Hutchinson.

Haskell, M. (1973) *From Reverence to Rape: The Treatment of Women in the Movies*, New York: Holt, Rinehart and Winston.

Herdt, G.H. (1987) *The Guardians of the Flutes: Idioms of Masculinity*, New York: Columbia University Press.

Herman, E.S. and Chomsky, N. (1994) *Manufacturing Consent: The Political Economy of the Mass Media*, London: Vintage.

Hobson, D. (1982) *Crossroads: The Drama of a Soap Opera*, London: Methuen.

Hodge, R. and Tripp, D. (1986) *Children and Television: A Semiotic Approach*, Cambridge: Polity Press.

Holland, D. and Quinn, N. (1987) 'Culture and cognition', in Holland, D. and Quinn, N. (eds) *Cultural Models in Language and Thought*, Cambridge and New York: Cambridge University Press.

Humphrey, N.K. (1976) 'The social function of intellect', in Bateson, P. and Hunde, R. (eds) *Growing Points in Ethnology*, Cambridge: Cambridge University Press.

Humphrey, N.K. (1982) 'Consciousness: a just-so story', *New Scientist*, 95, 474–8.

Jahner, E.A., DeMillie, R.J. and Walker, J.R. (1991) *Lakota Belief and Ritual*, Nebraska, University of Nebraska Press.

James, A. and Prout, A. (eds) (1990) *Reconstructing Childhood: Contemporary Issues in the Sociological Study of Childhood*, London: Falmer Press.

Jowett, G. (1976) *Film: The Democratic Art*, Boston: Little Brown.

Katz, E. and Lazarsfeld, P.F. (1956) *Personal Influence: The Part Played by People in the Flow of Mass Communication*, New York: The Free Press of Glencoe.

Kay, P. (1987) 'Linguistic competence and folk theories of language: two English hedges', in Holland, D. and Quinn, N. (eds) *Cultural Models in Language and Thought*, Cambridge and New York: Cambridge University Press.

Kempton, W. (1987) 'Two theories of home heat control', in Holland, D. and Quinn, N. (eds) *Cultural Models in Language and Thought*, Cambridge and New York: Cambridge University Press.

Kenny, M. (1968) 'Parallel power structures in Castile: the patron–client balance', in Peristany, J.G. (ed.) *Contributions to Mediterranean Sociology: Mediterranean Rural Communities and Social Change*, The Hague: Mouton and Co.

Lacan, J. (1977) *Ecrits: A Selection*, London: Tavistock.

Lakoff, G. and Johnson, M. (1980) *Metaphors We Live By*, Chicago and London: University of Chicago Press.

Landesco, J. (1929) *Organised Crime in Chicago*, Chicago: University of Chicago Press (republished 1968).

Lave, J., Stepick, A. and Sailer, L. (1977) 'Extending the scope of formal analysis', *American Ethnologist*, 4 (2): 321–39.

Lazarsfeld, P., Berelson, B. and Gaudet, H. (1944) *The People's Choice*, New York: Columbia University Press.

Lison-Tolosana, C. (1966) *Belmonte de los Caballeros*, Oxford: Clarendon Press.

Lull, J. (1990) *Inside Family Viewing: Ethnographic Research on Television Audiences*, London: Routledge and New York: Comedia.

Machin, D. (1996) 'Morbo, personhood, and the absence of a sensationalist press in Spain', *Journal of Mediterranean Studies*, 6 (2), University of Malta.

Machin, D. and Carrithers, M. (1996) 'From "interpretative communities" to "communities of improvisation" ', *Media Culture and Society*, 18.

Malinowski, B. (1922) *Argonauts of the Western Pacific*, New York: E.P. Dutton and Co Inc.

Mandler, J.M. (1984) *Stories Scripts and Scenes: Aspects of Schema Theory*, London: Lawrence Erlbaum.

Marin, I. and Otto, E. (1989) 'Establización y novedades en la prensa diaria', in Timoteo, J. *et al.* (eds), *Historia de los Medios de Communicación en España*, Barcelona: Ariel.

McCabe, C. (1976) 'Theory and film: principles of realism and pleasure', *Screen*, 17 (3).

McGuigan, J. (1992) *Cultural Populism*, London: Routledge.

McQuail, D., Blumler, J. and Brown, J.R. (1972) 'The television audience: a revised perspective', in McQuail, D. (ed.) *Sociology of Mass Communications*, Harmondsworth: Penguin.

Mead, G.H. (1934) *Mind, Self and Society*, Chicago: University of Chicago Press.

Merton, R. (1946) *Mass Persuasion*, New York: The Free Press.

Metz, C. (1975) 'Le Signifiant imaginaire', *Screen*, 16 (2).

Miller, D. and Slater, D. (2000) *The Internet: An Ethnographic Approach*, Oxford and New York: Berg.

Morley, D. (1980) *The 'Nationwide' Audience*, London: British Film Institute.

Morley, D. (1986) *Family Television: Culture, Power and Domestic Leisure*, London: Comedia.

Morley, D. (1992) *Television, Audiences and Cultural Studies*, London: Routledge.

Mulvey , L. (1975) ' Visual pleasure and narrative cinema', *Screen*, 16 (3).

Myers, K (1988) *Understains: The Sense and Seduction of Advertising*, London: Routledge.

Park , R. and Burgess, E.W. (eds) (1925) *The City*, Chicago: University of Chicago Press.

Peristany, J.G. (1965) *Honour and Shame: The Values of Mediterranean Society*, London: Weidenfeld and Nicolson.

Peristany, J.G. and Pitt-Rivers, J. (eds) (1992) *Honour and Grace in Anthropology*, Cambridge: Cambridge University Press.

Peterson, R.C. and Thurstone, L.I. (1933) *Motion Pictures and the Social Attitudes of Children*, New York: Macmillan.

Pitt-Rivers, J. (1954) *The People of the Sierra*, Chicago and London: University of Chicago Press.

Pttt-Rivers, J. (1965) 'Honour and social status', in Peristany, J.G. and Pitt-Rivers, J. (eds) *Honour and Grace in Anthropology*, Cambridge: Cambridge University Press.

Polanyi, M. (1946) *Science, Faith and Society*. Chicago: University of Chicago Press.

Polanyi, M. (1958) *Personal Knowledge: Towards a Post-Critical Philosophy*. London: Routledge and Kegan Paul.

Radway, J.A. (1984) *Reading the Romance*. London: Verso.

Radway, J.A. (1988) 'Reception study: ethnography and the problems of dispersed and nomadic subjects', *Cultural Studies*, 2 (4).

Riley, J. and Riley, M. (1959) 'Mass communications and the social system', in Merton, R. *Sociology Today*, New York: Free Press.

Said, E. (1979) *Orientalism*, London: Penguin.

Sant Cassia, P. (1991) 'Authors in search of a character: personhood, agency and identity in the Mediterranean', *Journal of Mediterranean Studies*, 5/1: 1–13.

Schank, R.C. and Abelson, R. (1977) *Scripts, Plans, Goals and Understanding*. Hillsdale, NJ: Lawrence Erlbaum.

Schramm, W., Lyle, J. and Parker, E.B. (1961) *Television in the Lives of Our Children*, Stanford, CA: Stanford University Press.

Schroder, K.C. (1994) 'Audience semiotics, interpretive communities and the "ethnographic turn" in media reasearch', *Media Culture and Society*, 16 (2): 337–48.

Schwartz, H. and Jacobs, J. (1979) *Qualitative Sociology: A Method to the Madness*, New York: The Free Press.

Shaw, C. (1931) *The Jack-Roller: A Delinquent Boy's Own Story*, Chicago: University of Chicago Press.

Shils, E. (1971) 'Mass society and its culture', in Rosenberg, B. and White, D. (eds) *Mass Culture Revisited*, New York: Van Nostrand Reinhold.

Silverman, S. (1975) *Three Bells of Civilization: The Life of an Italian Hill Town*, New York and London: Columbia University Press.

Silverstone, R., Hirsch, E. and Morley, D. (1991) 'Listening to a long conversation: an ethnographic approach to the study of information and communication technologies in the home', *Cultural Studies*, 5 (2).

Singer, J.L. and Singer, D.G. (1981) *Television, Imagination and Aggression: A Study of Pre-schoolers*, Hillsdale, NJ: Lawrence Erlbaum.

Stacey, J. (1994) *Star Gazing: Hollywood Cinema and Female Spectatorship*, London: Routledge.

Staiger, J. (1992) *Interpreting Films: Studies in the Historical Reception of American Cinema*, Princeton, NJ: Princeton University Press.

Starker, S. (1991) *Evil Influences: Crusades Against the Mass Media*, New Brunswick, NJ: Transaction.

Thomas, W.I. and Znaniecki, F. (1918–1920) *The Polish Peasant in Europe and America*, 5 volumes, Boston: Badger.

Thrasher, F.M. (1927 abridged version 1963) *The Gang: A Study of 1,313 gangs in Chicago*, Chicago and London: University of Chicago Press.

Tuchman, G. (1978) *Making News: A Study in the Construction of Reality*, London: Collier-Macmillan.

Tulloch, J. (1989) 'Approaching the audience: the elderly', in Sieter, E., Borchers, H., Kreutzner, G. and Wrath, E.-M. (eds) *Remote Control: Television, Audiences and Cultural Power*, London and New York: Routledge.

Tulloch, J. (1990) *Television Drama: Agency, Audience and Myth*, London: Routledge.

Tyler, S.A. (1986) 'Post-modern ethnography: from document of the occult to occult document', in Clifford, J. and Marcus, G.E. (eds) *Writing Culture: The Poetics and Politics of Ethnography*, Berkeley, CA: University of California Press.

Tylor, E.B. (1924 [1871]) *Primitive Culture: Researches in the Development of Mythology, Philosophy, Religion, Art and Custom*, New York: Brentanos.

Vygotsky, L. (1978) *Mind in Society: The Development of Higher Psychological Processes*, Cambridge, MA: London: Harvard University Press.

Wartella, E. and Reeves, B. (1985), 'Historical trends in research on children and the media 1900-1960', *Journal of Communication*, 35 (2): 118–33.

Watson, G. (1991) 'Rewriting culture', in Fox, R.G. (ed.) *Recapturing Anthropology: Working in the Present*, Santa Fe, New Mexico: School of American Research Press.

Wertsch, J.V. (1991) *Voices of the Mind: A Sociological Approach to Mediated Action*, London: Harvester Wheatsheaf.

Whorf, B.L. (1956) *Language, Thought, and Reality: Selected Writings of Benjamin Lee Whorf*, ed. John B. Carroll, Cambridge MA: The MIT Press.

Williamson, J. (1978) *Decoding Advertisements: Ideology and Meaning in Advertising*, London: Marion Boyers.

Willis, P. (1990) *Common Culture*, Milton Keynes: Open University Press.

Wilson, T.P. (1971) 'Normative interpretive paradigms in sociology', in Douglas, J.D. (ed.) *Understanding Everyday Life*, London: Routledge and Kegan Paul.

Wollen, P. (1982) *Readings and Writings: Semiotic Counter-Strategies*, London: Verso.

Ziman, J. (1978) *Reliable Knowledge: An Exploration of the Grounds for Belief in Science*, Cambridge: Cambridge University Press.

Zipes, J. (1997) *Happily Ever After: Fairy Tales, Children and the Culture Industry*, London: Routledge.

Index